Tony Laurence grew up safely and comfortably in the then largely unvisited, beautiful Dorset countryside, and was educated by the sea. He is one of the lucky generation and has lived happily in English peacetime.

He was a managing director for many years, controlling a dozen commercial companies involved in national and multinational businesses. He now lives quietly with friends and laughter in Europe.

Dedication

This book is dedicated to Jacqueline.

Tony Laurence

A CHEERLEADER IN INDIA

AUSTIN MACAULEY PUBLISHERS™

LONDON • CAMBRIDGE • NEW YORK • SHARJAH

A CIP catalogue record for this title is available from the British Library.

ISBN 9781787106796 (Paperback)
ISBN 9781787106802 (E-Book)

www.austinmacauley.com

First Published (2018)
Austin Macauley Publishers Ltd.
25 Canada Square
Canary Wharf
London
E14 5LQ

1
The Roller Skater

The year is 1992.

She is roller-skating along the sea front. Wearing shorts, a red shirt tied at the front and four-wheeled skating boots in white leather with white ankle socks. Around her wrists are strapped circles of weights. She is powering herself along with big strong strokes of her legs and swinging her arms to increase her momentum. Blonde hair, long limbs, muscles, about five feet eight inches tall. Her body is tanned to a honey colour. She looks strong. Her name is Kimberley.

Marcus Field watches her as she speeds past the seaside café. He is drinking an American coffee and looking through legal papers on the table. He is thirty-eight years old, dark thick hair, brown eyes with long eyelashes and full lips. About six feet two inches tall, he is slim but has the broad shoulders of a competitive swimmer – which he used to be. He is suntanned and wearing chinos and a blue cotton shirt. Dark brown loafers.

He is in Northern Florida. He is there to meet lawyers in Jacksonville to settle an English property dispute. Marcus is accompanied by his London lawyer, Alistair Bond. Bond has blonde hair, is aged around forty-five and wearing a biscuit coloured lightweight suit with a pale blue cotton shirt and a dark striped tie. He has sunglasses on. He is slim and serious.

"Athletic," said Bond as the girl skated past. She is moving more decisively than the other girls on the seafront who are skating around improving their suntans whilst wearing brightly coloured bikinis. Two of them have cold drinks in huge paper cups with straws sticking out of them. One of the girls is doing twirls on her skates in an attempt to attract the attention of someone inside the beach café.

"What a good life people have here," says Marcus. "I suppose the sunshine makes everything better." He is now watching four young men jogging along the sandy beach.

"Money is important here though," said Alistair. "Success, happiness, all judged by money. It creates a pressure for the young. They are driven to succeed. Without material success they have no self-respect. Do not know who they are."

"You make it sound like a race," replied Marcus. "The sandy beaches and the sunshine would defeat the ambitions of many Europeans. Coconuts and orange juice, cheap petrol and cars. Life could be easy here."

"Americans want more," said Alistair. "It is deeply ingrained in their culture. They are competitive; ever driving onwards and upwards. It is admirable. They believe that they can achieve anything, from a wooden house on the Mississippi to the White House in Washington. No limits. No class system. No inbred European limits on their expectations. The American dream. There is no English dream. Our education system flattens all of that. By the time you are twelve you know what your limitations are going to be for the rest of your life."

"Oh, I don't agree with that," answered Marcus. "There are plenty of self-made multimillionaires in Britain. Starting from modest backgrounds and succeeding against the odds."

"But the odds are in your favour here," said Alistair. "The whole country is designed for it. Start by selling ice cream, end up by owning six country clubs."

"I suppose that there is plenty of room here as well," says Marcus. "I've read that over a third of the United States has never been cultivated, never been disturbed. Apart from the cities there are vast areas of open space, long straight roads stretching into the distance. You don't find that in Europe."

"Maybe a bit in France," says Alistair. "Maybe a bit more on those big new roads through Spain, but you are right. There is nothing in Europe to compare to the vast land mass of the United States and the huge emptiness of parts of it."

"Lots of places to sell ice cream and lots of places to start country clubs," says Marcus with a laugh. "Come on, let's walk."

They stroll along the seafront.

Kimberley is skating back again. Pushing her body with long powerful strides, her arms still swinging hard.

She accelerates towards the two men as they saunter along with their backs to her. The rubber wheels of her skates are sports models. They bounce on a hard surface. It takes practice to control the extra spring but it increases her speed.

There are benches on the right hand side looking out at the sea. Two women are gossiping on a bench whilst their two small children are pushing each other playfully. Suddenly one of them pushes the other and then runs away across the promenade without looking. She is directly in the pathway of the skater.

"Hey kid," shouts Kimberley, and because there is no space left she bends her knees, gives a terrific spring and she dives over the child in a forward somersault, landing onto her skates again, but the dive has increased her speed.

9

Hearing her shout Marcus and Alistair turn around as Kimberley careers into Marcus, who catches her at the waist and spins around to break her speed before setting her down again, still holding her as she glides backwards and stops by putting her right boot forward onto its pad.

"Are you all right?" asks Alistair.

"All right," answers Kimberley, as she pushes Marcus's hands off her waist. "But I've spoilt my time." She glances at a stopwatch, which is clipped at her hip onto the waistband of her shorts. She glides slowly over to the two women on the bench. "Keep your kids on a leash," she says, and spins around, not interested in their reaction. "Catch one of those girls," she tells Marcus. She nods her head in the direction of the four girls in bikinis who are skating nonchalantly towards them, displaying their suntanned bodies. "They want to be caught," shouts Kimberley, as she starts again to power herself away along the hard surface towards the distant pier. In seconds, she is fifty yards away.

"She didn't thank us," says Alistair. "She could have fallen and hurt herself."

"We were in her way," says Marcus, "and we spoilt her time. That somersault she did would have increased her speed and her time. Pretty gymnastic move, don't you think?" He smiles.

"Tough girl," answers Alistair. "Our appointment is at two o'clock. We had better get back for some lunch before we get there."

Alistair and Marcus are in a lift inside a skyscraper office building.

"Oliver Gateskill is on the nineteenth floor," says Alistair. The lift speaks to them as it arrives at the floor.

"Nineteenth floor," says the lift, in a female American voice.

10

They get out and look at the doors along the corridor, Oliver Gateskill Law engraved on a stainless steel plate on an anonymous door. They enter and find themselves in a luxurious reception. Sofas, a coffee table with magazines, and a high reception desk with a smiling woman sitting behind it.

"Good morning. How can I help you?" she intones.

"We have an appointment to see Mr Gateskill," says Alistair.

"Your name, please sir," says the receptionist.

"Alistair Bond and Marcus Field," answers Alistair. "I am an English lawyer," he adds unnecessarily.

After a few minutes' wait they are shown into Oliver Gateskill's huge office. A very big rosewood desk, an expensive-looking big leather swivel chair and four smaller and lower chairs ranged in front of the desk. There is also a table with six chairs around. Big floor to ceiling thickly double glazed windows and in front of one of them is a powerful telescope, which is used to look at the moon and the stars.

"Welcome to Florida, gentlemen," says Oliver, "sit at the table." Oliver Gateskill is a short man with a very big bald head. He is wearing a double-breasted suit and a red silk tie with black anchors on it. "I'll get my legal assistant to bring in the latest papers on your little problem." He presses a button on an intercom and calls, "Please bring everything in, Kimberley."

Moments later the athletic roller-skater walks in, dressed in a smart conservative dark grey dress and carrying two thick files. She sits at the table opposite to Alistair and Marcus and next to Oliver. She shows no sign of recognising either of the two men.

Marcus, however, is certain that she is the same girl who was skating so competitively this morning.

They commence the meeting, Oliver giving them his opinion on events and Kimberley handing written reports to the two Englishmen.

The three men discuss the conflicting issues. The girl makes notes of the conclusions of the discussions. Alistair starts to say, "You don't need to go to court to get a tenant out of a commercial property if the tenant hasn't paid rent for six months. You just take possession and change the locks. Leave a notice on the door that any attempt to re-enter the building will be a criminal act."

Oliver looks at his watch. "One minute gentlemen, please," he says, getting up and walking over to the telescope. He looks through it, carefully adjusting the focus. "Yes," he shouts. "Oh yes." He goes on looking for another minute and then walks back to the meeting table. "No court action to get vacant possession in England, eh?" he asks. "English lawyers – solicitors you call them – tell me that the landlord has to go to court. Get a court order for vacant possession."

"They only say that to get the fees," says Alistair. "The reality is that the landlord can just take the building back. He doesn't need any court order."

"Okay," says Oliver. "Let's work on the basis that what you say is true. Kimberley, check it out, would you?"

The meeting goes on. Oliver rapidly goes through the problems, immediately offering answers and is altogether fast and aggressive in his approach. The meeting finishes after an hour and, whilst Alistair and Marcus are gathering their papers, Oliver takes another quick look through his telescope. "Aha," he says, "good day today." He then turns to usher his clients out of the office.

Marcus hesitates to thank Kimberley for her help. He puts his hand out to shake hers. She then shakes it quickly and pushes it away. She walks ahead of them out of the office, leaving Alistair and Marcus to say goodbye to Oliver. "I think we are going to visit the tenant's lawyers," says Alistair. "Not to say anything to give away our position but just to give them a look-over."

"The tenant's lawyer is a cowboy," says Oliver, "a complete cowboy, but I'll give you his address." He writes it down on a pad, tears the top sheet off and hands it to Alistair.

"Is Kimberley a lawyer?" asks Marcus.

"She is a paralegal assistant," says Oliver. "It's a professional qualification here, but she only works for me part-time. The rest of the time she is a cheerleader for the local football team. She will never make a success of a legal career. She doesn't care enough, but it suits me okay."

They walk into the main reception area and Oliver shakes their hands and goes back into his office. Marcus asks the receptionist, "Do you know who occupies the nineteenth floor of the building opposite?" He points with one hand.

The receptionist smiles mischievously. "It is the local dance club," she answers. "Their changing rooms and showers are on this side."

Marcus nods. "Thank you," he says. He and Alistair leave the building and take a taxi to the address which Oliver Gateskill has given them.

"Do you think that it is good judgment for us to employ a US lawyer who is a peeper?" asks Alistair.

"Well, he wasn't secret about it, was he?" answers Marcus.

"I don't know whether that makes it any better," says Alistair, frowning.

They arrive at another anonymous office building but this one is only twelve storeys high. There are metal nameplates just inside the lobby.

"We are looking for Peyton and Clarke," says Alistair. "Here they are."

The nameplate says fourth floor. Alistair and Marcus get into another lift. No speaking voice this time.

They ride up four floors and get out into a corridor. Walking a few feet Alistair sees a door marked Peyton and Clarke. "Here we are," he calls to Marcus. They both enter. They find themselves in what looks like a film set for an old western. A sheriff's office. There is an elaborate low fence across the last two-thirds of the room with a gate in the centre of it. Behind the fence there is old furniture in dark wood and leather and a coat rack fixed high on the wall. The wall is decorated to look like rough exposed brickwork. Hanging on the coat rack is a gun belt with bullets and a gun in a leather holster. Next to it hangs a Stetson hat.

In front of the fence is a battered wooden desk with telephones and a computer on it. A woman sits behind it. She is wearing a fringed leather skirt and short cowboy boots part way up her calves. She has on a white cotton shirt with a leather waistcoat over it in the same brown colour as her skirt. Her cowboy boots are red and white. She has a red Stetson hat on her head.

"Good afternoon, gentlemen," she says. "What can I do for you?"

"We called in to see whether Mr Peyton might be able to speak to us for ten minutes," answers Alistair. "Our names are Bond and Field."

"One moment, please," says the woman. She picks up a telephone. "Mr Peyton," she says. "Two men are here to see you. A Mr Bond and a Mr Field. Yes sir. Yes sir." She puts the phone down. "He'll be right out," she says. "Take a seat."

Against the wall is a long wooden bench. They both sit down. A few moments later a door opens and a Wild West sheriff walks out. Pointed cowboy boots, leather chaps, a gun belt, two six-guns. A maroon shirt that buttons across his chest, like a dentist. A neckerchief and a tall white ten-gallon hat. On the shirt glitters a silver five star sheriff's badge. The wearer of this costume is an ordinary-looking man, with grey hair and heavily lined face, modern steel-rimmed glasses and soft white hands. He is a small man and looks underfed.

"Peyton," he says in a loud voice. "What is to be done about the fix you guys are in? Shall we talk about a settlement or do you want to fight?"

"You act for Mr Baxter, the supermarket operator?" asks Alistair.

"Both Baxters," shouts Mr Peyton. "Both husband and wife are my clients. Yes, sir, and we are ready for you. Yes, we are."

"I am pleased to hear that," says Alistair. "We are calling at your offices simply as a courtesy to introduce ourselves. This is my client, Mr Field." Alistair indicates towards Marcus.

"You want to fight, Field?" shouts Peyton. "Because if you want to fight then we are surely ready."

"We just wanted to meet face to face because, of course, we already know Mr Baxter, although we do not know Mrs Baxter. Never met her," answers Marcus.

"And you never will," shouts Peyton, who seems unable to lower his voice. "She doesn't live with her husband no more. She is in Oregon. Yes, sir."

"It is good of you to spare the time to meet us Mr Peyton," says Alistair. "We shall not keep you a moment longer. Thank you so much."

"Settle then," shouts Peyton. "Let's talk about a deal. Settle."

"Well, not today, Mr Peyton," says Alistair. "We are short of time today."

"Won't take any time," challenges Peyton. "You name a figure. Come on. Numbers, gentlemen."

"So good to have met you," says Alistair. "We will be in touch with you. Goodbye."

"Goodbye?" shouts Peyton. "What the hell did you come here for? We can settle. Let's do it now."

"Goodbye," murmurs Alistair and pushes Marcus in front of him out of the door and into the corridor.

Peyton follows them out, bowing his head in the doorway to avoid knocking his tall hat off his head.

"No need to spend a lot of time over this," shouts Peyton. "This don't have to be no tennis match. We can do this here and now."

"We will let you know," says Alistair and he and Marcus step into the lift.

As the lift doors close they hear Peyton shout, "Come on now."

Alistair and Marcus walk out of the building onto the sidewalk. "He has no case," says Alistair. "He cannot come up with a single argument. Desperate."

"British," says Peyton to Miss Cross, who is the woman in his reception office. "God damn British. Don't say what they mean. So God damn polite that they cannot say anything. Can't second-guess them at all. I don't even think that they know what they think. British."

2
A Lunch

Marcus and Alistair are chatting in their hotel lobby.

"The whole of the property portfolio is well managed, I think," said Alistair. "I believe that the tenant Baxter has problems. His wife has left him, he is not paying the rent and his lawyer Peyton has revealed that their position is fragile. Lock him out, I think, and take the property back. Then we can ask our agent here to start looking for a new tenant."

"What about the prospect of building a new shopping mall?" asks Marcus.

"Okay, I don't like the USA," says Alistair. "It is all so tough here. My advice is to do something back home in the UK. The property market is thoroughly regulated there."

"Okay," answers Marcus, "whatever you think. Let's ask our lawyer here to meet us for lunch then we can tell them."

"I'll arrange it," says Alistair. "I'll meet you in the hotel reception at twelve o'clock."

They part company and Marcus takes another stroll along the seafront. There are lots of roller-skaters there but not the one he is looking for.

Later he joins Alistair again, who tells him that they have a one o'clock luncheon appointment at a beach restaurant two miles up the coast. They take a taxi and arrive early. Alistair chooses a table at the front overlooking the sea and shielded from other customers by a post and a big plant.

"Did you say that you were taking a long trip to India next month?" asks Alistair. "You are going with some student, you said."

"She doesn't want to go now," said Marcus. "I should never have asked her in the first place. She is much too young and she is a dreamer. Anyway she has met a boy at her college. He is younger than her and she is moulding him to her taste. Persuaded him to have a tattoo on his shoulder. A wolf, I think. His mother was furious when she saw it and when he told Amanda he cried."

"He should have had a poodle tattooed," said Alistair, "but what are you going to do? You told me that you had booked everything in advance and paid for all of the hotels and the travel arrangements within the country."

You have to book everything in advance," says Marcus. "You cannot just walk into a railway station and get on a train. All of them are booked up weeks ahead. It's the same with long distance buses and internal flights. There are so many people in India that you have to make arrangements in advance. The same with the good hotels. So I've already spent the money and now I do not have a travelling companion. You know how empty it can be to go somewhere astonishing and fabulous and to have nobody to share it with. Do you want to come?"

"No thanks," answers Alistair. "I've been to India before. It is quite an effort. You need energy and you need to be fit. I don't want to do it again and anyway I could not take seven weeks away from the office. Thank you for asking me, though."

"Okay," says Marcus. "I'll have to find someone else. I've only got two weeks until the departure date."

"You must know someone," says Alistair. "You know quite a few people."

"Yes, but nobody whose life is quite as fluid as mine. Some of my friends are married, working for big companies, or involved in some other way. Most of them don't even take two weeks' holiday. They are afraid that they will lose their place in the line."

"Go alone then," says Alistair. "It is a huge waste of money though because you have already paid for two. Will the student girl reimburse you?"

"No," says Marcus, smiling. "She has tattoos to pay for and a younger boyfriend to keep."

"I don't know why you bother with these young girls," says Alistair. "They are always so unsettled. Why can't you find somebody closer to your own age?"

"They are all married or divorced," answers Marcus, "and I don't know which is worse. I have lived an unconventional life and ended up outside the usual flow of society. I have missed all of the usual milestones."

"Okay, well," says Alistair, "a solution will present itself. It is not what you can call a real problem. Even if you didn't go at all it would not be a life-threatening disaster."

"I'll just go with the flow then," answers Marcus. "That is what people say, isn't it? Go with the flow and see what happens."

Oliver Gateskill arrives and once again he is accompanied by Kimberley, who is carrying files.

They all greet each other. Gateskill is missing his office and wants to get back to his telescope.

"Okay guys, what are we going to do?" asks Gateskill.

"Let us have lunch first," answers Alistair. "Then we can discuss it while we are in this pleasant restaurant looking at the beach."

"Yes, of course," says Gateskill. "I have to be back at my office within the hour. That should give us plenty of time and then Kimberley can stay here and make complete notes of all your requirements. Can you work within that timescale?"

"Of course we can," says Marcus. "Let us order some food and then while we wait for it we will tell you what we want to achieve."

"You won't wait long in an American restaurant," says Gateskill.

"That will be all right," says Alistair. "Our plans are simple and we do not need much variation. We know what we want to achieve."

The waitress arrives. A sort of breathless, excited-looking girl, with curly hair and sparkling eyes. She looks as if she has just heard a really funny joke.

"My name is Angie," she says, in a rhythmic singsong voice, "and I'll be your waitress today." She is carrying a large jug of water with many ice cubes floating in it. She deftly pours cold water into each of their glasses. "What would you all like to drink?"

"No alcohol today, thank you," says Alistair, "unless you would like some?" He looks at Gateskill.

"No, I'm fine," answers Gateskill.

"I'll have a freshly squeezed orange juice," says Kimberley, "no ice."

"I'll have the same," says Marcus, "orange juice whilst we are in Florida."

"Most of the orange juice here is frozen," says Gateskill. "I guess that is why Kimberley asked for freshly squeezed orange. She will know if it is not and she will send it back."

"Let's order some food," says Alistair.

"Chicken Caesar salad," says Gateskill.

"First of all, what would you like, Kimberley?" asks Alistair.

Kimberley looks at him for a moment, acknowledging his effort to emphasise that Gateskill did not wait for her. She knows, however, that Gateskill will not even notice Alistair's small courtesy. "I will have an avocado and spinach salad," says Kimberley, "no dressing."

"I'll have some fish," says Marcus. "Whatever is fresh today."

"I'll have the same," says Alistair. "Simply grilled with one green vegetable."

"Both of us," says Marcus.

They all hand the menus back to Angie, who looks delighted as if she is a four year old who has just been given a balloon. "Coming right up," she says and shimmers away.

The food arrives promptly and they eat slowly. Alistair starts to tell Gateskill exactly what he would like him to do and explains it step by step. Alistair is a lawyer who, when he sends a letter, has already composed the next three letters in his head. He tries very hard to impart this thinking to Gateskill whilst making it clear that neither Alistair nor Marcus are seeking Gateskill's advice but that they are directing him to carry out their strategy without variation.

Gateskill is not a man with an oversized ego. He does not mind that Alistair Bond wants to run the show. His only comments are to make it clear that Alistair and Marcus are not accepting Gateskill's legal opinion but that they are controlling events alone. Gateskill eats his Caesar salad quickly, showing that he is in a rush. Later Gateskill confirms in detail to Alistair in writing that Gateskill is following Alistair's instructions only. Gateskill's motive is to get himself and his legal firm 'off the hook' if Alistair's strategy fails.

In fact, after four weeks of exchanges, the strategy does not fail but succeeds absolutely. At this point Gateskill is pleased to take a full fee having enjoyed no liability and having done little legal work. He buys a bigger telescope.

Marcus stays out of the exchanges between Alistair and Gateskill, listening carefully to the precise exchange of words. Eventually Gateskill gets up from his restaurant chair. "I've got it," he says, "everything will be done as you describe. I will inform you of all responses and check with you for your replies. I have to go now. I'll see you before you leave. Thank you for lunch." He strides out of the restaurant quickly, leaving Kimberley behind. Gateskill has simply nodded to her to convey his wish that she should stay and write everything down. Kimberley has been writing everything down as the men have been speaking and she has it all clearly noted on her pad. She says nothing but starts to eat her healthy lunch, which she had left on her plate until after she had her comprehensive notes safely written in her notebook.

"I see that you have everything, Kimberley," says Alistair.

Kimberley looks a little shocked and mildly amused. It is difficult to read her expression. Momentarily she had thought that Alistair was commenting on her appearance, her body, but then she realised seconds later that he meant her work. "Yes," she says, without elaborating. She continues to eat her lunch, slowly chewing everything thoroughly. The food is vegetarian, raw and simple. She drinks her orange juice in sips.

Alistair and Marcus are finishing their fish and broccoli.

"Did you know that broccoli is an invented vegetable? Man made," says Alistair.

"Aren't they all?" says Marcus. "I mean all changed or refined, crossbred in some way since they were first discovered as a wild plant?"

"I suppose so," says Alistair. "I just know that broccoli was created recently. Late post-war."

"So if we had had broccoli pre-war then we could have defeated the Nazis more easily," says Marcus, smiling.

Alistair hesitates. He is a serious man and he knows it. He makes an effort to go along with the humour and teasing of Marcus's remark.

"Oh definitely," he says. "Broccoli would have cut two years off the British war effort."

"Only if the Nazis hadn't got it first," answers Marcus.

"My mother said it was rhubarb which won the war," says Alistair. "She didn't explain so I do not know now whether she meant speeches or fruit. I cannot ask her now. She died three years ago."

"We are a lucky generation," says Marcus, "not to have been obliged to live through a war or fight, lay down our lives for our country."

"My father said that most men in the 1939-1945 war did not find it hard to die in the conflict; whether they were brave or terrified it didn't matter either way when they were killed," says Alistair. "He said that it was the obligation to kill somebody which many of them found hard. Having to kill a man or men you did not know, men you had never met. That was the toughest threshold."

"Oh dear," says Marcus. "What do you think, Kimberley?"

"I have never thought about it, but now that you ask me I would guess that it could have been more difficult for the US forces. America was under no threat from Germany and Italy at all. No threat of invasion. So you could say that the US troops faced down reluctance to kill. That the US men were the bravest of all. The most courageous. Killing people they did not know and who were not threatening their family or their homes. They were fighting for the freedom of another set of countries. Another people. Fighting for the freedom of man. That would be what I think."

"Goodness me," says Marcus.

"It must have been a big step," said Alistair. "Even today only six percent of Americans have a passport and less than that number travel outside of the USA. It must have been very dramatic for the young men from America to cross the Atlantic in 1943."

"I suppose that they can ski on the snowy mountains of the north and sun themselves on the beaches of Hawaii and the south," says Marcus. "No need to leave their own country."

"Have you travelled, Kimberley?" asks Alastair.

"I travelled in the United States," answers Kimberley, "and I have travelled outside the United States as well."

"Europe?" asks Alastair.

"Not Europe," answers Kimberley. "Haiti and some parts of South America."

"That is impressive," exclaims Marcus, "was it dangerous?"

"It was dangerous if you allowed it to be dangerous," answers Kimberley. "If you drew attention to yourself or behaved carelessly. I did not find it dangerous. I went with a man. He was a tough guy. That can be dangerous. Trying to prove himself all the time to impress me."

"Was he your boyfriend?" asks Alastair.

"He was a guy I met," answers Kimberley. "Four of us were going and then at the last minute two of them dropped out. Fell in love," she says with a sarcastic lilt to her voice. She grimaced. "I had to go with the tough guy," she says. "I already paid for the ticket and gotten the time off work. So he and I travelled around Haiti and Venezuela and Costa Rica together. Tough guy got sick. I had to wait for him to get out of the hospital. Lost my part-time college job because I was late back."

"Why did you wait for him?" asks Alastair.

"I left with him so I had to come back with him," answers Kimberley. "That's the deal. Even if you don't like your travelling partner you gotta stick together."

"You didn't get sick?" asks Marcus.

"Careful about what I eat and drink," says Kimberley, "nothing that is not cooked right in front of you. No ice. Water from a bottle you have checked the seals of. No drugs. No funny smokes. I don't smoke anyway. Makes it easier."

"Did you enjoy it?" asks Alistair.

"Enjoy it more now than I did then," says Kimberley. "It was a rough trip. Bad accommodation. Cheap travel arrangements. All make for good memories afterwards, I guess."

"Marcus is going to India in two weeks," says Alastair, "but he is going first class. Comfortable hotels. Pre-arranged travel plans. He is going for seven weeks."

"You can't pre-arrange everything successfully," says Marcus. "You can pay for it but you cannot guarantee it."

"Why are you going?" asks Kimberley.

"I suppose the real reason is that I have never been there," answers Marcus. "India is a part of the British culture. The occupation of India affected the people who went there from England and then they changed things a little when they came home again. Habits acquired in India stayed with them. India became independent again in 1947 and then in the 1960s the Indians themselves started arriving in England. There are some strong opinions about it. I just want to go and see for myself. Previous visitors describe it as a unique experience, so I am going to take a look. I'm looking all over the country, south to north. West to east. All over the country."

"I'd go to India in a heartbeat," says Kimberley, "but I have to return to the office right now and get your wishes in order. You'll receive a call from us tomorrow. Thank you for the lunch. So long."

She gets up, nods at them both and walks out. Marcus notices that today she is wearing a different dress. Bright yellow. It contrasts attractively with her suntan.

"There is your travelling companion," says Alistair, "tough, independent and intelligent. And she just said that she wants to go to India."

"Hypothetically," says Marcus. "It was just a figure of speech. Agreeing with my wish to go. Anyway I don't know her at all. She could be looking after an old relative or involved in a complicated love affair or she could be a difficult personality. I know nothing about her."

"Except that she is a paralegal and a cheerleader and that she can roller-skate. We also know that she has travelled in difficult countries before and was loyal to her partner then," says Alistair.

"That's what she tells us," says Marcus. "We don't know the truth. Maybe she got sick and he stayed behind to look after her and then perhaps he lost his job by being late back. We don't know enough about her."

"You don't know a thing about half the girls who you take on holiday," says Alistair with a laugh, "and a lot of those turned out to be crazy or moody or demanding or just downright contrary. Of course most of them misunderstood why you had asked them in the first place. Why don't you advertise?"

"Advertise?" says Marcus. "What? Travelling companion to India? I might get a lot of British Indians replying because they want to visit relatives. Or a nutcase. I suppose at least I've met Kimberley and we have some point of reference with

Mr. Gateskill's legal firm. Okay, this is ridiculous. It would upset the whole business relationship if I were foolish enough to ask her. It would sound like a sexual proposition."

"Why do men like to take women away over long distances for sex?" says Alistair. "Much easier to do it at home."

"This is not about sex," says Marcus. "Let us not get sidetracked. I have a complete set of extra travel documents and tickets for a companion I do not now have. And we are talking about filling in the gap with a gymnastic legal assistant whom we have just met, plus the male conceit that we just have to ask her and she'll say yes. She has a job, remember, and a football team to support."

"I don't think that it is male conceit," answers Alistair. "I think she would say yes. There are your long eyelashes for one thing. And it is not the football season right now."

"She doesn't look like a girl who would care very much about eyelashes," says Marcus, "and they are not long. They are normal. Surely she has to rehearse or practise or whatever even if the football season is temporarily stopped?"

"It was just an idea," says Alistair. "Just as tenuous as a lot of your other endeavours. A cheerleader in India. Now there is a thought."

Marcus raises his hand to catch the attention of the waitress Angie and she comes skipping across to their table.

"Can I get you anything else?" she asks. "I have a delicious home-made key lime pie. Fresh today."

"Thank you. Nothing else for us today," says Marcus. "Just the bill, please."

"The bill?" answers Angie. "Okay, you mean the check. Sure thing. Coming right up." She skips away.

"Happy girl," says Alistair. "Hard work being a waitress but they get paid well."

·

27

"Do they get paid well?" asks Marcus. "I thought waitresses more or less got minimum wage."

"That is in the UK," says Alistair. "Here service businesses pay well. At least the customer pays well. In the United States it is customary to pay waiters and waitresses about one dollar per hour. They make the rest up on tips. The server, as they are called, works primarily for the customer. So if you hear a customer describe precisely how he wants his food cooked then the server tells the kitchen exactly that. If it isn't right you sometimes hear the server shouting at the kitchen staff, 'my customer doesn't want this. I cannot take it out to him. Do it again,' and so on. Making sure that the customer gets what he or she has ordered, and fast, means that the waiter or waitress can expect a tip of twenty percent on the cost of the meal. I would imagine that the smiling Angie earns eight hundred dollars per week here, maybe a thousand dollars. Enough for an apartment, a car and a good life in Florida."

"Well, well, well," says Marcus. "So I must leave a big tip?"

"The food will be cheap enough," says Alistair. "The tip just makes the price right."

"All right then," says Marcus, as Angie dances back to their table with 'the check'. Marcus pays with a credit card but then adds two fifty dollar bills for Angie.

"Thank you sir, see you again soon," she says, as she strolls away, storing up the tip in her moneybag.

Alistair and Marcus take a taxi, or a cab to use the US term, back to their hotel and Alistair goes up to his room to conclude the day's work. Marcus decides to go for a swim and then lie in the sunshine for an hour or two. He keeps thinking about his trip to India and Alistair's absurd suggestion that he should ask Kimberley to accompany him. Part of his irritation with Alistair's suggestion is the nagging realisation that he finds Kimberley physically attractive and he knows that that would be completely the wrong reason for inviting her. He intends to do nothing about his attraction towards Kimberley and nothing about Alistair's idea of asking her to come to India. "Stupid," says Marcus out loud, and startles an elderly couple that are walking slowly past him on the sand.

Marcus sits up and tries to think of something else. Images of the film 'Jaws' come into his mind as he gazes out across the sea, which is sparkling in the sunshine. Marcus shakes his head to clear his mind of the image and stands up to dress himself. Once ready, he strolls back along the sand and up onto the promenade. No roller-skaters there today. He reaches his hotel and goes inside. The receptionist hands him a note from Alistair. 'Kimberley has prepared all of the court papers and is bringing them here at four o'clock for you and I to check over,' says the note.

Well, that is pretty efficient, thinks Marcus, and asks the receptionist to ring Alistair's room.

"I'll meet you at the snack bar on the hotel terrace at ten minutes to four," he says. "Please tell Kimberley to meet us there."

"Will do," answers Alistair and he hangs up the telephone.

3
The Proposition

Alistair is already waiting at the hotel snack bar when Marcus arrives.

"Are you going to ask her?" says Alistair.

"She is a stranger," answers Marcus.

"All women are strangers," says Alistair, "at least to men anyway. You can be married to a woman for fifteen years and she can still surprise you."

"Are you speaking from personal experience?" asks Marcus. "You have been married for seventeen years."

"I married young," says Alistair. "I was Victoria's first boyfriend and I had little experience of girls myself. Too busy studying. We were both so new to the whole experience of mutual attraction that we married hastily. That is why it has worked out all right. We have no comparisons and neither of us want any comparisons. At least I hope not."

"But Victoria has still surprised you?" asks Marcus.

"I am not prepared to discuss it," answers Alistair, "mostly because I have not understood it myself yet, except that it is a good thing being pleasantly surprised by one's own wife. Yes, it is enjoyable. My point is that Kimberley may be as bad or as good as anybody else whom you could possibly invite at such short notice. Anybody could be a disaster or a bonus or neutral. At least Kimberley appears to be fit and strong and unlikely to weigh you down with ailments."

"I am not going to ask her," says Marcus. "Let us concentrate on finalising our few legal challenges here and then we can go home."

"All right," says Alistair, "here she comes."

Marcus watches Kimberley as she glides across the floor of the café. She is today wearing a maroon dress belted at the waist by a thin belt of the same material. She has wedge-soled sandals on her feet. She walks very smoothly, with all of the economy of movement that dancers and top athletes exhibit. Complete control.

Alistair greets her. "Good afternoon."

Both Marcus and Alistair rise from their chairs as she approaches. Marcus nods at her. He feels unaccountably wary of her after Alistair's recommendation of Kimberley as a travelling companion.

Kimberley sits at the table and starts to identify various legal documents to Alistair, explaining Gateskill's approach to the challenges and clarifying the strategy which Alistair had asked for.

"All of the moves will begin this week," confirms Kimberley, "and Mr Gateskill has asked me to assure you that I will be handling all of the work personally from now on. I'm on the case after today and will handle any new requests, of course."

"This all looks fine," says Alistair. "Please tell Mr Gateskill that I approve of all the proposed actions."

"What will you have to drink?" asks Marcus. Kimberley looks at him for a slightly extended moment.

"Tea," she says.

"Tea?" says Alistair. "That is not an American choice, surely?"

"Tea," says Kimberley again. "They have tea in India, don't they, Mr Field?" She looks again at Marcus.

"Yes, yes I suppose so," says Marcus. "What about you, Alistair?"

"I'll have coffee this afternoon," answers Alistair.

The snack bar waitress arrives. She is wearing a pink uniform dress, edged with inch wide white cotton. The skirt is short and the sleeves are just above the elbows. She is wearing white trainers.

Marcus orders two coffees and a pot of tea. The waitress trots away, swaying her hips provocatively at the two men.

"Have you decided on what to take to India?" asks Kimberley. "What luggage and equipment to take on your trip?"

"Well," says Marcus slowly.

"He hasn't got a travelling companion," says Alistair. "His friend let him down at the last minute. Now Marcus has nobody to go with."

Kimberley looks at Marcus carefully. "I don't really want to stand at the Taj Mahal and look at all of the other extraordinary spectacles all on my own," explains Marcus.

"There are millions of people in India," says Kimberley slowly.

"Yes, of course, but that makes it even more lonely," explains Marcus. "All of those busy people, rushing about attending to the daily tasks of their lives. No, it is much better if you have somebody with you to share the new experiences together and for their enthusiasm to reflect your own. Then you can enjoy it all."

"When do you plan to leave?" asks Kimberley.

"Well, I have tickets for two people," answers Marcus, "and the tickets are for flights leaving London in ten days' time. Now I am not sure what to do at all."

"Was your intended companion a man or a woman?" asks Kimberley.

"A girl," says Marcus, "but she has met a new boyfriend and now wants to stay in England with him."

"Did you want it to be a romantic trip? Romance between you and her?" asks Kimberley.

"Goodness no," answers Marcus. "She is a cheerful girl. Good fun to be with. I wanted to look at India and she wanted to come with me. So I booked everything. All of the cross-country travel arrangements and all of the hotels. It is already paid for and now I am facing the prospect of moving around India with an extra seat next to me and an empty hotel room in every place."

"Okay," says Kimberley. Looking at Marcus questioningly, "Mr Bond, would you give Mr Field here a good character reference?"

"Marcus, a character reference?" says Alistair. "Well certainly. He is a jolly good chap."

"I judge people according to whether I would want them in a lifeboat with me after the ship had sunk," says Kimberley. "Would they share for the good of everyone else? Would they do their part in rowing the boat or in bailing out? Would they help to collect fresh water? Would they be optimistic? The worse person you would want in your lifeboat is a screamer or a complainer or a doom person. We are all going to die type. How would you say that Mr Field would be in a lifeboat, Mr Bond?"

"Well, really," says Alistair. "This sounds like some sort of party game. Marcus would be a good man to have in your lifeboat, Kimberley, but I hope that none of us ever find ourselves in that kind of position. No, never. Mind you, I wouldn't let Marcus sing in your lifeboat to cheer people up.

No singing by Marcus. Other than that I know he would be all right."

"My singing is good," says Marcus.

"I don't think so," answers Alistair, smiling warmly at him.

"Okay then," says Kimberley. "I have an answer to your travelling problem, Mr Field. You can relax about it. I will come with you. I have some rules though."

"You have some rules?" says Alistair with astonishment.

"Yes. These are the rules," says Kimberley. "First of all I want a photograph of you and a copy of your passport. I will give them to my mother. Then if I get lost the American embassy will come looking for you. Second, the rule is that we have dinner together every night. That way we can keep a watch on each other. Make sure that we don't split up. So if you meet some little Indian girl, you are going to have to take her out for lunches. All of the dinners are mine. Thirdly, we come back together. Nobody gets left behind. Not even for a day. We travel out together and back together. Fourth rule. This is not a sex holiday. Not for you and not for me. This is an adventure holiday. Seeing the wonderful things that there are to see. No sex. Do you have any rules of your own?"

"Suggestions," says Marcus, who is overwhelmed by Kimberley's forcefulness and carried along by her momentum of speech. "Well, rules then, really. First of all bring two pairs of comfortable walking shoes. If you lose your shoes in India you won't be able to get another pair to fit you or at least not a pair which are any good. Don't bring a lot of clothes; we can buy them there. Secondly, bring your own first aid kit. In case you get sick. Thirdly, I need a photograph of you and a copy of your passport in case you get lost or disappear. I would need something to help me find you again. And fourthly, but this is not a rule. How are you able to get seven or eight weeks off work? And what about the football team?"

"I never said anything about a football team," says Kimberley. "I don't play football. Work, I'll just leave. I can get another job when I get back. I'm a little uncomfortable at Mr. Gateskill's office. No prospects for advancement."

"I see," says Marcus. He feels as if he has been bamboozled into something. At the same time he feels relieved. Now he has a travelling companion. God alone knows what she is going to be like but as Alistair has said she could be as bad or as good as anyone else. And the decision has been made for him. This is a new experience for him. He is usually in charge of everything he does. Just this minute he is not but it feels comfortable. "You have the answer to my travelling problem, Miss Judd," says Marcus. "Are we agreed on the rules?"

Kimberley puts her right hand out to shake Marcus's hand. "Sure," says Kimberley. "When do you want me to arrive in London? You are leaving from London, of course? I would like to get to London a couple of days before we fly to India and I will want somewhere to stay there for two nights."

Things are moving along very quickly, thinks Marcus, and he tries to regain control. "Alistair will get you return tickets to the UK," says Marcus. "You will have to let him have your copy passport first. Then in London you can stay in the Sloane Club in Chelsea. I will fix it up and I will meet your plane. Where can we get in touch with you here? We are leaving in two days. There is a lot to do."

"I will bring the copy passport to the hotel tonight," says Kimberley, "also my address and telephone number. I will leave it at reception for Mr Bond. Please leave your London address and phone number for me at reception and a copy of your passport. Then you can go home and start packing your two pairs of shoes. I will see you at the British airport in five or six days' time. Don't be late." Kimberley frowns at Marcus.

"Thank you, Miss Judd." Thank you, why am I thanking you? I am giving you a twelve thousand pound trip to India, thinks Marcus.

"Call me Kimberley," says Kimberley. "I don't want to go around India being called Miss Judd. Makes me sound like a secretary." She gets up and starts to walk away. She turns around. "Thank you, Mr Bond," she says to Alistair. "Be seeing you, Mr Field."

She walks quickly out of the café.

"She certainly knows how to close a deal," says Alistair. "Solved all your immediate problems. Your holiday problems at least. You should be so lucky."

"Lucky?" says Marcus. "I feel as if I have just been beaten up."

"You liked it," says Alistair. "She made the decision for you. Stopped you from dithering about. Now you know what you are going to do for the next eight weeks."

"Only in outline," says Marcus, "but you are right. I do feel better. In fact she has opened up the whole Indian trip to another dimension altogether. What will an American girl think of India? What will I learn from the American girl? The whole trip has just become much more exciting and I am glad that I didn't ask her. I would have messed it up. Made it sound like a proposal. Forced her to refuse. You are right. She has solved my holiday dilemma. Now I must suffer the consequences."

"Don't be a screamer," says Alistair, "a doom person. She has let you into her lifeboat on my recommendation, remember?"

"Don't worry," says Marcus. "I am looking forward to the whole thing. I am very happy. She is a smashing looking girl as well, isn't she? I wonder how old she is?"

"I will know tonight when I get a copy of her passport. I will tell you her age at breakfast. A smashing looking girl, eh? Would you be wanting to go with her if she was plain? And would she have had the rock solid confidence to invite herself if she were not a smashing looking cheerleader? Professionally displaying herself for the football fans. Assured of her own attraction. It is a no sex holiday as well, don't forget. No sex," laughs Alistair. "She certainly knows how to make herself attractive to you. Seven weeks in India with a no sex cheerleader. Day after day, night after night. Clever girl."

"Oh shut up," says Marcus. "It is a very sensible rule. I would have suggested it myself if she had not done so first."

"You couldn't have," says Alistair. "She is the girl. You could not have put forward such a rule without making it sound like a putdown. And insult. She could do it and she did it so swiftly that it didn't sound as if she had suggested or implied that there would be a sexual side to the trip. She just knocked it on the head. At the same time she has raised your interest a little bit more. Very experienced girl. I admire her. She could be much more than a paralegal. If she aimed for more, she could get it."

"Back to American aspirations again," says Marcus. "Come on, let's get out of here. I'll pay the bill, I mean the check!"

As they walk out of the hotel snack bar Marcus says, "I don't think that she was trying to raise my interest; she was just making everything clear at the start."

Alistair smiles. "It is your eyelashes, you know."

"Oh shut up," says Marcus, and they walk outside onto the beach promenade and look at the glittering sea in front of them.

Six roller-skaters whiz past them. Two men and four girls. All dressed for the sun. All fit and young and apparently carefree.

"Remember that Kimberley has never told us that she is a cheerleader," says Alistair. "We got that from Gateskill. So you don't know until she tells you."

"You know what they say here?" asks Marcus. Alistair glances at him. "Welcome to Paradise."

4
London

Six days later Marcus is waiting at the arrivals gate at Gatwick airport. The electronic displays tell him that Kimberley's plane has landed. He feels oddly apprehensive that she might not be on the plane. Of course she is on the plane you idiot, thinks Marcus, don't put yourself into the wrong frame of mind. Be positive. Act cool. Girls fly in from the USA for you every week. Pull yourself together.

Groups of people start arriving. Voices are raised as friends and relatives greet each other across the barriers.

Kimberley walks through on her own. She is dressed for a safari. Long white shorts and a pale blue shirt jacket with four big pockets, all with button-down flaps. Hiking boots. White ankle socks. Tanned, slim, muscular legs. She looks fierce. She stares straight ahead. She does not look around to find Marcus, she simply walks straight out.

Marcus finds himself walking quickly after her. "Kimberley," he says loudly. She stops. Turns completely around. "Welcome to England," says Marcus.

"Thank you," answers Kimberley. She is carrying a small leather holdall with external pockets and zips. The zips are locked with small brass padlocks.

"How was your flight? Are you tired?" asks Marcus, smiling because he is pleased to see her.

"Flights are always tiring," says Kimberley. "They turn down the oxygen in the passenger cabins to make the people docile. That makes the passengers tired. I will be fine as soon as I get some fresh air."

They walk through the huge airport towards the short stay car park. Marcus is carrying Kimberley's leather bag. He stops at the ticket machine to pay for the exit and then he leads Kimberley to his car. It is a steel grey Bristol car. Rather old-fashioned looking but beautiful coach-built bodywork and equipment. He opens the door for Kimberley to get in. "Is this your grandfather's car?" she asks, smiling.

"This is an English hand-made special car," answers Marcus. "This is a new car." Then he laughs, "Okay, it is a bit unusual but don't worry, it should get us into London." He turns a key in the ignition and then presses the start button. The big engine ripples into life. They begin their journey into the west side of London.

"We will check into the Sloane Club together and then if you want to you can have a sleep."

"I won't sleep until tonight," answers Kimberley. "I have to get my body clock right. Today I will stay awake. I would like to take a little walk around London. I have never been here before."

"All right," says Marcus. "We will get our rooms sorted out and then take a walk."

"Does the sky always look like this?" asks Kimberley. "It is like being inside of a grey plastic bag. It is not a dark sky but it is not a blue sky either. There is no sun to see, just a grey plastic cover."

"It does look like this often," answers Marcus. "It might be what drove the British to sail all over the world conquering

40

other countries, looking for blue skies. Grey plastic skies are responsible for the British Empire."

"Okay," says Kimberley. She settles into the comfortable leather seats of Marcus's car and closes her eyes. Marcus notices that she has done this and drives carefully. A lot of traffic makes the journey longer than it should be and throughout Kimberley sleeps. Eventually they arrive in Sloane Street, the very southern end of the street. There are two parking meters and one of them is free. Marcus parks quickly. Later he will arrange to move his car into the parking which the Sloane Club have arranged with the Chelsea barracks. Now he has stopped close to the doors of the club to save Kimberley from having to walk. Marcus gets out and puts some coins in the meter before walking to the passenger window and knocking gently on the glass.

"Okay," says Kimberley. "I'm awake. I was dreaming of blue skies." She sits up straight. "Where are we?" she asks. "Is this the place where we have rooms?" She looks at the long rows of the sash windows covered from the inside by opaque muslin cloth so that pedestrians cannot look in. The main walls of the building are six feet back from the pavement. There are black iron railings and a basement accessed by a small stone set of steps behind a locked iron gate. Kimberley and Marcus walk the few yards to the double black painted doors of the club. They walk inside. Kimberley's safari outfit is out of place. Marcus is more formally dressed with a dark blue blazer, grey trousers and black shoes. He is wearing a tie. Marcus deals with the necessary formalities at the club reception counter and then walks Kimberley to the lift.

"We are on their third floor," he says. "Quiet when you want to sleep."

The rooms are next door to each other and Marcus hands Kimberley the key to her door. "I will meet you downstairs in the club sitting room," he says and walks away.

Downstairs he makes arrangements for the parking of his car and drives it the half-mile or so to its secure space, off the road, and then he walks back to the club.

Plastic bag skies, he thinks and smiles, she is right.

Back inside the club Kimberley has found the sitting room. She is wearing an elegant dark blue woollen dress. The stretchy material makes onlookers aware of her body. She is also wearing smart dark blue shoes with slight heels. She looks expensive and exotic. Her blonde hair is brushed and it falls down her back.

She looks young and comfortable. There are no lines on her face. Her eyes are healthy and sparkling. London, she thinks, well, London first and then India. I want to get a really cool hat to wear in India. I wonder where I can get one.

Marcus walks in. Her appearance surprises and pleases him.

"Marcus, where can I buy a really cool hat?" asks Kimberley. "I want a really great hat to wear in India. Something light. Straw, with a big brim. That is, as long as India doesn't have grey plastic skies like here!"

"I am sure it doesn't," answers Marcus. "A hat. Well we will go to a hat shop. We will take a taxi, then you can look around."

The hat shop is in Mayfair. The shop assistant is imperious, grey haired; she wears an iron-grey suit and stands very erect.

"We are going to India," says Kimberley, "and I need a really cool hat."

"Yes madam," says the woman. "Please come this way."

Fifteen minutes later Kimberley emerges wearing a wide-brimmed straw hat with a dark blue ribbon. "I'll take it," she says.

"You'll have to wear it or carry it all the time," says Marcus. "It won't fit into your bag."

"It will fit into this tube," says the shop assistant. "It is made of the finest quality Ecuadorian toquilla straw and it rolls up. Here, I'll show you." She deftly rolls the hat and slides it into the tube. "There," she says, "and when you get it out it will be as good as new."

Later, both Marcus and Kimberley are standing on the pavement holding a bag which contains a hat rolled into a tube.

"A country with grey skies sells hats like these," says Kimberley.

"Hats for all over the world," answers Marcus. "It must be a leftover from the days of the Empire. Still selling the equipment for different climates. Provided of course that you are prepared to pay for them."

"You bet," says Kimberley. "I could almost buy a second-hand car in Florida for the price of my hat, but I love it."

"What now?" asks Marcus.

"I'm not so warm in this dress," answers Kimberley. "I need something to put over it, but not at the same price as the hat."

"All right," says Marcus, "off we go again – Peter Jones."

"Peter Jones?" says Kimberley. "Is that like a shopping mall?"

"You'll see," says Marcus, hailing a taxi. "We can get you a coat there and you can leave it in my car when we park at the airport hotel. Then you can put it back on again when we get back from India."

43

"Okay," says Kimberley. "So this is the capital city of the little country which created the greatest trading empire the world has ever seen. It all started here. Is that right?"

"Ended here too," says Marcus. "You'll see some of it when we get to India. After we get your coat I'll take you to tea at Fortnum and Masons."

"How did you know about the great British trading empire around the world?" asks Marcus whilst they are sitting at a table at Fortnum and Masons' top floor café, waiting for the tea to be brought.

"I've been reading up about it," answers Kimberley. "I wanted to know about the English India connection before I went there."

"What did you find out?" asks Marcus.

"You English were a greedy lot," says Kimberley. "Sailing into places and, because you had superior weaponry, you went ashore and took whatever you wanted."

"I think it was a bit more complicated than that," says Marcus.

"Oh sure. There was a lot of very clever mind games played by the British to establish themselves," said Kimberley, "and they were very good at it. Confidence, I think it was. They were sure that they were superior. Confidence like that gives people a lot of strength and impresses others."

"I don't know whether the British are very confident now," says Marcus, "or for that matter, who the British really are today. Our history seems to play no part in our everyday lives."

"Not today," says Kimberley. "Today we are preparing for an adventure. I have my hat for India and I have my Peter Jones coat for cold England. Now I am having an afternoon tea. I am having a great time."

"I'm pleased," says Marcus. "Now we have tomorrow to look around and visit whatever you would like to see. The following day we are flying to India and the plane leaves early in the morning. So tomorrow night we will have to go to bed early. Tonight we could go out for dinner. What would you like?"

"Something typically English," says Kimberley.

"All right, I will try to get us a table at Rules," says Marcus.

"British Rule you say?" replies Kimberley.

"No. Not that," answers Marcus. "It is a restaurant which serves game."

"Game?" says Kimberley. "Sounds sexy."

"I mean birds," says Marcus. "Pheasant, partridge, grouse, that sort of thing. Also venison and wild boar. It is English. It is no good my taking you to an Italian or Chinese restaurant or many others because you have them all in the States. I'm trying to think of something, which you can only get here. I'll try to get a table."

"Okay," says Kimberley.

"It is the right time of the year for game," says Marcus.

"I guess so," says Kimberley, and smiles.

That evening they both arrive at Rules in a black taxi. Kimberley is wearing her simple Peter Jones overcoat and a scarf, both of which Marcus had paid for in a mood of generosity. Marcus is wearing a dark blue suit underneath a Crombie overcoat. They enter the restaurant and the cloakroom attendant takes their coats. Under her coat Kimberley is wearing a short, low-cut black dress with spaghetti straps at the shoulders. With her shiny blonde hair, honey skin and healthy glow, she looks magnificent. Marcus tries not to show his surprise as he walks behind her when they are led to their table by the maître d'. She has a fantastic body, he thinks.

They are shown to their table, which has banquette seating. A semi-circular red velvet sofa behind an elaborately laid table with a snow-white linen tablecloth.

"You look wonderful tonight," says Marcus to Kimberley.

"Thank you," she says. "You look very handsome, and the restaurant is magic."

"What would you like to drink?" asks Marcus.

"This is an English evening, okay," says Kimberley. "Grey plastic skies and a magic restaurant. What should I have to drink? This is my night off before we start our adventure."

"Champagne?" says Marcus.

"That is a bit of a cliché, isn't it?" says Kimberley. "Think of something else."

"Puligny-Montrachet please," says Marcus to the wine waiter.

"What year would you prefer, sir?" asks the man.

They haggle for a little whilst Kimberley gazes around the restaurant. This is the real thing, she thinks, this is two hundred years older than any restaurant back home. Has a kind of wise feel to it. Like it's seen everything. And Marcus looks good here. More English looking here in London. An old-fashioned angular look to his face like those movie stars in the pre-war British black and white films you would watch on the movie channel. Wide shoulders. Thick hair. She looks around again. We are the best looking couple here, she thinks, I like that.

"What have you ordered, Marcus?" asks Kimberley. "And what if I don't like it?"

"We are about to embark on a journey around India, Kimberley. I have ordered a French white wine. Strong flavoured but special. It may be a good aperitif to your meal. If

46

you don't like it, don't drink it," answers Marcus. "I have chosen it because it is special."

"Thank you," says Kimberley. "Decide on everything, please. This is your town and this is your great-grandfather's favourite restaurant. You decide. Except, please, no oysters."

"You don't like oysters?" asks Marcus.

"Oh yes I do," answers Kimberley, "but I don't want to take the risk the day before our flight."

"Very sensible," says Marcus. "I will order for us both."

The wine arrives. Marcus approves it and a glass is poured for Kimberley. "Oh boy," she says when she has tasted it. "Special." She does not say whether she likes it or hates it, she just smiles. "Go ahead," she says. "I'll try whatever is specially English."

The menu arrives; Kimberley leaves hers closed on the table in front of her whilst Marcus makes his choices carefully.

"I'm ordering dishes that you probably won't get so often at home," he says, "and also some things which are particularly old English taste. If you don't like anything then please don't eat it to be polite."

"I won't be polite, Marcus," answers Kimberley "but I do want to try new things, no old English poisons, please."

"The poisons are on a separate menu," says Marcus. "They give those menus to couples who are going through nasty and painful divorces."

"This is a forward thinking country then," says Kimberley.

"Only in some things," answers Marcus. "I have ordered a red wine to go with the main course. Like the Montrachet, it is fairly strong but I think that you will find it a softer flavour. I do advise that you drink only a glass or so of each wine to save me from having to carry you home. I'm introducing you to the combination of flavours. The wines, of course, are French, which is what the English prefer."

"I'm abandoning myself to you as my guide," says Kimberley. "Can we have some water as well?"

"I have already ordered Malvern water," says Marcus. "It is the clean water that the Queen drinks. Don't put it in your wine, please."

"Please," says Kimberley. "I am allowing you to guide me through your English customs. Hats made from toquilla Ecuadorian straw and coats made of cashmere. Now hard tasting white wine like smooth Greek retsina, to be followed by a poor little roasted bird. I am enjoying the experience, Mr Field, I mean Marcus, and now I get to drink the same water as the Queen. It is a classy first evening, Marcus. Do you think that you can keep it up?"

"I am going to do a lot better than this," says Marcus. "Give yourself up to it. It can only get better."

"What a seducer you are, Marcus," says Kimberley.

The food arrives. Kimberley eats sparingly of each course and drinks a glass of each of the wines. "You ordered whole bottles," she says.

"You get better wine in whole bottles," answers Marcus. "In fact you get the very best wine in very big bottles and the lesser flavour into progressively smaller bottles. The French vineyards put the best wines into the bigger bottles."

Kimberley pretends to fall asleep, then jolts and sits up. "Have you stopped talking now?" she asks. "There is nothing very specially English about mashed potatoes. I can get that at home."

"I had to make sure that there was something that you could eat," says Marcus. "Mashed potatoes and water."

They both had a small glass of Muscat Beaumes de Venise with their desserts.

Kimberley proclaims the meal to have been "outstanding."

"Now carry me home," she says.

Marcus consciously avoids allowing his eyes to flicker over her breasts, which are defined perfectly against the black silk of her dress. He looks directly into her eyes whilst thinking, I would love to carry you home and peel off your dress and kiss you from head to toe. Pull yourself together, he thinks. Discipline. We are travelling companions. That is all.

"Not tonight," he says to Kimberley and she picks up a little of the telepathy of his thoughts. "We can walk a little. We are close to the centre of Covent Garden market. It will give you the chance to see where we are. Tomorrow I'll take you to Portobello Road because it is Saturday and there will be a street market there."

"Have you thought about setting up a business called Marcus Tours of London?" asks Kimberley.

They collect their coats. Marcus helps Kimberley into her coat, admiring the skin of her neck whilst he does so. They walk outside and saunter along towards the centre of Covent Garden.

"So this used to be a vegetable market?" asks Kimberley.

"Yes, that's right," says Marcus. "It was a wholesale vegetable market. Vegetables from England, from the professional growers. We call them market gardeners. Then the shopkeepers called greengrocers would come here early in the morning and buy what they wanted to sell in their little shops all over London."

"And now it's a shopping mall," says Kimberley. "Where do the little shops get their vegetables now?"

"There is a place called 'New Covent Garden' now," says Marcus, "a little way out of town, a big new warehouse building. The other thing which has changed, is that most of the small greengrocers' shops have closed down. Now people buy their vegetables from supermarkets and the vegetables come from all over the world, sometimes from places where the local people haven't got enough to eat. The vegetables are often days old, whereas here, in the old Covent Garden, the vegetables had been growing only hours before they were sold. Growing in British soil, eaten by British people."

"Sounds like a bad change," says Kimberley.

"Money," says Marcus. "Everything is justified because of profit. These clothing shops and the others here pay big rents, much more than a wholesale vegetable seller could pay, and the supermarkets have ninety percent of vegetable sales now, so little the men are all gone. What you have now are street performers and classical music recitals downstairs. It all looks spontaneous, but it is the result of an audition process and careful screening by the 'authorities'. They decide on the music and they decide on the street performances. So what you see is pre-arranged. Censored if you like. Certainly controlled. A vegetable market here would be closed down anyway today. Health and safety would not approve of the handcarts, great sacks of root vegetables. Everything rolling around on these stones. No, London is now antiseptic. Controlled. Legalised. Except for the homeless people living on the streets. They are invisible. They do not exist because they do not have an address. Without an address the local authority have no responsibility for them and do not have to count them."

"Holy cow," says Kimberley, "you make it all sound like a corporate horror movie. Lighten up, Marcus."

"It is a corporate takeover," answers Marcus. "Look at all of these shops. All multiples. Some of them multinationals. Owned by shareholders, run by corporate management unanswerable to anybody and the profits they make do not get spent in London, they do not even stay in the country. They

50

are moved around the globe for favourable tax arrangements. And most of the stuff they sell comes from all over the world. Mostly Far East. Lots of it is made by children earning fifty dollars a month. Not British clothing makers. It is economic progress. A lot of British people's hobby is shopping for things that they will never need."

"Shall I pick up a wooden box for you to stand on?" says Kimberley. "Come on Marcus. Don't be a revolutionary or you will have to go and live in Cuba. Okay, so people go shopping now instead of having world wars. Maybe that makes us a lucky generation. I just got a hat and a new coat, better than an incendiary bomb. Hold my arm, Marcus. Let us live for today. Try to be happy."

"I am happy," says Marcus. "I apologise for raving about the inevitable greed and impatience."

"Okay, that is enough, Marcus. I have had a wonderful dinner, with strange new wines and I got to wear my little cocktail dress. Thank you, Marcus. Now shut up or I will have to break a shop window as a protest, and I will say that you told me to do it."

"Strange wines?" says Marcus.

"The white wine was like a strong flavour and the red wine dried out my mouth," answers Kimberley, "but I am pleased to have had the experience. California wine will taste better from now on."

"I am glad to have helped," says Marcus. "Look, there is a taxi with his yellow light on. Let's go back and go to bed. I will be more fun tomorrow."

"You have been fun today," says Kimberley. "It was refreshing to hear you explaining things to me like I didn't know. Like I didn't grow up with them. There is always someone who wants to own everything. Make your own world and live in it. That's what my dad says. Ever since the

51

Pharaohs, the Greeks, the Romans and Adolf Hitler people have always wanted to own everything. They can't. They are going to die, that's why. You know that the North American Indians could not understand how the invading white man thought that he could own land? Just laugh and dance and be happy. We are here for a good time not here for a long time. I'll race you to the cab."

Slipping her shoes off into one hand she races across the pavement, pausing only to give a piercing whistle to stop the taxi. Marcus is running behind but she is faster.

They get into the taxi.

"Sloane Street, please," says Marcus, "the southern end of Sloane Street."

"You have to get fitter, Marcus," Kimberley punches him on the arm. "Exercise stops you from thinking. That's why all those soldiers are kept fit. Then they can run into danger without thinking," she laughs.

"You slipped out in front before I was ready," said Marcus. "I was catching you up."

"No, you ate every course of your dinner. You were weighed down with food and that caused nostalgia. Very heavy, Marcus. Hey, what is that over there?" Kimberley points to Buckingham Palace.

"That is where the Queen lives," says Marcus.

"I wouldn't want to clean all of those windows," says Kimberley, "with all of the traffic going by and messing them all up every day. Do we get to see her? The Queen. Does she come out and wave or anything?"

"The American Embassy has asked her to come out and wave for you," says Marcus, "but she has made her own world and is living in it."

"Some world," says Kimberley. "I've heard that she doesn't have a passport, so for all we know there could be three or four Queens travelling around the world. Taking turns."

"We will never know," answers Marcus. "Look, we have arrived."

5
Skipping

The next morning Marcus is up early. He showers, shaves, dresses and goes downstairs.

The receptionist says his name, "Mr. Field. The manager would like to speak to you, sir. May I tell him that you are here?"

"Certainly," says Marcus, who is a little surprised.

The manager is a tall slender man with beautifully coiffed grey hair. He is wearing a black frock coat and grey and black striped trousers. He has a grey dove tie.

"Mr. Field. Good morning, sir. Do you have a moment, sir?"

"Certainly," says Marcus, wondering whether he has forgotten to pay his membership fees.

The manager ushers Marcus into a small but luxuriously appointed office behind the reception desk.

"It is your guest, sir."

"My guest?" says Marcus.

"Yes, sir. Miss Judd. We believe that she is making something in her room, perhaps with a hammer. There has been a tap, tap, tap noise from her room for the last forty minutes, sir. The guest in the room below has complained, sir. It would be helpful, sir, if you were to ask her to stop."

Marcus is startled. What can she be doing?

"Of course, I will do my best," says Marcus.

"Sir, what I mean is that she must stop."

"Yes," says Marcus. "Excuse me."

He leaves the little office and travels upstairs in the lift. Outside Kimberley's room he hesitates. He really doesn't want to disturb her. He steels himself and knocks on the door. He can hear a definite tapping noise. He knocks again.

"One minute," calls Kimberley. She opens the door wearing one of the club's white dressing gowns. On the bed is a skipping rope. "Marcus," she says, "what's up?"

"Please excuse me," says Marcus. "The club manager told me that another guest had reported a tapping noise from your room. He, ah, asked me to ask you, if it was you."

"You couldn't kill your husband in this club could you?" says Kimberley. "Another guest would hear you. Come in." She pulls Marcus by the sleeve. He walks in reluctantly. "I've been skipping," says Kimberley. "I skip every morning for half an hour or sometimes forty minutes. I was travelling yesterday and missed my routine. So I'm doing it now."

"In your room?" says Marcus.

"Well, I sure as hell wasn't going to do it out on the sidewalk. Not in my underwear and not under grey plastic English skies. Do they have a gym here? I can do it there." She smiles. "Has the other guest survived or died of shock?" She smiles again. "I had to skip for forty minutes this morning to get over the depression I had thinking about all of that world capitalism bullshit you told me last night. It worried me for as long as four or five minutes, but I am all better now. Are you here to take me to breakfast? Give me fifteen minutes. I'll meet you downstairs. Tell the club manager that you smashed me to death with a chair to stop the tapping." She smiles delightedly and goes into the bathroom.

Marcus leaves the room and walks downstairs, wondering what to tell the manager. He smiles. I don't think I'll tell him that I've smashed her to death, he thinks. He smiles again. She must be fit, he thinks. Forty minutes is a very long time to skip. So is thirty minutes. He doubts whether he could skip continuously for ten or fifteen minutes, and the club manager reported a tap, tap, tap noise. He, Marcus, heard a tapping noise. She must be light on her feet. Gateskill said she was a cheerleader. So how fit does a cheerleader have to be? Marcus doesn't really know. He has only seen them jumping about for two minutes on the TV but they form human pyramids as well, I think. That doesn't take forty minutes of jumping. Maybe she is a nut about it. All of that roller-skating with a stopwatch.

The club manager is standing in the reception area looking stern. Marcus speaks to him. "Mr. Waverley, my guest was mending one of the legs or feet on the bed in her room. Somehow it had broken, so she was hammering it back on with her shoe."

"She should have called reception," said Waverley. "Maintenance would have attended."

Marcus steps closer to Waverley and lowers his voice. "The thing is, Mr. Waverley, she is embarrassed and did not want me to find out about it, in case I had somehow booked her into an inferior place. A place where things were broken. I believe that she was shy about that. A complete misunderstanding, of course. You and I both know what a splendid club this is but as my guest she was embarrassed, you see?"

Mr. Waverley pursed his lips. "So that is the explanation, Mr. Field," he said.

Marcus was not convinced that Waverley believed the explanation. At that moment Kimberley arrived.

"Miss Judd," Waverley says. "I regret to hear about the leg, Miss Judd, but I understand from Mr. Field that you managed to remedy it."

"Sure did," says Kimberley, "both legs. Come on, Marcus, breakfast."

She pulls Marcus away and they both walk towards the club restaurant, which is laid for breakfast. They are shown to a table.

"What was all that about my leg?" asks Kimberley, and when Marcus explained she breaks into laughter. "So if I want to skip tomorrow morning, I'll have to say that the other two legs broke. If we were staying here a week I'd have to smash up the whole room. Now you've got yourself into trouble, Marcus, you could have just told him that I was skipping, right?"

"I suppose so," said Marcus, "but he may not have liked that."

"Like it or not it would have been the truth," says Kimberley. "Now we have to make a couple of bed legs loose to back up your story. You're turning me into an accessory to the crime, Marcus, and I am a paralegal. What kind of a trip are we going to have? 'Billy Liar's tour of India'?"

"Look, Kimberley, I did not," starts Marcus.

Kimberley interrupts him harshly. "Marcus," she says, "I am enjoying it."

The breakfast waiter appears at their table. Marcus is usually in control of his life. Authoritative and confident. Mildly amused by some other people's clumsiness. Marcus sees himself as a 'cool guy', but Kimberley flusters him. She treats him as mildly amusing and she does not recognise that he has any authority at all. Of course, Marcus knows that he has made himself sound like a geek by continually explaining things in a boring way. That has got to stop, thinks Marcus. No more history stories.

6
Portobello Road

Later Marcus and Kimberley are at the northern end of Portobello Road.

"What's the deal, Marcus?" Kimberley asks.

"We walk down the road and look at things and buy things if we want to," answers Marcus. "It is a Saturday market selling everything."

"Okay," says Kimberley, "no multinational problems here then?"

"Oh, shut up," says Marcus pleasantly.

"What is that?" asks Kimberley.

"That is a pith helmet."

"Did you say what I thought you said?" says Kimberley.

"P.I.T.H. A pith helmet," says Marcus. "They were worn in hot countries by the British army one hundred years ago."

"I gotta have one," says Kimberley. "Are they heavy? Could I wear it when I'm roller-skating? What do you think?"

"It looks big to me," says Marcus. "A big size. Try it on."

Kimberley steps up to the military cast off stall and picks up the pith helmet. She puts it on and it comes right down over her head until it is resting on her nose. She pulls it off again.

"Couldn't see any blue skies with that thing on," she says. "Thank you, sir," she calls to the stallholder.

"I can let you have a German army helmet," he says.

"No thank you, sir. Too hot for me," answers Kimberley.

"Nothing here is hot," retorts the man. "It is all kosher."

"Thank you," says Marcus as he guides Kimberley further up the road.

There are second-hand stalls selling jewellery, watches, fur coats, hats of all descriptions, all kinds of different clothing. Vintage dresses and coats, feather boas, leather riding boots, pre-war dancing shoes. Ancient long length gloves and interspersed with all this are modern things. Souvenirs from TV shows, t-shirts with characters from the Simpsons on them. Charlie Brown and Peanuts t-shirts. Mirrors with mottos engraved onto them. Heaps and heaps of goods for sale. Kimberley is delighted and stops to look and pore over almost everything, laughing now and again.

"Do you think that the Queen gets her people to throw some of her old stuff out and then it ends up here?" she asks Marcus.

Marcus has decided at breakfast not to be boring.

"She has her own stall here in the very early morning," answers Marcus. "She is usually here from seven a.m. until eight thirty a.m. Then she goes back to the Palace for breakfast."

"Get out of here," shouts Kimberley.

"No really, if you hadn't lingered over breakfast, we would have seen her horses and carriage," says Marcus with a deadpan expression.

"Shut up," says Kimberley. "I believe you just like the club manager believed you this morning."

"I may never be able to stay at the club again," says Marcus.

"Why are we staying there anyway?" asks Kimberley. "You have your own place in London, don't you?"

"It has only one bed," says Marcus. "A very big bed, but only the one."

"Okay," says Kimberley. "Then we just have to go on fooling the club manager."

"You could do stretching exercises," says Marcus.

"I do those as well," says Kimberley, "but I need aerobic exercise every day."

"You'll have to do it at the airport tomorrow," says Marcus. "We are catching an early flight."

"Well, that's fine," answers Kimberley. "Everything is a little crazy at airports. Nobody will notice me."

"I'm going to buy this old tweed flat cap," says Marcus, picking it up. "It's a bargain at a pound and then I can use it to collect money from all of the people who will crowd around to watch you skipping at six thirty a.m. in the departure lounge."

"I'll dress for the crowd," Kimberley answers, "but we get to split the money, right?"

She never backs down, thinks Marcus. "This should interest you, Kimberley," he says. "Snowshoes."

"And what in the hell do I want with snowshoes?" cries Kimberley. "I live in Florida."

Marcus walks on without answering until he stops at a stall selling china. Kimberley is standing next to him. "Do you have a left-handed moustache cup?" asks Marcus.

"A what?" says Kimberley.

"The man will show you," answers Marcus, wishing to avoid playing the boring schoolteacher role again.

"If madam will observe," says the stallholder. "A fine bone china teacup with a ribbon of china crossing the cup over a third of the opening with space between."

"What for?" asks Kimberley.

"When English gentlemen had moustaches they could drink their tea without getting their moustache wet. Alas, all of

61

these examples are for right-handed tea drinkers. Your friend, he was asking for a rare left-handed moustache cup, which regrettably I do not have."

"Darnation," says Kimberley.

"Come along," says Marcus. "There is a stall here selling old roller-skates and roller-skating boots. It also sells ice skates and ice-skating boots which were used for dancing on ice."

"Another thing I can't do in Florida," says Kimberley. "We got no ice. Look, here is a place selling dolls' furniture but I think that is not right."

Kimberley is looking at glass cases which contain miniature scissors, penknives and miniature purses. None of these things are more than one inch long and many are less than that.

"Come on, Marcus. What is all this junk?" asks Kimberley.

"Why do I have to explain everything to you?" asks Marcus. "Makes me into a schoolteacher. I don't like it."

"You do it too, Marcus, because this is your country," says Kimberley, "and it seems like everything here is from some long time before. You do know everything, Marcus. You are so clever."

"So when we leave this country I don't have to explain anything," says Marcus. "In fact you will then have to tell me all about the USA. What a homecoming queen is and the prom and all those things."

"That's a deal," says Kimberley and puts up her hand to slap Marcus's hand. "Now what are all these little things?"

"They are travellers' samples," says Marcus. "The manufacturers who made knives and scissors and shears and other things. Probably manufacturers from Sheffield in the north of England. They didn't send out catalogues in those days, they sent salesmen who visited all of the little hardware shops in towns in England and showed them these miniature samples of what their company made. Then they took purchase orders. Then the manufacturers sent the real full size stuff to the shops after they had received the orders. Wholesale selling. Of course that has all gone now."

"How do you know all this stuff, Marcus? Are you making it all up?" Kimberley asks, "Because they are great stories."

"Of course I'm not making it up. My father was an auctioneer," says Marcus. "Specialised in antiques. Mainly porcelain and glass and silver. What you call portable stuff. So over the years of my childhood I couldn't help but remember some of it."

"Okay, but it's yesterday right?" says Kimberley, "and this whole Portobello Road is yesterday."

"Most of Europe is locked into yesterday," answers Marcus.

"We don't care about yesterday in the USA," says Kimberley. "We care about tomorrow."

"Tomorrow you are going to give a skipping exhibition at the airport to collect spending money for our trip," says Marcus. "I suspect that India might look much older than England does. I hope you will be all right with that."

"I'll be okay," says Kimberley. "What is this thing?"

She points to what looks like a glass ornament.

"One more schoolmaster lesson," says Marcus, "and then I'm going on strike. That thing is a lacemaker's lamp. A glass bowl with a wide hole in the top, all on a long tall glass stand. The lacemaker lit a candle inside the glass bowl and then held the lace the other side of the bowl while he worked. This circular shape acted as a magnifying glass and made the work easier to do."

"Jiminy Cricket," says Kimberley, "and that's all gone as well."

"It is still here today," says Marcus.

"Yeah but just so somebody can put it in their house as a dust collector and then bore all their friends with it," says Kimberley.

"It is true that it is only worth money now because so many of them have been smashed or thrown away. So now the ones which are left sell for more money," says Marcus.

"Okay, so what's next?" asks Kimberley. "And why did you bring me to a museum anyway?"

"I thought you'd like it," answers Marcus.

"Okay, so I do like it," says Kimberley.

Kimberley is wearing white jeans, blue trainers and a blue pullover. She looks lean and fit and she shuffles and dances on her feet as she moves along. Some of the younger stallholders look admiringly at her as she passes.

"My father could walk the length of this road, buy things and sell them again and make enough money to buy lunch," said Marcus.

"How did he do that?" asks Kimberley.

"Because most of the stallholders don't have any real training about what they are selling. They buy goods somewhere and add a profit and sell them again. If there is something really special then often they don't know. My father would buy and then further on he would explain to a well-to-do stallholder what he had and sell it to him for more money. He just did it casually, simply because he knew so much. He could also tell you that over fifty percent of the stuff was fake. Certainly in the furniture."

"Why the furniture, Marcus?"

"No, I am on strike," says Marcus. "You're going to start seeing me as a tedious old scholar and I am not that. So the lessons are finished."

"Meanie," says Kimberley, and laughs.

"Hurry up," says Marcus. "If we get up to the top of the street the market changes into food stuff."

"Food stuff? Okay, great," says Kimberley.

They walk further on towards Notting Hill and after some time they arrive in a thriving food market selling plantains, yams, pawpaw fruit, kiwis and star fruit as well as coconuts, pineapples and other exotic produce.

"Oh boy," says Kimberley. "Do they give out free samples? What do I have to pay for it?"

"You have to pay," says Marcus. "These people have to earn a living."

They stroll about separately between the stalls, Kimberley engaging the West Indian stallholders in friendly banter whilst Marcus looks on from a distance.

"I want to buy everything," says Kimberley. "I'd love to have a coconut but when am I going to eat it? On the plane?"

"We could buy a monkey nut," says Marcus, "and then you could look at it through the glass of the lacemaker's lamp and maybe it would look like a coconut."

"Stupid," says Kimberley, and punches him on the arm. "What are we going to do now? Are you going to feed me or give me a coffee at least? I have to keep my energy up, you know."

"Coffee," says Marcus. "Do you want to go on the tube or on a London bus?"

"What the hell is a tube?" asks Kimberley. "A London bus for sure, but I want to sit upstairs. A red bus? Yes."

"We will have to walk a little way," says Marcus. "Out of this market towards the road where the bus stop is."

"I can walk," says Kimberley.

They make their way through the market until they get to the bus stop, where they stand with three other people waiting for a bus.

"We want the West End," says Marcus to the people waiting.

"You need a number forty-two then," says a lady with a shopping trolley. "Should be the second bus along here."

"Thank you," says Marcus.

"Here is the bus Kimberley," says Marcus, "Tell him we want to get off at Park Lane, near the Hilton Hotel."

"Sure," says Kimberley. "You going to get me coffee in the Hilton, Marcus?"

"No," says Marcus. "We are going to a different place."

The bus pulls up after the first bus has left and Kimberley and Marcus climb up the small curved stairs to the top floor.

"Let us sit at the front," says Kimberley, who notices that the front seats are empty.

"All right, but you are not to stamp on the driver's head," says Marcus.

"What?" says Kimberley, "the driver is right underneath us?"

"Of course he is," says Marcus, "so don't stamp your feet or he may have an accident."

"He will be used to people on his head," says Kimberley. "Where are we now? What is that over there?"

Marcus explains the sites as they pass them and Kimberley enjoys everything like a child on a birthday outing. Eventually they arrive in Park Lane and the bus stops. They get out.

Kimberley says, "There is a huge park over the road. I saw it from the bus."

"That is called Hyde Park," says Marcus.

"Like Dr. Jekyll and Mr. Hyde?" asks Kimberley.

"I suppose so," says Marcus.

"Well, how do people get across the road to the park?" asks Kimberley.

"There is an underpass," answers Marcus, "a pedestrian tunnel under the road from one side to the other. I know a funny story about it, too."

"Tell me a funny story, Marcus," says Kimberley.

"Once I had an office around here and there is an enormous car park underneath the park."

"Underneath all these trees?" says Kimberley.

"It is deep enough to miss the tree roots," says Marcus. "Anyway we used to leave our cars there and walk through the underpass every day."

"Okay," says Kimberley.

"And the underpass had a couple of people down there busking," says Marcus.

"Busking?" asks Kimberley.

"Entertaining people for money," says Marcus, "playing a guitar or a violin or something with a hat on the ground for people to throw money into. One day there was a man with a saxophone and his music was very good."

"Yes," says Kimberley.

"So my friend decides to make a tape recording of the saxophone player. He does and after that he plays the tape to his friends. Well, one of his friends works in the music business and says that he thinks the playing is so good that maybe a record could be made. You know, a CD. So my friend asks him how much money could be made and the man from the recording studio tells him at least £50,000. So that night my friend rushes back to the underpass and looks for the saxophone player. He could not find him. So he asks the guitar player who is at the other end of the tunnel. 'He gave up and went home,' says the guitar player. 'Where is home?' says my friend. 'I don't know, I think Humberside or somewhere like that. The man is a welder normally,' says the guitar player. 'A welder?' says my friend, 'he could have made £50,000 as a saxophone player'."

"I don't think that's a funny story," says Kimberley. "I think that is a tragedy."

"Life is a comedy or a tragedy," says Marcus.

"Not my life," says Kimberley. "My life is an adventure. An expedition. An exploration of happiness. Where are we going now?"

They walk past the Hilton Hotel into Hertford Street and from there they walk until they are in Shepherd Market.

"Wow, this is cute," says Kimberley.

"Prostitutes work from here," says Marcus.

He doesn't know why he said that; perhaps to damp down Kimberley's puppyish enthusiasm for everything. He likes her enthusiasm though, so he has made another mistake. Said the wrong thing.

"You gonna get a prostitute, Marcus?" says Kimberley, smiling mischievously. "I did not guess you were feeling like that. Can I get a coffee whilst you are busy?"

She smiles delightedly as a statuesque curvaceous black girl in a tight leather skirt insinuates her body unnecessarily close to Marcus as she slides past.

"Course you may not take long enough for me to drink a coffee," says Kimberley, and skips away laughing as Marcus takes a threatening step towards her with his fist raised.

"You really oughta work that kind of aggression off, Marcus." Kimberley is laughing now. "That girl would help you. No...," she cries as Marcus starts to chase her down the little street. He catches her by the shoulders and turns her around.

"Coffee," says Marcus. "We are having coffee in Richoux's in South Audley Street. This way please, Miss America."

They walk away from Shepherd Market past Curzon Cinema, past Crockfords Casino until they reach the southern end of South Audley Street.

"Are you okay?" asks Marcus.

"Okay with what?" asks Kimberley.

"All of this walking," answers Marcus.

"I thought we were walking all over India," says Kimberley. "I brought my walking legs with me. The Mark III luxury legs. They are working just fine. Want to run?"

"It is undignified to run in the West End," says Marcus.

"You just did it in Prostitutes Market," says Kimberley. "I thought it was undignified when you did it, but I thought you just felt horny."

"Coffee, Kimberley," says Marcus.

"That will be lovely, Marcus," says Kimberley.

They are walking past extravagant shops now and on the other side of the road is a gun shop.

"Shall we get a couple of guns, Marcus?" asks Kimberley.

"What for?" asks Marcus.

"We could go into Jekyll and Hyde Park and shoot deer," answers Kimberley.

"We are getting on a plane first thing in the morning, Kimberley. We will not have time to eat a deer."

"We could give it to your friend at the club, Marcus," says Kimberley. "Make peace with him."

"Coffee, Kimberley," says Marcus.

"Yes, Marcus," says Kimberley, and gives him a Girl Guide salute.

They have arrived at Richoux's and Marcus opens the door for Kimberley to walk inside.

A scene of artificially created Edwardian splendour greets them, but it is splendour on a small scale. Banquette seating in dark green leather around the walls, and small tables and small chairs arranged in the centre of the room. There is a glass counter at the entrance forming a chicane so that customers must wait to be seated by the staff. The glass counter displays chocolates. As they are led into the room by a Thai waitress they walk past a table laden with exotic-looking cakes. The high ceiling of the small room has three glittering chandeliers hanging from it. The whole place is cool from air conditioning. They are seated on one of the banquettes and menus are handed to them immediately.

"This is a crowded country, Marcus," says Kimberley, "everything close together and everything small. It is very rich in here but it is also kinda small. When I was flying in over England every patch of it looks like somebody owned it and was tending to it regularly. A patchwork of ownership. Cold with grey skies but the Brits have made the place so that everybody wants to live here. How can that be?"

"I really don't know," says Marcus. "Houses cost a fortune here. Tiny flats cost a fortune."

"Flats?" says Kimberley. "You mean like a flat tyre?"

"It is the English word for apartments," says Marcus. "Apartments here are amongst the most expensive in Europe and for that matter everything else is expensive as well and yet hundreds of thousands of new people are arriving here every year."

"You've got sea all around you," says Kimberley. "Why don't you stop 'em from getting here? Give yourselves a bit of space to breathe?"

"I don't know, Kimberley," says Marcus. "The more people there are here the more people to pay taxes to keep the Queen in five palaces and to keep all the hangers-on who get paid to do very little and have huge pensions at the end of it. It is all politics. The more different all of the people are, the less everyone looks at how the politicians are spending our money. No matter how many people are here, we never seem to have enough money to pay for the public services. Libraries without enough books, parks with no flowers or public toilets, fire brigades who don't want to put out fires, policemen who don't walk the streets anymore, hospitals which are too small to serve the people they are built for, schools which are too small for all of the children. Prisons which are primitive, barbaric and which house more prisoners in each cell than they were designed for one hundred and fifty years ago. And all of the time more and more people getting overpaid to administer all of the public services which are being reduced."

"Hell Marcus, you are getting into one of your negative trances again," says Kimberley. "I think you should go and live somewhere else. You could be a lumberjack in Canada. You have the shoulders for it and Canada has plenty of room."

"They won't let us in," answers Marcus. "None of the big countries with lots of space will let us in. Australia, New Zealand, Canada, USA, all of these places have shut their borders so all of the hordes have come here."

"I think you need a cake, Marcus. Maybe you should have been a customer in Prostitute Market. You need something to lift you up, Marcus, or you are going to be a heavy weight to carry all around India."

"I'm not going to be a heavy weight. I don't want to be thrown out of your lifeboat, Kimberley," says Marcus. "It is just that you keep asking me questions and I would like to say that it is a wonderful democratic fair and free country but regrettably I no longer believe that it is and I wish that it was. Look at Abba, the successful Swedish group who earned more money than Volvo. They stayed in Sweden, paid all of their taxes because they said that they loved their country."

"Perhaps they were idiots," says Kimberley brightly. "What are we going to have here, Marcus?"

"You wanted coffee, didn't you?" answers Marcus. "Would you like something to eat, a cake or something?"

"What the hell is a Welsh Rarebit?" asks Kimberley, looking at the menu.

"It is cheese on toast all toasted together with a poached egg on top," answers Marcus.

"Boy, that will fill a person up," says Kimberley. "No, I don't want to eat, thank you."

Marcus orders the coffee, which arrives in two little cafetieres.

"That is sweet," says Kimberley.

"Child size coffee jugs. There are two little child size jugs of milk as well."

"When we have drunk our coffee is there any place or thing which you would like to see here, Kimberley?"

"I'm thinking about that, Marcus," answers Kimberley. "How about that museum where they have the complete skeleton of a dinosaur or a trip up the river or a look at Chelsea?"

"What about all three?" says Marcus. "We can take a trip down the river to Greenwich where we can have a light lunch. Then we come back and go and see the dinosaur, then get a taxi to the World's End."

"Whoa there, Marcus," says Kimberley. "The World's End?"

"It is what they call the end of the Kings Road," says Marcus. "We can start from there and walk up the Kings Road, Chelsea until we get to Sloane Square at the top. That is where we bought your coat yesterday. You've got your Mark III walking legs with you, don't forget."

Kimberley smiles at the mention of her Mark III legs.

"Great attitude, Marcus," she says. "Given three choices you choose all three. I like that. You are cheering up, Marcus, shaking off all of that negative Britishness. I'm glad to hear it. There is a lot to see in the Kings Road, is there?" she says, smiling.

"There is always a lot to see in London. It is a matter of taste whether you find it interesting or not. There are colourful people to see in the Kings Road and when we get to Sloane Square we are only one hundred yards from the club."

"Are we really going back there, Marcus? Ooh, you are brave. We could smuggle our things out and sleep in your flat apartment."

"It is either called a flat or an apartment," says Marcus pedantically.

"I'm taking your new bright attitude, Marcus. I'm choosing both," says Kimberley. "I'm going to look at those chocolates."

Marcus drinks his coffee and looks around the café. A lot of Arab ladies are here today, he thinks. Kimberley comes back.

"No chocolates?" asks Marcus.

"I was looking," says Kimberley, "not buying or tasting."

Kimberley drinks her coffee. "Not that awful," she says. "Strong flavour. Guess that is why they don't give you refills."

"Are you ready?" says Marcus. "I'll pay on the way out."

"I already paid," says Kimberley. "You have to save your money in case I break another bed."

She walks out onto the pavement, whistles loudly and stops a cruising taxi. "Hurry up, Marcus," she says, as she gets in.

Marcus and Kimberley have a delightful last day in London. They take a riverboat to Greenwich and Kimberley gazes at all the buildings they pass by. She is particularly impressed by David Lean's house off Narrow Street in the East End. The vehicle and pedestrian entrance is concealed behind a big solid metal gate painted rust colour whilst the river view has lawns running down to the river, behind which is an extraordinary large Georgian house. Kimberley remarks on how many bridges there are across the Thames.

"People can't make up their minds, I guess," she says. "Just keep on crossing back and forth. We don't have that many in New York."

At Greenwich they look at the Cutty Sark, the fastest tea clipper in its time.

"You guys sure wanted your tea quick," Kimberley says. "Pretty boat. It would be kinda cool to have it in Florida. Float around the beaches."

They have lunch in a colourful vegetarian restaurant with plants on every conceivable surface. Kimberley eats a big lunch. Afterwards they take a boat back to the Houses of Parliament and then take a taxi to the Natural History Museum. Kimberley stares at the dinosaur skeleton for a very long time.

"I'm thinking about him or her," she says. "Wondering if he had a good life. You know, whether he was happy living all that time ago. Makes you feel kind of small thinking that he is maybe from a time like two million years ago. Doesn't seem like it's worth saving up for anything. May as well just do it all now."

"You could be buried with your roller-skating boots on," says Marcus. "Then if you were discovered in two million years' time they might have a fine puzzle writing about how people used to go about on wheels."

"Shut up," says Kimberley, smiling at him. "I don't want to see anything else here, Marcus. Do you mind? I only wanted to see the dinosaur."

"It is your day," says Marcus. "Now we are going to the World's End."

"I can tell my friends I've been to the World's End," says Kimberley, "tell them that it was scary but that I was brave."

"There is an old lady who lives in local authority housing there. Well, at least in a flat, not a house. She was once responsible for bringing down the government in 1963."

"Wow," says Kimberley, "like Monica Lewinsky."

"Monica Lewinsky embarrassed a president," says Marcus. "This woman caused a government crisis."

"Go on. Tell me," says Kimberley. "What was her name?"

"Christine Keeler," answers Marcus. "She was having an affair with the minister for war in the British government and she was also having a liaison with a Russian diplomat at the same time. It was interpreted as a scandal. The assumption was that she was telling the Russian national defence secrets which the minister for war was telling her."

"Was that true?" asked Kimberley.

"It is as difficult to see the truth now as it was then," answers Marcus. "The girl was a simple relatively uneducated girl who liked a good time. She was also physically attractive. She was probably completely innocent. The main problem was that the minister told a big lie to parliament. He said that he had never met the girl. Once he had told that lie everything began to escalate. I think that the British public enjoyed it all at the time, reading about the rich and privileged being naughty with the pretty girls. Anyhow the point is that the pretty girl, who is now old, lives here in the World's End. She never made any success out of her fame. She just faded away."

"I never heard that story," says Kimberley. "I guess it was a British scandal. Back home in 1963 everyone was bothered about race riots and Kennedy getting shot. Nothing like the good fun of a pretty girl and a couple of guys on opposite sides."

"There was another man as well," says Marcus. "A black man, who got jealous and shot a gun at the house where the girl was living."

"She attracted a lot of men," says Kimberley. "Jealous Othello types and important government guys. Do you think that she got a good time out of it?"

"I don't think so," says Marcus. "I would say that all of the men used her and she got nothing out of it at all. I think that she went to prison for a short time."

"What happened to the government man? Did he go to jail as well?"

"No," says Marcus. "He resigned from the government and devoted himself to working with the poor in the east side of London."

"Oh boy," said Kimberley. "I bet that annoyed the hell out of the poor. Being ignored all the time and then suddenly being useful to some rich guy who wanted to make himself look good for a while. He used the poor as a smokescreen to conceal the fact that he was a bad man."

"Yes," said Marcus thoughtfully, "and the girl went to prison."

"And now she lives at the World's End," says Kimberley. "This is my last London treat for today. Walking up the Kings Road. Let's go."

They stroll along together and Kimberley examines everything. She stops at Christopher Wray's lighting shop.

"Can we go in?" she asks Marcus.

"Of course," he replies.

Kimberley looks at all of the different lamps and shades and brass fittings and spot lighting.

"Okay," she says to Marcus and they walk out again and go further up the road. Kimberley looks over to the other side. "That looks like an old United States filling station," she says, pointing at the Bluebird Café.

"That is exactly what it was," says Marcus, "at least it was a 1930s English garage.

"What is it now?" says Kimberley.

"A café restaurant," says Marcus. "A café on the ground floor and a restaurant upstairs. It used to be a Saturday morning gathering place for classic American cars when it was still a garage. Owners of the cars used to meet up there and then drive down the Kings Road in a procession."

"That's cool," says Kimberley. "They do that in a lot of towns back home."

Kimberley is looking in all of the dress shops and the shoe shops. "Expensive here," she exclaims.

"You can buy a lot of the same stuff in the East End from market stalls," says Marcus, "but you don't get a super paper bag with handles and the name of the shop written all over it."

"I don't want to buy anything," says Kimberley. "I am window-shopping."

"Leche-vitrines," says Marcus.

"What?" says Kimberley.

"That is what the French call window-shopping," answers Marcus. "Licking the window is what it means."

"The French," says Kimberley. "Holy cow!"

"Talking about the French," says Marcus, "there is a little French restaurant on the other side of the road called Thierry's. The food there is actually quite delicious."

"Did you say actually, Marcus?" asks Kimberley. "I had heard that the Brits use that word for emphasis, but I didn't believe it. Ectuelly." She emphasised the letters as 'E's.

Marcus looks at her. "Holy cow," he says.

Kimberley slips her arm through his. "Walk me further, Marcus," she says.

"You are my official London walker. You know that rich ladies in New York have their New York walkers to go out with. You are my London walker."

"All right," says Marcus. "A few hundred yards from here there is a house which Dickens used to visit to see a friend of his. It is called Carlyle's House. The house is in the same condition and with the same furniture that it was in 1834 when Dickens used to visit. There is no electric light and no modern plumbing. Like a little museum. Do you want to see it?"

"Why not?" answers Kimberley. "Let's go find it."

They walk quite a long way to Carlyle's House, which is on Cheyne Row. They come upon a flat-fronted Georgian terraced house with sash windows and a rather plain panelled front door painted black. There is a sign fixed to the wall at the side of the front door showing opening times for the house. They go inside. Immediately it seems to be very quiet. The house is absolutely full of furniture, rugs, pictures and ornaments on every surface. There are also a lot of books on shelves.

"They sure had a lot of stuff," says Kimberley.

"Most Victorian households seem to have had a lot of clutter," says Marcus. "I suppose that they had servants to clean and dust everything. They had open coal fires as well so there could have been an amount of coal dust everywhere."

Kimberley is walking around looking at everything. "Are we allowed to go upstairs?" she asks.

"Of course," says Marcus, "but you might find the house manager in bed with someone," he smiles.

"Get out!" says Kimberley. "I'm going upstairs."

She is very curious about how people had lived in the house. She looks at the small beds and the ornamental clutter in the rooms and the elaborate curtains and lace. Marcus is downstairs looking at Carlyle's desk and the pens and paper on top.

Kimberley comes downstairs. "We are in the centre of a busy city," she says. "I wonder why it is so quiet in here?"

"Do you feel that the place is haunted?" asks Marcus. "I don't mean in any active or malevolent way, just gently haunted in its atmosphere from the people who lived here before."

"Nothing has been changed," says Kimberley. "That might make you think that you have stepped back in time. Through a door in time."

"A friend of mine went to Alaska," says Marcus. "She said that she missed the feeling of a human history there. She felt that she was in a place where nobody had lived before. Here in Europe people have lived everywhere before. Many generations have been here before us and in some towns in England and, of course, in Europe it goes back two thousand years to the Romans."

"That is a lot of ghosts," says Kimberley, "if you believe in ghosts. From what you say even when we burst out of this house into sunshine we are still in a city full of the spirits and influences of all of the people who have lived here before. We cannot escape. Can we run off somewhere, Marcus?"

"We can go tomorrow," says Marcus, "but you still have one night left here. What do you want to do, remembering that we have to get up early in the morning?"

"Marcus, I have one great dress left which I haven't worn here yet," says Kimberley. "I brought three dresses and I've worn two of them. I want to go somewhere especially English so that I can wear my third dress and knock 'em all out."

"Can you dance?" asks Marcus.

"Can I dance? Oh boy," says Kimberley.

"I see," says Marcus cautiously. "I will take you for cocktails in the Savoy and then, if I can get a table, I'll take you dancing in a nightclub called Tramp."

"Tramp?" says Kimberley. "Is that an insult, Marcus?"

"It is a London club," answers Marcus. "It would be an authentic tourist experience for you and you could show them your dress. We can also get supper there. The restaurant is very good."

"Okay, Marcus," says Kimberley. "I want to go there now."

Marcus is wondering about Kimberley's dress.

"Let's go back now," says Kimberley, "and leave this dusty stuffed haunted house."

They walk outside into the sunshine and begin to stroll home. Kimberley starts to spring along in sort of dance steps.

"Keep up, Marcus," she says. "I am losing my last day."

Marcus smiles and quickens his pace. He is a very fit man but he is not going to start running down the street. He doesn't have to because Kimberley keeps dancing back to him and then away again, keeping in reach of him all the time. She stops suddenly.

"I feel better now," she says. "Boy, that house was a downer, Marcus."

"I'm sorry," says Marcus.

"Don't be sorry," answers Kimberley. "It was an experience."

They are nearing the Sloane Club now.

"Sir Laurence Olivier used to live in that house there," says Marcus.

"Who is Sir Laurence Olivier?" asks Kimberley.

"He was an actor," says Marcus.

They walk into the end of Sloane Street and make their way towards the club.

"What time shall we go out?" asks Kimberley. "I have to get ready."

"If we are going to have cocktails first, and we have to get over to that side of London, then let's meet in reception at seven o'clock. Does that give you enough time?"

Marcus is erotically wondering whether Kimberley has to oil her body to slip into her dress and he cannot imagine why his mind is running in this direction.

"That's fine," says Kimberley. "I'll meet you here."

She bounds off up the stairs leaving Marcus to take the lift. Once inside his room he calls the reception desk, using the telephone next to his bed, and asks them to have a taxi waiting outside at seven o'clock.

"Certainly, Mr Field," says the receptionist.

7
A Night to Remember

Kimberley and Marcus meet in reception. Kimberley is wearing a dark red wine-coloured dress which fits her closely. The back of the dress is made of one inch wide ribbons of the same material which is crisscrossed over her otherwise bare smooth suntanned back. The dress is about two inches above the knee. Kimberley is carrying her warm overcoat.

Marcus cannot decide whether the good dress makes Kimberley's body look superb or whether Kimberley's superb body makes the dress look good. He decides that it is the latter. He feels a kind of envy inside him and he doesn't know why.

"You are beautiful," he says to Kimberley, without thinking about it first.

"I know," says Kimberley. "I am lucky, aren't I? Thank you for telling me."

"I am proud to be your companion for the evening," says Marcus, who is wearing a charcoal grey suit with a faint chalk stripe, a brilliant white shirt and a dark blue tie. He has polished black shoes on his feet. Marcus does not intend to take any of this clothing to India. He will leave it behind in the boot of his car.

"A taxi is waiting for us," says Marcus.

"Thank you kind, sir," says Kimberley. "I am very proud to be your guest tonight, Marcus," says Kimberley graciously, and smiles at him. "You look handsome."

"I know. I am lucky, but thank you for telling me."

"It is not luck for men or women," says Kimberley. "It is the work that you put into keeping yourself fit. You know how little children run about everywhere and flap their arms and skip? Well, they grow up and they get trained out of it. Brainwashed into sitting still and not moving around. So they get a little more flesh on them every year and they get a little more stiff and unable to move as easily as they did when they were little. Adulthood is combined with dignity and unfitness. You Marcus, look good. You must move around more than most people." She puts her warm coat on.

"Yes," says Marcus. "When I am alone I run around and flap my arms a lot and skip. It is why I look so cool today."

"Okay," says Kimberley. "I believe you and it is a very clear explanation."

Marcus opens the taxi door for Kimberley and asks the driver to take them to The Savoy. The driver pulls away from the pavement. As they enter the short road which leads exclusively to The Savoy Hotel, Kimberley shouts to the taxi driver, "You are on the wrong side of the road!"

The driver tells her, "This is the only road in London which you enter on the right-hand side and leave on the right-hand side."

"Why?" asks Kimberley.

"I don't know, Miss," answers the driver, as he stops outside the hotel doors.

A doorman dressed in livery steps forward and opens the door. "Good evening, madam, sir," he says, as he helps Kimberley out of the back seat of the taxi and then notices Marcus following. Marcus pays the taxi driver and tips the hotel doorman. They walk inside. Marcus leads the way up a soft tread staircase on the left and along a passageway to what is called the American bar. Inside there is a piano on the left side of the room with a black piano player seated at the keyboard. He is playing ragtime music softly. A waiter greets them and takes Kimberley's coat from her shoulders. She emerges tanned, lithe, fit, tall and exceptionally beautiful. This causes the waiter to lead them to one of the best tables in the room.

Kimberley is delighted by the room. It sparkles with the art deco decoration marquetry and lighting. It looks rich and comfortable.

"What may I get you, sir?" asks the waiter.

Marcus looks at Kimberley. "I'm gonna get a Blue Lagoon," she says.

"It will match your eyes," says Marcus.

"Oh sir, you do say the darnedest things," says Kimberley, in an exaggerated Texan accent. She looks at the waiter. "Maybe he is angling for a favour later in the night."

She slowly winks her eye at the waiter, who acts as if she has said nothing and done nothing.

"I will have a champagne cocktail, please," says Marcus, "to give me courage for later." He grimaces at the waiter who still acts as if nothing untoward has been said or done.

"Yes sir, madam," the waiter says, and walks towards the bar.

The piano player starts to play 'The way you look tonight', singing softly in a very deep voice.

"Marcus," says Kimberley, "thank you."

"The evening is not over yet," says Marcus.

"Okay," says Kimberley.

The waiter walks towards them carrying a tray. He places their drinks on paper napkins on the very small table in front of them together with two little bowls of mixed nuts and olives. He pivots and walks away.

"Didn't give me a chance," says Kimberley.

"A chance for what?" asks Marcus, but he already knows the answer.

"A chance to surprise him with another dumb remark," says Kimberley, "and another wink of the eye."

"He is on his guard against you now," says Marcus. "Now. It is your turn to start explaining things about the United States to me."

"I am not working now, Marcus," says Kimberley. "I am off duty now. I have my off duty dress on. And you said that you wanted to ask me all of those things in India. We are not in India yet."

They sip their cocktails and watch as the bar starts to fill up. Customers are dressed well and all seem relaxed and happy. The piano player starts to play a different tune to which he does not yet sing. Kimberley feels privileged to be in such a grand place; such a different style to Florida, which is an out of doors place, whereas London is cold and grey and it is an indoors sort of place. She is enjoying the luxury of the surroundings. She is also feeling more relaxed about Marcus as a travelling companion. Only a few days ago she had never even met him, and when she first came to London he was a bit shy and formal. He seems to have lightened up a lot, thinks Kimberley. I had not expected to like him. A stiff Brit, but I could like him if I wanted to now. I have become more used to his manner and he is a very warm person underneath the Englishness. Now she is accompanying him on an extraordinary trip. Marcus is obviously more relaxed with her now. Kimberley recognises that Marcus has assumed the responsibility of being a guide and a host to her in London. She has never been here before but she knows enough to know

85

that the London which Marcus has, and is, still, introducing her to, is the first-class part of the town. She feels warm and spoilt. She glances at Marcus, who is sitting calmly looking at the new people arriving in the bar. Kimberley acknowledges to herself again that Marcus is a physically attractive man. He is obviously at home in this environment and everywhere he has taken her for the last two days and nights has been the best of what is available. Kimberley wonders if Marcus lives like this all the time or whether he is just making this effort for her. A person couldn't live like this all of the time, thinks Kimberley. He is doing his best to give me a good time here. I must do my best to be a good travelling companion for him in India. It certainly won't be as luxurious as it is here. She turns towards Marcus.

"Are we taking a tent with us to India, Marcus?" she asks him in a sweet little girl voice. "If we are you will look after me, won't you?" She exaggeratedly flutters her eyelashes at him like a silent movie star.

Marcus grins at her. "You know that we are travelling across the country," he says, "and that everywhere we will be staying in the best hotels which I have been able to arrange. It is a hot, dusty, overpopulated country and so I intend that we shall at least have clean and comfortable rooms to sleep and be able to make a recovery from our daily adventures."

Kimberley is pleased to hear this again. She recalls Marcus's lawyer Alistair Bond describing the arrangements which Marcus has made for the India trip, and Kimberley admits to herself that the efforts made to provide comfort in India had been largely responsible for her inviting herself. I am looking forward to it, she thinks, and smiles to herself.

"We have booked a table at Tramp for nine thirty," says Marcus. "It is across town, we will get a taxi. Would you like another drink or shall we go?"

"Let's go," says Kimberley, and gets up.

The piano player, who is still playing softly, says in a deep carrying voice, "Coats, coats," and the waiter nods at the piano player and fetches Kimberley's warm overcoat. He holds it for her to put on. Marcus and Kimberley leave the Savoy.

"I am wearing my dancing legs tonight, Marcus," says Kimberley.

"Cocktails and dancing?" asks Marcus. "Will you be able to get up early in the morning?"

"We will be fine in the morning," says Kimberley.

They walk along side by side. They make an impact on some passers-by because they look very well together. Kimberley feels very confident tonight. She knows that Marcus admires her looks and it pleases her. They hail a taxi and get in.

When they arrive in Jermyn Street in the West End of London the taxi drops them outside the nightclub door, which is a fairly anonymous entrance. A tramp is sitting on the pavement outside. He appears to be wearing a lot of clothes. He certainly has two overcoats on and big nailed ankle boots. He is also wearing a Manchester United football scarf. He has an unkempt grey beard and matted hair.

Kimberley looks at him with interest.

"Is this the entrance to Tramp?" she asks.

The tramp replies, "This is my nightclub, miss. Welcome."

Marcus gives him a five pound note. Marcus and Kimberley walk through the door to the reception area. A pretty girl is sitting behind the desk.

"Mr. Field," she says, "we have not seen you here for a long time. Your guest's name is?"

She smiles at Kimberley, who confirms her name and is given a one night pass, dated and stamped. Marcus and

Kimberley walk downstairs to the lounge area. The dance floor of the club is adjacent. They are greeted by a pretty hostess wearing a modest party dress. She speaks as if she has known them well for years.

"We have a table free against the far wall," she says confidently. "It has a view of the dance floor."

Marcus thanks her and he and Kimberley sit down. Kimberley, as usual, looks all around the room. She sees a well-known pop star at a table close by. The star, who is certainly in his late forties, is sitting with a very young and curvaceous girl, who is wearing a small dress made from shiny material which looks as if it has been sewn onto her body. The girl has a sulky, sexy look and listens to the pop star as if he is a fount of all wisdom. Crossing and re-crossing her bare fake-tanned legs, she is managing to hitch her short dress higher up her thighs.

Holy cow, thinks Kimberley.

At the well-stocked bar on the other side of the large room a middle aged man, who appears to have the same hairstyle which he would have had at twelve years old, and who is wearing a tweed suit with a yellow waistcoat, is flipping a huge wad of fifty pound notes from one hand to the other whilst talking seriously to one of the happy hostesses. The hostess looks to Kimberley as if she is making a positive effort not to pick up the message which the man is trying to convey to her. She smiles brightly at the man and then abruptly walks away. Kimberley stares at the man; idiot, she thinks.

There are young people on the dance floor and there are couples at tables in the room who appear to be utterly absorbed in each other's company. One young man and woman are holding hands so intently that it seems to Kimberley as if they could be alone in the room. There is a table where four men are having a serious conversation. They all look dark and angry. There is a table of six girls who are dressed for an evening out and are all laughing uproariously together. Other groups of friends are laughing and gossiping merrily. The room is exceptionally well-appointed and luxuriously furnished.

Marcus gets up and turns towards Kimberley. "Miss Judd?" he says.

"I'd love to," says Kimberley.

Marcus takes off his suit coat and his tie and leaves them on the chair. He undoes his top shirt button.

They move onto the dance floor. Marcus swings Kimberley around on the dance floor and she matches him step for step. She allows him, in fact encourages him, to lead in the dances and she intuitively follows him without hesitation or error. She is a real team player, thinks Marcus, as he whirls her around the floor. She dances on her toes and is extremely light on her feet.

He is quite masterful, thinks Kimberley with amusement, and he moves extravagantly and confidently in the dances. He is certainly a very fit and fluid man.

Both of them were pleased with the partnership. Neither of them wanted to leave the dance floor. They were oblivious to the other dancers who stepped the floor politely and in a disciplined and controlled style.

Holding Kimberley's hand, Marcus stepped off the dance floor onto the carpet of the lounge area and asked one of the hostesses to enquire if the man controlling the music could please find some rock'n' roll from the USA in the 1950s. "We want to dance to it," Marcus tells her, pressing a twenty pound note into her hand.

"I will try, sir," she says, "but we don't get much call for it. What do you want?"

"We want real music," says Marcus, "so that we can swing and dance the Lindy Hop and Jitterbug."

She hurries away. Marcus stands with Kimberley, smiling. Neither of them shows the slightest sign of exertion. They are breathing softly and they stand together.

There is suddenly a change in the music coming through the speakers. The clever soundproofing of the dance area muffles the volume of the music but as Kimberley and Marcus move onto the dance floor the sound increases. The music is real 1950s rock.

"Can you do the Lindy Hop and Jitterbug?" asks Marcus.

"I certainly can," says Kimberley. "Get ready, I want the whole thing."

Marcus shows himself to be an accomplished dancer of the American steps. Kimberley drives him further and further until she is doing the dip and the double-dip around his hips with her legs off the ground. As the energy and excitement between them increases he takes a swift to look into her eyes as a question, then, having seen her daring look back, he does the stick wad wraparound. Kimberley is laughing as the music comes to an end. They walk off the dance floor together.

"You are a surprise, Marcus," says Kimberley. "I thought that we were going to dance like Fred Astaire and Ginger Rogers."

"I'm not good enough for that," says Marcus.

"Good, because nor am I," says Kimberley. "The dances we did were just great. Where did you learn?"

"I only have three secrets," says Marcus, "and I have to save them for our long trip. Would you like a little supper here before we leave for the Sloane Club? The food is simple but good."

"Sounds just like me," says Kimberley. "Food would be great and something to drink. Water maybe. All that dancing makes me thirsty."

They move into the nightclub dining room where they are greeted by another happy girl in a pretty party dress. She shows them to a corner table.

"Mineral water, please," says Marcus.

"We have an Evian or San Pellegrino," says the hostess.

"Is Evian that stuff your Queen drinks?" asks Kimberley.

"No, that is Malvern water," says Marcus. "Evian is French water."

"French," says Kimberley. "Okay, I'll take the San Pellegrino."

The hostess notes and walks away. There are two menus on the table and a wine list. Marcus looks at the menu.

"What do you think you would like?" he asks.

"Marcus, I don't know. You choose something," says Kimberley, "but something British, not French."

"Well, it's quite late," says Marcus, "so how about something simple like caviar and toast followed by strawberries and cream?"

"Sounds great," says Kimberley, "but I would like my strawberries with black pepper."

"All right," says Marcus, who decides not to ask about the black pepper. Perhaps she doesn't eat cream, he thinks, to keep herself slim.

The hostess comes back with the two bottles of water.

"Would you like wine or a strong drink?" asks Marcus.

"No, I'm good," says Kimberley. "I needed this water. I never thought I'd dance the Jitterbug with a Brit in London."

"Imagine what can happen in India," says Marcus.

"I know already," says Kimberley. "You are going to climb up a rope and then disappear at the top."

"I can't do that trick," says Marcus. "Not now that you know."

"Is that one of your three secrets blown?" ask Kimberley.

"No, they are still safe," answers Marcus.

The caviar arrives with a big rack of hot toast.

"Here I go," says Kimberley. "I've never eaten caviar before. I put it on the toast, right?"

"Right," says Marcus, "and be generous with it."

"Okay," Kimberley murmurs, and takes a bite. "Mmm, salty," she says. "But I kinda like it. Are you having some?"

They eat silently for a few minutes until the caviar is finished.

"You had more than me," says Marcus.

"Are you going to be like this all over India?" asks Kimberley. "You have had caviar before. I was trying to get used to it."

"I quite understand," says Marcus.

"Marcus, what is a quite?" demands Kimberley. "You said it before. You said it is quite late. Now you say, you quite understand. I want to know. I speak American. You speak English. So what is a quite?"

"It is a form of measure," answers Marcus. "Quite late is not completely late, it is only a bit late."

"A bit late?" asks Kimberley. "So does that mean that you understand me a bit? Not a lot, just a bit? That is discouraging for a girl, Marcus. Don't say it again. Say that it is late and that you understand everything. Then I will think that we speak the same language. Even if we don't."

Marcus smiles. "I think that we understand each other," he says.

"You think we do?" says Kimberley. "Come on, Marcus. Say that we understand each other. Is there anything about what I say that you don't like?"

"I like everything about you, Kimberley," says Marcus.

"Clever," says Kimberley. "Now I am the bad guy."

The strawberries arrive in one big bowl and the hostess places a smaller glass bowl in front of each of them. A jug of thick double cream is put onto the table. Kimberley asks for a pepper grinder. The hostess goes to a sideboard to fetch one for her. Marcus heaps strawberries into Kimberley's glass bowl and then Kimberley grinds black pepper over them. Marcus takes the pepper grinder from Kimberley and places half a strawberry onto the tablecloth and grinds a little black pepper over it before popping it into his mouth whole.

"Sweet and peppery," he says. "Just like you, Kimberley."

"And your strawberries and cream are sweet and smooth, Marcus," says Kimberley.

Marcus looks thoughtful, then he smiles.

"I will not have coffee," says Marcus, "because I need to get some sleep before five o'clock in the morning, but would you like coffee?"

"No, thank you," says Kimberley. "I am happy to go back to our beds whenever you're ready."

They depart from the club, catch a passing taxi and are in the Sloane Club fifteen minutes later.

"Five o'clock in the morning?" asked Kimberley.

"Meet me here in reception at five thirty," says Marcus. "I have to walk over and get the car."

"Yes sir," says Kimberley. "See you later." She bounces up the stairs two at a time.

8
The Airport

Waiting at the airport is boring. After they have cleared immigration they have breakfast in the departure lounge. They choose a Café Rouge because the menu looks better than most of the others.

"Where are our seats on the plane, Marcus?" asks Kimberley.

"We are in business class," says Marcus. "Slightly bigger seats and we are sitting just in front of the wings on an exit."

"An exit?" says Kimberley.

"You get more leg room on the seats next to an exit," says Marcus. "So we can stretch out. Do you want to look in the bookshop here and get magazines for the flight?"

"Sure," says Kimberley.

They finish their breakfast and walk across a huge departure lounge to an open-sided WH Smith shop. Once they have made their choices they walk to a long row of seats joined together.

"If we had our own private jet we wouldn't have to wait," says Kimberley. "We could just arrive in a long quiet car and then get onto our plane. Then, whoosh, we would be off and away."

"If only I had known that, I would have sold my toy train set to buy a plane," says Marcus.

"Or I could have sold my rocking horse," says Kimberley, "but we forgot."

Their seats are back to back to another row of seats and behind them are sitting two twenty year old girls. Side by side and two seats away from them is a boy in his early twenties dressed in the Hollywood image of Jesus including open sandals displaying his white bony feet.

He leans over to the two girls and says, "Everything is safe in India. Just do what the locals do and you won't get ill. Drink a little bit of the local river water on the first day, then a little more the next day and so on. By the end of the week your immune system will be working well."

Kimberley leans over the back of the seat. "You lying little punk," she tells him. "You have never been to India, have you?" She turns towards the girls. "If you want to die then listen to this idiot," she says. "But if you want to have a good time follow the information in your guide book and never speak to this retard again." She sits back in her seat again.

Jesus gets up and walks away in search of more disciples.

"Good advice," says Marcus. "Holiday makers can get unwell in India if they forget the rules."

"He was a punk," says Kimberley. "I hate that sort of guy, pretending that he was an experienced traveller so that they would look up to him and admire him, and giving them dangerous advice."

"Forget about him," says Marcus. "You have done your good deed. The man has ego problems. He has to work them out on his own. Maybe he never will."

"I don't care about him," says Kimberley. "I spoke out because of those young girls, sitting there looking all innocent on their own. Like a target for every predatory male."

"I hope that they are tougher than you think," says Marcus. "We will never know how they would have dealt with him. He has wandered off now."

"You are right, Marcus," says Kimberley. "Maybe they would have beaten him to a pulp. Maybe they are real tough."

The two girls sitting with their backs to Marcus and Kimberley have been very quiet. The younger-looking one leans back and says to Kimberley, "We were not talking to the hippy, Miss. He was talking to us. We are not travelling to India anyway. We are going to Spain for a karate meeting. I was runner up in the championship last year. My friend, Yvonne, is the champion. I started with judo before I changed to karate. More discipline."

"Discipline," says Kimberley. "Holy cow! Okay, I'm sorry I interfered."

"Thank you," says the girl. "Have a safe time in India."

The two girls walk slowly away.

Marcus laughs, "What time is it?"

Kimberley is wearing an impressive diver's watch with a luminous dial. "Nine twenty," she tells him.

"That is a very professional diver's watch, Kimberley," says Marcus.

"Well, I can't scuba dive," says Kimberley. "I just thought that the watch looked real cool. I am not a good swimmer even though I live near the beach. I was more interested in track sports when I was a kid."

"I am a good swimmer," says Marcus. "I won competitions when I was younger and I swim fifty lengths every day in the local pool. So if your ball blows into the sea I can swim out and get it back for you."

"What a relief," says Kimberley.

"Judo," says Kimberley. "Karate."

"You were right," says Marcus, "those girls are real tough."

"Okay," says Kimberley, "I'm not rescuing anyone else."

"Perhaps not today," says Marcus. "I'm going to look at the departure board to see what gate we have to wait at."

He walks away and ten minutes later he comes back. "It is gate thirty-four," he says, "and we may as well wait there."

"Okay," says Kimberley, "let's go."

9
The Flight

Thirty minutes later they have boarded the plane and are sitting comfortably in their seats.

"I don't really like flying," says Kimberley. "Never have. It's dangerous."

"Not as dangerous as driving a car," says Marcus. "Anyway, it's too late now."

"What is the pilot's name?" asks Kimberley.

"He will tell us soon," answers Marcus. "But I happen to know that his name is Percy and he has a wife and six children so he wants a safe flight as well as us."

"Percy the pilot," says Kimberley. "That is a bullshit name, Marcus. You are going to be found out when his name is announced."

"All right, I admit it," says Marcus. "I was just trying to make you feel better."

"Thank you," says Kimberley. "Telling me the truth might make me feel better. Six children! That doesn't comfort me. He would be tired out. What is the first class area like?"

"You can take a look once we have taken off and the seatbelt signs are off,' says Marcus. "I know a story about a first class passenger."

"It had better not have a bad ending," says Kimberley.

"A rich and famous footballer is catching a flight to Germany," says Marcus, "and he usually travels first class, but this time the whole of the first class is full up and he has to go into the second class area with all of the holiday people. 'I don't travel second class,' he says. 'I am playing football against Germany tomorrow.' The older air hostess tells her colleagues that she will handle the situation. 'Today, sir,' she says, 'the first class is not going to Germany.' 'Oh, I see,' says the footballer, 'thank you.'"

"All of your funny stories are a bit weird, Marcus," says Kimberley. "Wake me up when we get to India."

"We are going to Dubai first," says Marcus. "The plane has to refuel there."

"Holy cow," says Kimberley, "two lots of taking off and landing. I am going to try to sleep through this. Wake me up when they serve lunch, okay?"

"Yes," says Marcus. "I will."

He settles down and starts to read one of the magazines he bought.

At lunchtime Kimberley produces a lot of fruit from her hand luggage.

"Better for your body when you are on a plane," she says.

"I'm sure you're right," says Marcus, watching as Kimberley puts orange peel into the elastic pocket on the back of the seat in front. Kimberley offers Marcus an orange but he is content to eat the vacuum-packed plastic food provided by the airline. The food looks a little better on the china plates of business class and Marcus finishes his meal with a coffee. Black, hot, slightly coffee-flavoured water, he thinks, as he drinks it.

They both sit quietly again for the next few hours of the journey, Kimberley getting up regularly to walk briskly up and down the aisles between the seats in the second class compartment and then right through to the front of first class. Marcus also has a walk after Kimberley has sat down. They are both bored.

After four hours the plane starts the descent into Dubai airport.

"All passengers must disembark for refuelling," says the captain, who they now both hear is really called Jack Bailey.

Marcus and Kimberley get off the plane and enter the departure lounge in Dubai. It is very clean, very white and very big. There are shops and big white sofas. Kimberley and Marcus feel a sense of liberty at being able to walk about freely in a building with lots of space and an enormous ceiling height. There is a shop selling nothing but caviar and Kimberley stops to look. An Arab is behind the counter.

"What is the best caviar?" Kimberley asks.

The Arab looks at her. Kimberley is wearing her safari outfit in readiness for India; long shorts, white ankle socks, Timberland boots and a khaki-coloured cotton shirt with big pockets. She still looks attractive. Her toned figure and natural glow shine through her adventurer disguise.

The Arab answers her question thoughtfully. "All caviar is very much the same," he says. "Sturgeon eggs. Fish eggs. Some people talk about Beluga caviar and say that it is the best but that is really because of the fictional man James Bond, who asked for it in the films. You can buy any caviar I have here and it will all be excellent."

"Thanks," says Kimberley. "Good afternoon."

She walks away and sits down on a big white sofa. Marcus has wandered off and she is sitting on her own. A tall, fierce-looking but elegant Arab sits at the other end of the sofa. He is wearing a white robe. Kimberley looks at him.

"Good afternoon," says Kimberley.

The Arab nods his head.

100

"What are your robes made of?" asks Kimberley.

The Arab looks sternly at Kimberley and notices her expedition clothing and her American accent. He decides that she is innocent, so he replies in a deep sonorous authoritative voice. "The thawb is made of the finest quality cotton," he says. "It is double, so that a vacuum is created between the two layers, assisting the wearer to help keep cool, or in the winter, warm. Here in Dubai it is always warm."

He stops speaking. Kimberley then asks him, "What do you wear underneath?"

The Arab has an impassive face. "We do not wear European or American clothing," he replies sternly.

"So nothing then," says Kimberley, brightly.

"As you say," the Arab replies. "I would not, however, ask you what you are wearing."

"I guess not," says Kimberley, and smiles at the Arab, "but you can see what we wear in the movies. We don't get any movies about your people."

He looks at her face and smiles. His brown angular face is broken into an amused kind smile and Kimberley feels the warmth of his personality.

Kimberley thanks the Arab for talking to her and gets up and walks away. He does not look at her as she leaves. He sits with a ramrod straight back and looks straight ahead.

Kimberley finds Marcus in the airport bookshop.

"What are you doing?" she asks, as she creeps up behind him.

"Just walking around," Marcus answers. "How about you?"

"Asking questions," says Kimberley. "What time do we have to get back to the plane?"

"Another question," says Marcus. "We have half an hour left before we should go and find the plane. Do you want anything?"

"I am going to try to buy some more fruit," says Kimberley. "I have seen pineapples but they are difficult to eat without a big knife. I have seen bananas but they are boring."

"Let's ask," says Marcus, approaching the cash desk. Five minutes later they are at an exotic fruits stall, which is hidden around the corner from the caviar bar. Kimberley buys oranges, kiwis, nectarines, blueberries and a mango.

"I'm not sure about the mango," she says, "but I am going to try to eat it on the plane with a plate and a knife from the stewardess. You know, the one who likes you?"

"I have not noticed," says Marcus.

"Yes you have," says Kimberley. "You know you have."

Marcus shrugs his shoulders.

"If we get the same stewardess when we get onto the plane again I'll introduce you," says Kimberley. "Say you are my cousin. That way she can make play for you without worrying about me."

"You behave yourself," says Marcus, "or I will introduce you to somebody and say that you are Miss August. This is a no sex holiday, don't forget."

"Marcus, what can you mean?" exclaims Kimberley.

"They drink mint tea here in Dubai," says Marcus. "Would you like one?"

"I sure would," says Kimberley. "Are we making peace now?"

"Always," says Marcus. "Come on."

They sit in the little airport café with thick squat glasses of mint tea in front of them. It is refreshing and clean.

10
Cheerleaders and Marcus

Fifteen minutes later they are back on the aeroplane, occupying the same seats as before.

"Another takeoff," says Kimberley. "I am closing my eyes."

The takeoff is smooth and the flight uneventful, comfortable. Marcus and Kimberley watch a movie shown on the little screens in the back of the seats in front of them. They are each wearing headphones in order to allow them to hear the film. The story is about a group of cheerleaders who have witnessed a murder and are being looked after by the local police force before the trial of the suspected culprit.

"They are not cheerleaders," says Kimberley.

Marcus takes out his earphones. "What did you say?" he asks.

"Those girls are not cheerleaders," says Kimberley.

"No, they are actors," answers Marcus.

"I know that," says Kimberley, "but they are not physically right for the roles."

"They are all young and slim and pretty," says Marcus.

"Yes, that's not fit," says Kimberley. "They couldn't run very far or jump or do cartwheels, look at their skinny arms! No muscle. And their legs. Long and thin. No muscle. No strength. They could not do the job. They could never be professional cheerleaders."

"What is a professional cheerleader?" asks Marcus. "We do not have such girls in England."

"Football teams or baseball teams and other sports teams, if they are in the big league, they pay the cheerleader squads to cheer them on from the sidelines," says Kimberley.

"They pay them?" replies Marcus. "You mean it's a full-time job? A career?"

"Maybe not a full, full-time job," says Kimberley. "Unless it's one of the big-earning US teams, but even with medium-sized clubs it's maybe three days a week and then training days and rehearsals. The whole squad has to learn and practice how to work together. All of the moves are choreographed. So that when we, I mean they, do their pyramids, all their somersault moves, every girl has to be in the right place, sometimes to catch the other girl or to throw her."

"Throw her?" asks Marcus.

"Yeah, maybe up the pyramid or in some other somersault move. The girls all have to be tough, strong, gymnastic and athletic. It is no job for an unfit girl or even an average girl. They all have to be top of their game. Peak fitness. That is why I say that these actresses in this movie are badly chosen."

"Perhaps they were chosen for their acting," says Marcus.

"Oh sure, I can see that," says Kimberley, "but it is all talking about lip gloss and nail varnish and waxing. Not like real cheerleaders."

"Don't real cheerleaders do all of that?" asked Marcus.

"Yeah, but they don't talk about it. Hardly at all. They talk about lap times and takeoffs and aerobics. Weights and muscle strengths. They have to keep their backs supple and flexible and their weight under control and their fitness at top level. Maybe they compare hairdressers or clothing but mostly they talk about guys. The guys they want, or the guys they have, or the guys they are gonna have next week. I guess it's all fitness, dancing and guys."

"It all sounds marvellous," says Marcus. "Just the kind of life I should have, except for the guys, of course, for me it would have to be girls. The one I had, the one I want, or the one that I was going to have next week. Fitness, dancing and girls and getting paid for it."

"They don't get paid a lot," says Kimberley. "Nothing like the big money that the players get. Most girls in the smaller league teams have another job to help to pay the bills, but I guess it's a good life. They are famous. Envied by other girls. Chased after by all the guys. They can have their pick of eligible men. New girls get looked after by the older girls. Told to take it slowly. To be choosy about guys. To keep on refusing them even if they are a great catch. Cheerleaders are a prize catch. The girls have to learn to be able to select a top guy. A guy who deserves a cheerleader. The girls only have a short window. Maybe ten years, possibly twelve, before they are thrown out of the squad. So they have to be careful. A couple of mean guys who boast about sex with a girl in the squad can set her back. Maybe even ruin her chances to make a good marriage.

The best move is to get a guy who wants to marry you so much that he tells you that you have to leave. Stop being a cheerleader once you have married him. Then you play it tough. Real reluctant until he promises you all the things you want. Then you marry him quick and leave the cheerleaders behind on your wedding day. That counts as a real win. That is what most of the girls are working for. Course, there are always some losers who go for the bad boy sort of guy. Then get knocked up and chucked off the squad. End up fat in some trailer park with a baby they don't want. The bad boys move on to another girl."

"Sounds like trapeze walking," says Marcus. "One wrong move and you've fallen but if you make it to the other side then you are safe.'

"A lot of the girls have a tough time with men," says Kimberley. "A cheerleader is not a real person to most men. Just a sexual fantasy. Some girls make it to the centrefold of Playboy magazine. Makes them even more unreal to men. So you have to get yourself a confident man. You cannot rescue some sensitive nerdy weak guy. Your man has to be a winner. Enough of a winner for him to know that he deserves a cheerleader. That he is the cheerleader's type. So he has to have money, a good business and some sports prowess of his own. Everything that puts him up on a level with the cheerleader. So that she is not reaching down. Better yet if she is reaching up."

"It sounds like a tough life," says Marcus.

"Life is tough, isn't it?" says Kimberley. "Life is about making yourself the best you can be and then finding a man who has been doing the same thing. Making himself into an eligible man. A strong man. Then you join up and use all of your strengths together. You have to keep trying all the time. Pushing yourself. You can't just watch the scenery. Watch the clouds go by. You have to keep up. Hit every target date. Husband, babies, fortune. All on time. Takes a lot of work, but it's all there if you want it."

"It makes me feel exhausted," says Marcus. "I don't think that I have kept to the rules. I have spent time watching the scenery go by. Wondering why we are all here."

"Don't wonder that, Marcus," says Kimberley. "We are here and we have to make the most of ourselves. We have to live the best lives we can. Wondering about it is wasting time.

Doing it is all that matters now that we are here. Doing it all really well before we get to the end of life. Before we have to leave. Wondering about it is no use. Like all of these scientists working to try to explain everything. Why? Everything is as it is. Live with it. There is a lot to enjoy in life. The world is designed for happiness. Take it."

"Goodness me," says Marcus. "I have a lot of catching up to do. Where is that air hostess that you said liked me? I think I might take her into the bathroom and ravish her. I have so much left to do. I must start now."

"She is pushing the drinks trolley now, Marcus. One of the other rules is that you cannot take your happiness at the expense of other people. Wait until the passengers have had their drinks," says Kimberley. "And this is a no sex holiday, remember?"

"Another rule," says Marcus. "You had better give me a list."

"They are all obvious," says Kimberley. "You live a good life anyway, Marcus. Why have you never married? It is time for you to marry. You will be too old for your children if you wait. Children need guidance. You need a lot of energy for the job."

"I feel as if I am being dragged out of a hot bath," says Marcus. "Made to face my shortcomings. Told that I am too late for almost everything. We don't have any cheerleaders in England so I cannot get one of those. Even if we did have cheerleaders I am not sure that I would qualify for one. I might not measure up to requirements. Oh dear. I felt all right until you told me about all of the targets."

"Don't feel so bad," says Kimberley. "I've missed targets too. The man I went to Haiti with and Venezuela. I told you when I first met you. He was my bad boy. He looked handsome and strong on a Harley Davidson but it wasn't true.

107

At least I didn't get knocked up and have to live in slum housing. All I had to do was get rid of him. He was my missed target."

"Perhaps he was a lesson for life," says Marcus. "Without an experience like that how can you set the right example for the daughters you are going to have? Your sons as well for that matter. Now your experience can help their values."

"Okay Marcus," says Kimberley. "What about you?"

"This is like talking to a stranger on a train," says Marcus. "You know how you tell all your secrets, thinking that you'll never see them again?"

"So now I'm a stranger on a train?" says Kimberley. "We are past that, Marcus. Now we are travelling companions. Travelling out and travelling back. So if you have secrets don't tell me because you cannot get off this plane at the next station. Now, marriage, Marcus."

"I accept," says Marcus. "I would be foolish not to since you know all the rules and I do not."

"Give, Marcus," says Kimberley, smiling.

"How long till we land?" asked Marcus. "How long have I got?"

"Four hours," says Kimberley, "only three really because I am going to eat my fruit. You must be quick, Marcus. Just yes or no."

"Well, no," says Marcus. "Two hours, fifty-eight minutes left," says Kimberley, "even with the fruit. You had better give me a longer answer."

Marcus thought for a few minutes. "It is a matter of ego," says Marcus. "You know those men who are sure of themselves, confident? I don't know whether they are or whether they pretend to be and maybe it's the same thing. If you pretend to be brave then maybe you are brave. Anyway, those sorts of men get a girlfriend who they call, 'my girlfriend', or even, 'my girl'. Later it's 'my fiancée' then it becomes, 'my wife'. Always an adjunct to the man. A man who worked for me said one day, 'okay, the wife has put out a red tie for me today'. He had just noticed it and I realised then that he thought that her job was to serve him. Wash and iron his clothes and put out what he was going to wear every day. There are lots of men like that. They don't wonder about what the wife is thinking about just so long as she cooks and cleans and washes his clothes.

When they have children they become, 'my son' or 'my daughter'. They don't really get to know them. They don't realise that they are new people who have arrived with their own characters and their own personalities. No, to this type of man, most men, they are 'my son' and 'my daughter' and altogether 'my family'. Always separate from him. 'Me and my family'. So he is important and his family are a kind of fan club in his own mind. Of course he loses them eventually and he never does understand why. The best times for him were when the children were little and treated him like a kind of God. As they grow up and move away from him, then he thinks that they are wrong and prides himself on not understanding them. Often prefacing his comments by saying, 'I don't understand him, her' and saying it as if it gave him a superiority. That he was right.

These men in England are in all walks of life: carpenters, doctors, lawyers, plumbers. Ego is what they have and it is that which protects them.

I don't have that sort of ego. I don't seem to have much ego at all. I've never felt like saying 'my girl' about anyone, even though I have, of course, had girlfriends and I never wanted to say, 'my wife' even though I have wanted one. The girls, the women I've met though seemed to want to be somebody's wife. They seemed to want a man who didn't understand them and who had a hobby or something which kept him busy. The women would wash his sports kit the day before he went off to play some activity with his friends. Sporting men call each other 'lads' in England, you know? Me and the lads are going up to London. And sports teams are all called lads. 'The lads did a good job today'. Anyway the women like to understand their men. They like to know where they stand. They never seemed to understand me or even to like me after a while. I did not make them feel safe. I was not one of the lads. And my career is very patchy. I run around to find a site, a piece of land, then I run around to get the money. Then I build something. Then I sell it, make a profit, pay a lot of tax, buy a new car or something and go on holiday often with a girl who doesn't really understand what I do and why I don't have a job. She sets about trying to compartmentalise me and I'm trying to cooperate but I seem to fail the tests. I've even had girls come back to me a week before their marriage to suggest that we have sex one more time. I have asked, 'Why did you not marry me?' And they reply, 'Don't be silly, Marcus, girls don't marry men like you.' They said it as if everyone would understand and that I should understand. So I have become used to being sort of outside it all. I don't completely understand why I'm not married except that I now understand that it was always up to me to do something about it. English women don't suit me anyway. The middle class women come with such a long list of requirements, the type of house, furniture, car, three blond-haired children and a Volvo estate car. The man's role is to provide it all. And once he has provided everything on the first list, his English wife provides a second list and then a third. The lists are never-ending: private education for the children, a holiday house, and then university for the children. When the children have left home the wife starts on herself. Adult education."

"You mean like porn lessons?" asks Kimberley.

"No," Marcus laughs. "I mean gardening, interior design, yoga, creative writing. You see the husband has to be kept occupied paying for everything or he might start to think about what he wants. As it is, he is kept so off-balance that he hasn't a chance. He never gets on top of his finances."

"That is misogynistic stuff, Marcus," says Kimberley.

"Okay, I'm not misogynistic in world terms. I'm just talking about the English middle classes. About the wives. Not the working class girls, they have more honest appetites. No, I'm describing the class of women who considered me. They don't wonder about anything. They have a pretty clear idea of what they want and they are certain that they are so sexually desirable that their husbands are straining at the leash to get at them. By a kind of telepathy autosuggestion process, the husbands fall into the same belief. 'Oh, Bernard is looking forward to the holiday. Seeing me in my swimming costume, eh Bernard? He will have to stand in the sea to cool down.' None of that really appeals to me. And the English women seemed to know that I was not suitable material."

"You talk about your people as different types. So what about your top type of people?" asks Kimberley. "Your dukes and kings and all those."

"They are the ones who marry for land and property," answers Marcus. "They pride themselves on the fact that they do not work for money. That is their status. So they married to increase their money which is mostly always in land and property."

"Do you want to get yourself one of those?" asks Kimberley.

"They wouldn't want me," says Marcus. "Not enough land and property. Also I am not the right sort. My family is not an old family. Besides, a lot of the women in the top

111

families are pretty unattractive to look at. They do not marry for romance."

"So who do you want then, Marcus?" asks Kimberley. "Who have been your best girls?"

"The important relationships for me were with a Cambridge theological student who robbed sub-post offices with a revolver all over the Midlands in England until she had to disappear to France and then elsewhere, and a burlesque dancer who was fifteen years younger than me and outrageous in her social behaviour, flirting and playing footsie with strangers in restaurants or getting drunk and swimming naked in swimming pools. I loved her very much. Nearly married her, in fact. Both of these girls offered me companionship, equality and a mutual attraction. We had a genuine desire for one another and as a consequence a great sex life and a friendship. It was perfect. They were real people."

Kimberley thinks for a long while. "Would you have had children with these girls?" she asks. "So you want a real person, Marcus," says Kimberley. "You are in more trouble than you think. It is not that you do not have any ego, Marcus. It is that you have got far too much ego. You are like a man with the fatal gift."

"The fatal gift?" says Marcus. "What is that?"

"Somebody wrote a book about it a long time ago," answers Kimberley. "It is a person who is good-looking, talented, clever, naturally athletic. A person who does not have to try for anything in life because it all comes easily. Gradually the lack of trying becomes a state of mind and as the years pass all of the lesser people, the ones who have had to try, begin to overtake him. Their achievements become more than his. But this does not concern him. So confident is he that he honestly believes that their having to try so hard puts them on a level below him. Even if by now they are richer and better placed than him, he still feels superior. He feels detached, you see, and it is this steadfast detachment which is his enormous ego. How could a girl possibly love him? There is no room for her."

"This is not a train, you say?" says Marcus. "So I cannot get off?"

"We are together for weeks, Marcus, and neither of us can get off," says Kimberley, "and we are not judging each other. We are supporting each other. I will give you something. Do you know that I am a professional cheerleader for a team in Jacksonville? So that it was my life I was talking about. I tell you because you were talking about your life and so you should know about mine."

"Not Miss August, though, Kimberley?" says Marcus.

"I have never been asked," answers Kimberley.

"Has it occurred to you that for all of our policy and beliefs and efforts, life may be nothing to do with us? That we are not directing our own lives?" asks Marcus.

"God helps those who help themselves," says Kimberley. "So you have to try."

"I know that God supported the poor," says Marcus, "but I didn't know that he supported shoplifters."

Kimberley hits him on his upper arm. "Idiot," she says.

"The cheerleaders won, did you notice?" asked Marcus. "The film has ended and the cheerleaders won. I am so glad."

"Shut up, Marcus," says Kimberley. "Listen, this marriage thing. It is a partnership. You have to have somebody on your side to help you and so together you work to build up your own little fortress. Do you want children, Marcus?"

"Yes," says Marcus. "Lots of them. To keep me young and involved in life but you are talking about an American partnership and working together. I am talking about the

113

English version where the woman takes everything she wants from the man."

"Maybe she figures that without her, the man would stay in a one bedroom apartment playing football on Saturdays with his grown-up school friends. Achieve nothing at all. Maybe she is doing what her mother did. She thought her father was happy. Maybe it is just a different way of looking at it. The woman is helping the man. The truth is, Marcus, that you are scared of it all. It is a commitment to life. Building a nest. Having babies. Growing old. You are still fighting it, Marcus. Burlesque dancers and armed robbers, you cannot build a nest with those girls. So you are back in your apartment with your one big bed. Empty."

"I wonder if they have a psychiatrist's couch somewhere on this plane?" says Marcus. "I feel faint. I need a professional to tell me that I am normal."

"I can tell you, Marcus," says Kimberley. "You are not normal. Nor am I. That is why we are going to India together. That is why we do not have nests and babies. Because we are not normal people."

"At least I am not alone," says Marcus.

"Not for the next few weeks," says Kimberley. "After that you may be alone."

"Well, I will live for today," says Marcus. "I'm going for a walk up and down the plane."

"Don't talk to any burlesque dancers or armed robbers," says Kimberley. "You have to take a few weeks away from all that."

"I will save my strength," says Marcus.

"We don't know what India is going to be like," says Kimberley.

Kimberley starts to eat her fruit. She makes a mess with her mango even though she has a plate and a sharp knife. She puts the peel and the big stone into a strong bag she finds in the seat pocket in front of her. She has some San Pellegrino water and she washes her hands with a little of it. She has cut the mango into slices but now realises that she is going to get into another mess eating the slices with her fingers. A hand comes over the back of her seat holding a fork. It is Marcus.

"I noticed that you had forgotten the eating bit," he says.

"Thank you. I had forgotten how I was going to get the pieces into my mouth," says Kimberley.

"You should have eaten the blueberries," says Marcus. "I'm going to have lunch. An airline lunch."

Gradually they advance towards India. Slowly the plane starts to descend.

"What is our programme?" asks Kimberley. "How are we travelling around? What places?"

"All right," says Marcus. "First we are going to have five days on a beach. To take it easy. There will still be lots to do and see. After that we are going to Bombay for four days, then to Agra to see the Taj Mahal and after that we go to Delhi for a look and then on to Udaipur where we will stay in a hotel on a lake. Five weeks later we go back down south to a three-bedroom bungalow we have rented on a beach. It is not the whole of India. That would take us two years. It is just a taste of India."

"It sounds fine," says Kimberley.

"Then we get five days of sunshine and swimming and then back to London."

"Not more planes I hope," says Kimberley.

"Trains, a coach, and then one flight back from right up north to right down south again. Then a rest and then back to the world again. Your world and my world. Both different worlds."

"I'm ready for all of it," says Kimberley. "Are we going to see elephants? I've always wanted to see an elephant."

"I promise that you will see an elephant," says Marcus.

"Gee," says Kimberley.

The plane comes in to land. Kimberley closes her eyes and the plane touches down and taxis towards the arrivals gate. A set of steps is waiting. The plane stops.

"Are we down?" asks Kimberley.

"Down and stopped," answers Marcus.

All of the passengers take a long time gathering their things together, getting their overhead bags down. Many of them look surprised that there are other passengers trying to get their bags at the same time. One man pulled his bag down and then slammed the overhead locker shut, almost catching another passenger's hands.

"Sorry, you are getting off here as well?" he said, in a puzzled voice.

The other passenger did not answer.

Eventually they leave the plane. Marcus and Kimberley make their way towards immigration and after that baggage and then customs. There seem to be a lot of uniformed officials.

"Creating jobs," says a formidable English woman in her sixties. She is dressed for safari with big brown boots and a large man's hat. "Government jobs, you see. Three people to do one job. Employment. Feeding the population. Airport job. Good position. Expect everything to take time. Always does in India. No need to rush. Good luck."

She moves forward in the queue for immigration.

"Well, it's nice to stand up," says Marcus.

"Yup," says Kimberley, "but we should still have got our own jet."

"Next time," smiles Marcus, "next time."

116

They shuffle through all of the procedures. The airport is dark and painted inside with dark grey paint. The customs officers take a long time, looking in fascination at Marcus's and Kimberley's clothing and possessions. Eventually their bags are marked with chalk and they are free to leave the airport. Marcus walks into a little office next to the airport to change English money into Indian rupees. Kimberley follows him in. Marcus changes several hundred pounds into rupees.

"It is not allowed to bring rupees into India and it is not allowed to take them out of India," he explains to Kimberley.

"Okay," she says. "I'll change some dollars."

The moneychanger is very pleased with the business and Marcus and Kimberley emerge into the sunshine. They are in Goa in southern India.

"Smells rich," says Kimberley. "Kinda strong, like newly born animals and maybe a little sweet."

"Powerful smell," says Marcus, "but not unpleasant."

"Where do we go from here?" asks Kimberley.

"Well, I arranged everything through an agency," answers Marcus. "Scott and Harvey. I believe there should be a coach waiting for us."

"To hell with that," says Kimberley. "You find your Scott and Harvey rep and tell him we are getting a taxi. While you find him I will get a taxi. I'll be over there." She points at the long row of waiting taxis. "I will take the luggage."

"Can you manage the bags?" asks Marcus.

"I am a strong girl," says Kimberley.

Marcus walks away and finds a bored-looking young woman holding up a board, which says 'Scott and Harvey India Tours'. Marcus explains the decision to her and she asks him if he has the name of the hotel.

"Yes, the Excelsior," answers Marcus.

"That's right," says the woman and crosses two names off her list. "Have a good few days," she says. "I'll pick you up next Friday morning at ten o'clock at the hotel."

"All right. Thank you," says Marcus, and walks to the taxi rank.

Kimberley is waiting. "The bags are all in the trunk," she says.

11
Southern India

They both sit in the back of the taxi and Marcus tells the driver where they want to go. He asks the driver to drive slowly.

They both look out of the windows at the passing scenery. Away from the airport they are driving through the countryside. There is a lot of very long grass on either side of the dusty beige-coloured road. Fields with wheat or corn or barley and many trees. People are walking along the road either alone or in twos and threes. They all seem to be carrying bags or baskets of foodstuffs. Fruit and large misshapen vegetables.

"The people here are small," says Kimberley. "The size of children."

Marcus says nothing, noticing the calm old faces on the people as they walk along. They are not talking to each other; they are just quietly attending to their different tasks.

"Is it a long way to the hotel, mister?" Kimberley asks the taxi driver.

"Oh no, no. It is not far. Not far at all," answers the driver.

"How soon do we get there?" asks Kimberley.

"Very soon indeed, madam. Oh yes, very soon."

They travel for another hour, passing through a town which seems to be called Mapusa. It is bustling with people.

The main road through the town is very wide, covered with grey Tarmacadam. There are many side roads and the buildings vary enormously in quality. A lot of them appear to be made of concrete and are four or five storeys high. Some windows have air conditioning units sticking through them. Other buildings are constructed of a variety of materials, including what the English would call wattle and daub. Some of the more simple buildings have roof tiles scattered randomly and held down by heavy stones. There are many giant posters and advertising boards and everywhere they look there are people and children. People on bicycles, pushing handcarts with strange-looking vegetables or fruits on them. There are horses pulling laden carts with their driver sitting on the cart. There are motor scooters, often with two people and a child riding on them. There are small yellow buses, completely open at the back. Women herding goats along the roads. There are big old-fashioned British motorbikes. Men riding side-saddle on ponies with tin buckets of milk. Camels loaded with goods being led along by women who are also walking in groups, wearing the most colourful ankle-length outfits with long sleeves. Pink, green, orange, red, blue. The women wear large headdresses and apart from plain colours they wear every variety of pattern. Women here have oval-shaped faces and are attractive. There is a baby camel following its mother. There are three-wheeler taxis, motorised tricycles with the driver in front and two passengers sitting under a little canopy over the back two wheels. There are schoolchildren wearing blue uniforms and carrying smart square briefcases on their shoulders held there by straps. There are trees growing at the side of the roads and there are market stores selling a wide variety of foods. Large heaps of grain, pulses, lentils, great sacks of flour and above the stalls there is washing hanging out to dry.

They drive past a shop which has buckets hanging outside and leather trouser belts, fishing rods and electric fans. There is a bony black cow ambling past the shop.

"Holy cow!" says Kimberley.

"That is exactly what it is," says Marcus. "A Holy cow. Cows are sacred here. Nobody is allowed to kill one."

Kimberley notices that most of the men have rich dark moustaches and thick black hair. None of them are wearing hats. They move with dignity, going about their business. A handcart is pushed by a man. The cart is covered by long green vegetables, like extra big, very pale green courgettes. They pass more stalls protected by cotton canopies held up by spindly wooden struts. The stalls are heaped with five or six different kinds of nut and piles of white garlic, green vegetables, onions and misshapen tomatoes. The roads are full of people. Marcus notices that the people do not look at each other. They all move straight ahead as if they are alone. Unless they are running a shop or a stall, the Indian people in Mapusa behave as if there is nobody else near them. They are aware of each other because they do not bump into other people but they do not acknowledge their presence. They simply walk forward in a self-contained manner. Some of the men wear turbans. Babies are everywhere, playing in the dust or being carried casually by slender women. In fact almost everybody is slender. Marcus has not seen a person who is carrying any excess weight. The taxi they are travelling in is an old British model Morris Oxford, now made new in India. They pass slowly through the town whilst Kimberley watches the passing scene. Slowly they emerge from the other side of the town and are in the countryside again. More trees and this time there are palm trees and coconut trees and groups of women sitting cross-legged on the ground behind piles of fruit, which they are selling.

"The beach is there," says the taxi driver, pointing with one hand to a place behind the women. "A very fine beach indeed." They drive three hundred yards further. "And here is your very fine hotel," says the taxi driver, pointing at a big rectangular concrete building boldly painted in a striped pattern of dark blue and white, like a gigantic English ice cream hut.

The taxi stops and two uniformed men run down the hotel steps to greet them. Their bags are carried into the hotel. Marcus pays the driver. Gives him a generous tip and follows Kimberley to the hotel reception. Marcus asks to see the manager. The request causes much consternation but after Marcus has reassured the reception staff that he has no complaint, one girl hurries away to find the manager.

"What are you doing, Marcus?" asks Kimberley.

"Be patient please. Say nothing," answers Marcus.

The manager emerges from his office, exquisitely formally attired and carrying an air of excessive dignity.

"I am booked into your fine hotel," says Marcus. "My name is Mr. Field and this is my guest, Miss Judd. I simply wanted to meet you and thank you for giving us such excellent rooms, sir." Marcus stretches out his right hand and the manager takes it in a handshake.

The manager instantly feels the large thick Indian banknote, which Marcus has passed to him with the handshake. The manager swiftly and discreetly puts the note into his right-hand trouser pocket, realising as he does so that the rupee note is of such a size as to represent four weeks of his entire salary.

"I am pleased that you have chosen our hotel," says the manager. "I will check your booking." He seizes the hotel register away from the girl receptionist and, with the pen which he has whipped from his pocket, draws a line through the two rooms which have been designated for Mr. Field and Miss Judd and substitutes them for larger air-conditioned rooms on the quieter fourth floor. The rooms are adjacent to each other and have adjoining balconies. The manager taps the bell on the desk and the hotel porter runs up.

"Mr. Field and Miss Judd are special guests," says the manager. "See to all of their requirements."

"Yes sir," says the porter, and shows Kimberley and Marcus into a metal cage lift which, with them aboard, cranks slowly upwards. The luggage is in their rooms.

When they have both settled in, Kimberley knocks on the door of Marcus's room.

"What do you want to do tonight, Marcus?" she says.

"Okay, let's just take it easy," says Marcus. "Walk around this little village a bit and go and look at the beach. I suggest that we eat here in the hotel tonight then get a good night's sleep. What would you like to do tomorrow?"

"Go in to Mapusa in the morning," says Kimberley. "Have a look around and in the afternoon we can go to the beach."

"That settles that,' says Marcus. "How long do you need to get ready?"

"I am ready now, Marcus," says Kimberley.

Marcus and Kimberley walk out of the hotel and onto the village road. It is quiet, with very little traffic, and many small children playing. The children look boldly at them as they walk by. They reach a place by the side of the road where the three women are sitting cross-legged behind large piles of fruit. Watermelons and bananas are what they are selling most of.

"I wouldn't recommend the watermelons," says Marcus, "because of the water."

Kimberley looks at him. "Okay," she says.

They notice that the women are in front of the pathway which leads to the beach, and so they walk around the women and start down the beach path. The time is about five-thirty in the afternoon. The beach is very wide and very long and sandy. The sea is crashing onto the sand with big waves. There are groups of people lounging on the sand. Along the beach there are wooden huts with roofs made from palm leaves.

"I think they are snack bars," says Kimberley.

They walk one hundred yards down the beach towards the last one and Kimberley walks inside. The interior has a rudimentary kitchen with two gas rings fuelled by cylinders of gas, a scrubbed wooden table covered with food and a long deep box which contains an enormous block of ice. Earlier in the day bottles and cans of drink had been placed on top of the ice and now at five-forty the bottles and cans have sunk down into the ice in deep holes. The proprietor is a man of indeterminate age. He has a happy face and is accompanied by a little boy.

"My grandson," he says proudly, and ruffles the boy's dark hair. "Have you come to eat?" the owner asks.

"No sir, we have just arrived here and we are looking around," answers Kimberley.

"Then come to eat tomorrow night," says the man. "I will make you crab curry. Very special. Just for you. Come at seven o'clock."

"Okay," says Kimberley. "We will."

"What would you like to drink when you come?" asks the man. "I can get anything you want."

"Then I reckon we will have good French wine," says Kimberley, thinking about the incongruity of her suggestion as she says it.

"Certainly," says the man, "and how many friends will you bring with you?"

"We have only just arrived," says Kimberley. "Just the two of us. We have not made any friends yet." She looks at the man's grandchild. "Can you bring four friends?" she asks.

"Oh yes madam, most certainly," says the boy.

"Then I guess we will have a dinner for eight people," says Kimberley. "See you tomorrow night. Goodbye." She walks out.

"We are going to a dinner party tomorrow night, Marcus," says Kimberley.

"All right," says Marcus. "You arranged that very quickly."

"It is all for you, Marcus," says Kimberley. "For you to meet new people."

"What made you decide on that place?" asks Marcus.

"The owner has a happy face. He works with his grandson who is lovely and the place is clean," answers Kimberley. "We are having crab curry and French wine."

"That's settled then," says Marcus, smiling.

They turn to look towards the restless sea. A large red sun is setting into the sea and it is becoming dark rapidly.

"What time is it?" asks Kimberley.

"Just about six o'clock," answers Marcus.

"So it gets dark early here. Same as the Caribbean. That must be the only thing which is the same as the Caribbean," says Kimberley.

They begin to walk back along the beach whilst the light is fading fast. Marcus looks carefully along the edge of the trees and long grass to find the entrance where they came in. He sees it.

"Look over there," he says. "That is where we must head for."

They walk towards the gap in the vegetation and reach it at the same time that it becomes completely dark.

"Can you see all right?" asks Marcus.

"I'm putting my hand on your shoulder, Marcus," says Kimberley. "You guide me."

They both walk carefully into the beach pathway and onwards to the village road. The women fruit sellers have gone. There are no lights in the village except for the lights of their hotel shimmering in the distance. The hotel lights give them confidence and they walk briskly towards the welcome of the bright building.

"Dinner at seven?" asks Marcus.

"Sure thing," says Kimberley. "I will meet you in the bar."

They move towards the lift and when they have reached the fourth floor they part company at the doors to their rooms.

Later – early evening, Marcus makes his way downstairs to the bar. He is wearing dark grey trousers, his usual loafers and a pale blue shirt. Over this he is wearing a beautifully tailored cream linen jacket. He looks like a rich international traveller. The area of the bar extends to include tables and chairs set well back from the edge of a large, irregularly shaped swimming pool, tiled with white tiles and with low lighting around it. Exotic gardens extend into the darkness beyond. The dining room is on the other side of the swimming pool and Marcus walks over to make reservations for dinner at eight o'clock. The dining area also extends out into the gardens and each table has a little lamp on it. Marcus requests an outside table. He walks back to the bar area and is just in time to see Kimberley walk in. She looks like a movie star on a red carpet arriving for a film premiere. She is wearing a black cocktail dress, which Marcus had first seen when she wore it to Rules restaurant in London. Tonight, under the warm moonlit sky of India, Kimberley looks exciting. Her tanned skin is glowing in the soft lighting and her hair shines with health. Her long, bare tanned legs are displayed from mid-thigh and she is wearing simple expensive-looking black shoes with four inch heels. Marcus is proud to be with her. He remembers the pretty student he had originally invited on the India trip and now feels lucky that she let him down. Kimberley is a tough character. Strong, fit and intelligent. Marcus is pleased to be with her now.

"Good evening," says Marcus. "You look like a film star."

"A film star? Who is the heroine or the villain?" asks Kimberley, as she sits down at a small table.

"Some of the most beautiful film stars have played villainess parts," answers Marcus. "I think that you could play it either way."

He sits opposite to her.

"Correct," says Kimberley with a grin, "and now that all of the horrible flying is over for a few weeks I am going to get me a real drink. What about you, Marcus?"

The bar waiter walks up to their table. Marcus asks the waiter how the ice is made in the hotel bar.

"The ice, sir, is made from the very best most clean bottled water, sir," says the waiter. He has soft brown eyes and a beaming smile with even white teeth.

"Are you telling the truth now, mister?" Kimberley asked him. "You know that God is watching you. If you tell lies to us tonight you will come back as a dog."

The waiter continues to smile. "I am most confident about the ice, madam," he says. "I made it all myself and so I am most confident." He shows no sign of being offended or insulted by Kimberley's attack on him. He is used to the eccentricities of the hotel guests. He treats them as uneducated people who cannot possibly know how to behave correctly. So he forgives their rudeness. Indeed he does not notice their rudeness. He has worked in the hotel for five years and he believes that the English and northern Europeans who stay in the hotel for short intervals must in fact live in most unpleasant countries with savage and cruel customs and behaviour practiced every day upon citizens. The waiter, if he thinks about his customers at all, which he rarely does, simply feels superior to them. He continues to smile. "What do sir and madam desire this evening?" he asks obsequiously.

Marcus is looking at Kimberley at this moment and shamelessly acknowledges to himself what he desires this evening. Again Kimberley picks up Marcus's thought and looks directly at him conspiratorially with an understanding smile on her face.

"Better have a strong drink, Marcus," she says. "It will help you to settle down." She smiles again without any hint of condemnation and as if she is accustomed to receiving sexual admiration and is comfortable with it.

Marcus becomes aware of the blood rushing to his face. He conquers his feelings of embarrassment and answers the waiter. "A large vodka and tonic, please," he says. "Kimberley?"

"Brandy and soda," says Kimberley.

"At once," says the waiter and hurries away.

"I don't know what kind of food we are going to get here," says Kimberley. "I don't trust the chickens or the four-legged meat. I guess I'll get vegetarian."

"You are right," says Marcus, "although you organised crab curry for us tomorrow."

"That will be fine," answers Kimberley. "The man has no freezer. Just a simple hut. The crabs will be alive when we arrive."

"Now I feel like an assassin," says Marcus.

"Don't," says Kimberley. "In the seas and oceans of the world everything eats everything else. They got no vegetables down there."

"I suppose you are right," says Marcus.

The waiter arrives with their drinks. Both of them relax and sip drinks and savour the peace, tranquillity and the abundance of nature all around them, which contributes to their sense of calm.

"This sure is different," says Kimberley. "Long way from home. I like it today. I don't know how I'm going to feel later."

"We have lots of different places to visit," says Marcus. "You will like some of the places more than others."

"I guess that's right," says Kimberley. "Now that we have stopped moving I feel comfortable and I'm enjoying the alcohol."

"I'm pleased to hear it," says Marcus.

"If I was going to Venice or Paris or maybe the Caribbean, for the first time, I would have a very clear idea about what I expected and what I would see, but India, I never thought about India. I have no expectations at all except food poisoning and heat," says Kimberley.

"We are going to avoid food poisoning," says Marcus, "and we are going to enjoy ourselves on this trip."

"That's for sure," says Kimberley. "You order dinner now, Marcus. Then everything can be your fault."

They eat a companionable dinner of curried vegetable dishes, rice, spicy naan bread and green tea. Afterwards they walk through the hotel gardens and go upstairs to bed in their separate rooms. Marcus misses Kimberley as soon as her bedroom door closes and Kimberley thinks about Marcus whilst she takes her clothes off and gets into bed naked. He looked smokin' tonight, she reflects just before she falls asleep.

12
The Market

In the morning of the following day they meet at the dining area around the swimming pool. The tables are prepared for breakfast. Kimberley is there first. It is eight a.m. She is drinking fresh orange juice and looking around at the other guests, mostly English couples and families who have come here for a beach holiday. Cheaper than Spain and more interesting. Keeping the children settled on the long flight is the worst of it. Now that they are all here parents don't have to worry about their children. There are calm, confident Indian babysitters employed by the hotel, who take the children for adventures in the hotel gardens, and organise tennis and bowls and painting competitions, so that the parents can relax on the beach.

Marcus arrives. He is dressed casually with Panama Jack boots on. Kimberley is wearing her usual safari outfit and looks ready for anything.

"Good morning, Marcus," she says. "Did you oversleep?"

"It's early, isn't it?" says Marcus, "and no, I did not oversleep. I have been organising a taxi for the day."

"For the whole day, Marcus? What for?" asks Kimberley.

"There is a long line of taxis parked across the road from the hotel. The drivers are asleep inside their taxis. If we pay one for the whole day then he is pleased and will look after us and carry anything we may buy in the market today and we get a free guide. So I chose a man who spoke reasonable English and was clean and his taxi looked okay. Now he is waiting for us. He can also speak the language to the local people and help us that way."

"Perfect," says Kimberley. "This orange juice is good, try some." She hands her glass to Marcus, who takes a sip.

"Delicious," he says. "Is there a menu for breakfast?"

"I guess so," says Kimberley, "but the waiter said that we can get anything we like."

"What would you like?" asked Marcus.

"Remember those kind of curry spicy potatoes we had last night with herbs on them?" says Kimberley. "I am going to get me some of those with eggs. And with coffee. Do you think they have coffee?"

"I expect so," says Marcus. "Let's find out."

The waiter arrives at their table smiling. "A beautiful day, sir and madam," he says. He says this to all of his guests every morning because it pleases them. He has read a book about the weather in Northern Europe and certainly the English visitors to India seem to talk about the weather every day. The waiter wishes his customers to be happy. "Very good weather," he says, still smiling.

Marcus tells him, "We would like breakfast."

"Certainly, sir. Of course, sir. Very rapidly, sir. What do you desire?"

The word 'desire' reminds Marcus of his thoughts last night. Kimberley is dressed this morning as a kind of colonial owner of an African plantation. Big shorts, khaki shirt, white ankle socks and boots. To Marcus, however, she still looks very desirable.

"What do I desire?" Marcus says. "Kimberley?" He turns to look at her.

"Sure," says Kimberley, and tells the waiter what she wants. Marcus orders a more conventional breakfast with toast and tea.

"I want to buy spices in town today," says Kimberley. "What about you?"

Marcus looks up. "I'm taking a camera," he says. "I want to create a record of the trip. I will never remember all the details without photographs."

"Okay," says Kimberley. "When you are ready I will meet you outside the hotel, say around nine o'clock?"

"Fine," says Marcus, who is still enjoying his breakfast. "Why does food taste better when you eat it out of doors in the open air?" he asks.

"I have never eaten curried spicy potatoes and eggs before. Inside or outside, so I can't say," answers Kimberley.

After they have both visited their rooms again to prepare and to collect the things they want for the morning they meet downstairs outside the hotel and walk across the empty dusty road to the taxi. The driver springs out and opens a rear passenger door for Kimberley. He leaves Marcus to get in on his own.

"Where may I take you, sir?" asks the driver.

"I want to buy spices," says Kimberley, "and Marcus wants to photograph everything and everybody."

Marcus has a large canvas bag over one shoulder. It contains six spare films. His Leica camera is hanging from a strap around his neck.

"Driver, please stop where the women are selling fruit at the entrance to the beach," says Marcus. "I want to buy some."

The driver stops as requested and Marcus get out to buy two large bags of oranges and two large bags of small bananas. He gets back into the taxi and they drive towards the town of Mapusa.

"You gonna feed the five thousand, Marcus?" asks Kimberley, with a grin.

"I hope so," says Marcus.

The taxi stops outside one of the entrances to a big covered market. The driver gets out and opens Kimberley's door. When Marcus and Kimberley are together the driver tells them, "I am coming with you, to show you the best places. Follow me." He walks in front of them through the thronging market, which appears to sell every possible kind of food. Except of course that it is all fresh and there are no processed foods or preserved foods at all. Just stall after stall with baskets lined with worn hessian sacks containing vegetables, beans, rice of different kinds, lentils, pulses, herbs and after twenty yards, stalls which sell spices. There are separate heaps of spices contained in large open ceramic bowls, each about two feet in diameter and each with different brightly-coloured powders and leaves. The taxi driver stops. "Very good place," he says and stands back.

Kimberley kneels down to look at the produce and two women who are sitting cross-legged tell her the names of the different spices. The women do not seem to know any English words or expressions. The taxi driver steps forward to help. Kimberley wants to buy a small quantity of every different spice and a medium size packet of saffron. The taxi driver negotiates for her and the purchases are packed into thick brown paper packages. Marcus stands back and looks at the market taking deliberate photographs and taking care to photograph Kimberley as she looks through all of the spices.

After about fifteen minutes she gets up and says, "Okay, I'm done."

The taxi driver takes the packages from her. "I will carry," he says.

"Please show us the market," says Marcus.

The stalls extend over about two acres. It is nearly all women who are selling and tending to the stalls. They wear bright colours and their clothes cover their bodies almost completely. Everywhere there is the rich dark thick hair of the women shining in the bright sunshine. Stalls have umbrellas shading the women who are working. Men stroll by displaying confidence and an air of superiority. The men wear long trousers, brightly-coloured cotton shirts and sandals. The men do not do any work but look important. A small gang of five or six children are now following Marcus and Kimberley as they follow the taxi driver. They come across a fish stall. All of the different kinds of fish are laid out separately in rows on top of basket lids. There are four or five old-fashioned black umbrellas over a lot of the fish. Marcus and Kimberley walk on, with the taxi driver in the lead. They pass a meat stall. No flies were attracted to the fish stall. The fish were very fresh. The meat attracted no flies as Kimberley and Marcus passed it.

They come upon an empty space with what seems to be a barber's chair. As they draw closer they realise that it is a dentist's chair and that the dentist has five patients waiting on low chairs whilst he attends to a man sitting in the dentist's chair. There is a drill, which is attached by cables to a bicycle, which is raised up with its back wheel off the ground. The dentist's drill cables are connected to the hub of the back wheel instead of the bicycle chain. A young man is pedalling vigorously to keep speed up in the drill which the dentist is using inside the patient's mouth.

"Aah, aah, aah," the patient is gripping the arms of the dentist's chair tightly. The dentist is wearing a white tunic, which is flecked with blood.

"Rich patients come in the morning," says the taxi driver. 'When the young man is fresh. The poorer patients come in the afternoon when the young man is tired."

They all walk on, Marcus sucking his teeth thoughtfully. The three of them are still followed by children. When they are out of sight of the dentist and can no longer hear the patient's cries, Marcus stops.

"Wait," he calls to Kimberley and the taxi driver. Marcus reaches into his big canvas bag. "Here," he calls and throws each of the children who have been following an orange and a banana. The children sit down at the side of the walkway and begin immediately to eat the fruit.

The taxi driver, Marcus and Kimberley walk on. They emerge from the other side of the market and see three cows, two standing and one sitting. They are being watched by a single woman. One cow is white and the other two are brown. They look well fed. Marcus and Kimberley walk on until Marcus sees a shop which sells fireworks. A motorbike passes them, ridden by a man in grey trousers and a white shirt with a woman sitting side-saddle on the back with her handbag secured under her arm. When the motorbike has gone by Marcus says, "Come on. I want to look in here."

The taxi driver walks in with them. Kimberley is astonished to see a vast stock of fireworks, some of them very big, being kept five feet away from a roadway and twenty yards from the busy market. The firework shop is inside a wooden building.

"We will blow ourselves up if we buy any of those, Marcus," says Kimberley.

"No, we won't," says Marcus. "We will get the people in the shop to set off all of the fireworks we buy." He turns to the taxi driver. "Please tell the shop owner that I want a very big firework display on the beach tonight, just opposite to the last food hut. The one which is the furthest walk from the hotel. And we want the fireworks show to start at eight thirty tonight. I will pay this much." Marcus hands the driver a bundle of Indian rupees and watches and listens as the driver bargains with the shopkeeper before handing over the money. Marcus hears figures discussed.

"I will give him half the money now," says the driver, "and half after the show tonight. I look after you, sir."

Marcus looks at him. "Thank you," he says. "Now there is one more thing I want. Can you please tell all of the families? All of the children from the hotel village, that there will be fireworks and food on the beach tonight."

"Food also?" says the taxi driver. "Where do we get the food?"

"You can help me with that," says Marcus. "I want kebabs. That is, meat and vegetables cooked on sticks, so that people can eat it easily. And I want enough for forty people."

"Yes sir," says the driver. "I can arrange to have pieces of chicken cooked with peppers and onions and served with naan bread."

"That will be great," says Marcus. "Be generous and then tell me how much it will cost. I will give you the money at the hotel at three o'clock today."

"Yes sir," says the driver, who wonders if Marcus is a little mad or simply very rich and trying to buy himself a better karma. The driver is pleased. His own children and their friends will be happy.

"Now we want to go somewhere for lunch," says Marcus.

"Yes sir," says the driver. "What would you like?"

"Something that is cooked fresh in front of us," says Kimberley. "Something light. We are going on the beach this afternoon and we do not want a lot of food."

"Yes madam, I know the place," says the driver. "We will go there in the taxi, madam."

When they have walked back to the taxi, Marcus has already taken many photographs. They are both glad to sit in the back of the taxi. It gives them a little privacy from the relentless throng of people walking all around them and from the children who are always following them.

Marcus's bag of fruit is almost empty now. Only four oranges remain. The taxi drives away towards the direction of the hotel village. On the outskirts of Mapusa the driver stops the car. "We are here, sir," he says, and gets out of the car.

They enter a large restaurant furnished with dark wood tables and chairs. Along one wall of the restaurant is a long polished metal barbecue, hot plate and grill.

"Food is cooked here, sir," says the driver. "I will tell the owner what you would like. Goat, possibly. Goat meat is very good. Goat grilled with onions and courgettes, sir. Very good. Served with spicy rice sir. All fresh, sir."

"What do you think?" Marcus asks Kimberley.

"You promised no food poisoning," says Kimberley. "I guess goat is all right. I've had it before. Tastes like lamb."

"Yes, that will be very good," says Marcus, "and some Indian beer as well. Very cold. Is beer all right with you, Kimberley?"

"You are the boss," says Kimberley. "I am happy to be inside in the cool."

The lunch is fiery hot and spicy. Marcus asks the waiter why it is so hot. The waiter fetches the manager, who explains. "Hot chillies, sir, are in the food. Good for the stomach, sir, in hot weather. Good for the stomach of a visitor to India, sir. Helps to keep stomach calm."

"Thank you," says Marcus.

He and Kimberley eat with more confidence now the spices have been explained.

They enjoy their lunch. Kimberley wants to go to the beach. "I want to lie on the sand, Marcus," she says.

"Have you done your exercises today?" asks Marcus. "Have you been skipping?"

"This morning," answers Kimberley. "I skipped on the terrace next to the pool. I wore my gym clothes so that I would not upset the staff. And I did all of my stretching exercises. What about you, Marcus? You are going to seize up."

"I will go swimming this afternoon," answers Marcus, "in the sea."

"What about sharks, Marcus?" asks Kimberley. "There may be sharks and barracuda."

"I don't know," says Marcus. "I will ask someone."

They finish their lunch and take the taxi back to the hotel. Marcus pays the taxi driver for the whole day and also for tonight's food arrangements. "Are there any sharks in the sea here?" asks Marcus.

"I have not ever been in the sea, sir," says the driver. "I do not know."

13
Fireworks

Marcus and Kimberley go inside the hotel and change for the
beach. They meet again outside and walk towards the beach
path. It is three forty-five p.m.

Once on the sand they stroll along the shoreline, moving
away from the crowds of people and further up the beach, just
past the wooden hut where they have arranged supper. There
are gypsy women on the beach moving in groups of three or
four. They are carrying very thin cotton blankets, embroidered
with swirling patterns of coloured thread, and with tiny
mirrors sewn into the cloth. The women carry the blankets
folded up small and when they approach a group of
holidaymakers they flick the blankets to open them. The
blankets are very large. One different colour after another.

"We are not buying anything," holidaymakers say
politely.

"No, no," the gypsies say. "We want to show you these
things. Only to show you."

A charming patter of description follows. The gypsies
explaining that the work is done by the very oldest women at
their camp. Women who cannot walk now. Cannot do any
other work. They make these things to sell for pocket money,
the gypsies say. Only for themselves. For their little pocket

money. The gypsies are so warm in their manners and so open in their dark faces that before long they have sold five or six blankets. They give the purchasers profuse blessings as they move away. Walking backwards and blessing the holidaymakers with high emotion. The holidaymakers are left feeling very pleased with what they have done.

"Do you notice that as soon as somebody says that they will buy one," Marcus says, "the gypsy claps her hands together very loudly? One loud crack. It stops the process of introduction and ends the sales talk. Smack. The deal is done. There is no more talking. It is a very effective technique."

"Come on, Marcus," says Kimberley. "Relax. Maybe you could pay a gypsy to go swimming in the sea. To test for sharks."

Just as she says this four teenage Indian girls run past them towards the waves. They are all dressed in very thin cotton, which covers their bodies and legs. They start to swim in the sea whilst wearing these thin clothes. It is very modest and dignified. Kimberley thinks about the yellow bikini which she is wearing beneath her summer cotton dress.

"Maybe the dresses protect them from sharks, Marcus," says Kimberley. "Do you want to borrow mine?"

"I'm going to lie in the sun for a while," says Marcus. "If you hear screaming and splashing let me know, please."

"They are screaming already," says Kimberley. "I think it is happiness and excitement. I'll tell you if the sound changes." She slips off her sandals and her wide-brimmed Panama hat and then her summer dress. She lays her towel onto the sand and lies down.

"You cannot use suntan oil on a sandy beach," Kimberley says. "So I'll have to time myself. Thirty minutes either side."

"What will you do then?" asks Marcus. "Pull a switch and put the sun out?"

"I will go into the hut and drink a lot of water," says Kimberley. "Friends told me to drink a litre of bottled water every day here. We have not done that yet. The heat can dehydrate you, they said."

"I will buy a lot of bottled water tomorrow," says Marcus. "Today we will have to survive on alcohol," he laughs.

They both lie quietly for a long time. Marcus is sunbathing in dark blue swimming shorts. He has his money buttoned up inside the pockets. He hopes that Indian rupees can survive seawater. He has decided to swim because he has been sitting around a lot recently in planes and taxis and restaurants. Marcus tells Kimberley that he is going swimming and he gets up and runs into the sea. Marcus takes a shallow dive into the water and begins to swim powerfully for one hundred yards in each direction parallel to the shore. He swims tirelessly up and down and up and down. Kimberley props herself up on her elbows and watches him. He is moving very fast through the water and his pace is constant. After looking for a few minutes Kimberley turns onto her front and starts tanning her back. Marcus continues to swim for about forty minutes until he stops and walks out of the water. He feels exhilarated and vibrant as he walks up the sand towards Kimberley. She hears or feels his footsteps approaching and turns over to look at him.

"The sharks did not catch you?" she asks. "They prefer girls," says Marcus, "so they are waiting for you."

"They are going to have a long wait," says Kimberley. "I am staying here."

She turns over to lie on her stomach again and reaches back to undo the back strap of her bikini top.

"I don't want strap lines on my tan," Kimberley says.

"Why not take the bottom off as well?" asks Marcus.

"That would be an insult to the Indian people," says Kimberley. "It would be rude."

Marcus takes a big tube out of his bag. "Suntan cream," he says. "It is easier to use on a sandy beach than suntan oil. Lie still and I will rub some onto your back."

Kimberley gives him a knowing look but then puts her head between her arms and lies still.

Marcus rubs the suntan cream into Kimberley's skin. Her back is muscled and her skin is as smooth as satin. His hands massage her lower back with cream and he reaches her bikini bottoms. Decisively he puts more cream onto his hands and starts to rub it into the calf of her left leg. Kimberley lies still but raises her leg a little so that Marcus can do a thorough job. I could cream my own legs, she thinks, but I kinda like having Marcus do it. It is sexy, but I am not going to acknowledge it. I am pretending that I have not noticed.

Marcus continues his task; reaching the back of her knee he swiftly moves on to her thigh. Kimberley says nothing, pretending to be asleep. Marcus massages sun cream into her thigh to the very top and then briskly moves to her right leg. He massages cream into the firm calf muscle again and lifts her leg slightly to complete the task. Then without hesitation he proceeds to massage her long smooth thigh, marvelling at how hard the muscles are. Marcus lingers over the job and Kimberley joins in the conspiracy by continuing to pretend that she is asleep. Marcus reaches the top of her thigh and massages the inside of it. His hands stay there a moment longer than necessary and Kimberley has to try hard not to move although her leg wants to quiver. Marcus stops and sits back.

"All done," he says.

"What?" says Kimberley. "Oh, I'm sorry Marcus, I was asleep."

"No strap lines," says Marcus, gazing at the physical perfection of her body as it is stretched out on a towel in front of him.

"Okay," says Marcus, and stands up, wishing to break the spell and to stop his thoughts from racing. "I'm going to walk up the beach a little bit and look at those gypsy girls again. Will you be all right?"

"I'll be all right," says Kimberley, and stays still.

Marcus walks away and when he has gone fifty yards Kimberley lets out a sigh. "Oh boy," she says out loud. "That was special. Good hands. Strong hands. Mmmm!"

She turns onto her back and picking up the sun tan cream which Marcus has left behind she starts to smooth it into the front of her body, releasing her breasts and rubbing cream into them. He will be gone awhile and there is nobody at this end of the beach. The Indian girls who were swimming have gone. I don't want to get white patches. She finishes the task and after rubbing cream into her stomach and the tops of her thighs she lies back, closes her eyes and smooths cream lightly into her face and forehead. Putting the back of her head onto the sand she screws the cap onto the tube of cream, throws it onto Marcus's towel and falls asleep, her body enjoying the embrace of the warm pleasant sunshine and the clean sea air she smells in the breeze as it blows lightly over her body. She falls into a deep sleep.

Marcus has bought four of the large cotton blankets from the gypsies and is now walking down the beach showing the blankets to English holidaymakers. After he has sold two of them and accompanies the sales with a loud clap of his hands, he decides to keep the remaining two blankets. He puts them under his arm and strolls slowly back to the place where he left Kimberley. When he is one hundred yards away he starts looking at the sea. Big rolling waves are still crashing up the beach. There are no swimmers in the sea now. He draws closer to Kimberley and suddenly notices that she is not wearing her bikini top. He doesn't want to walk up to her unexpectedly. He stares self-interestedly for a moment at what he considers to be the perfect breasts and then when he has had a good look he turns and walks towards the sea, whistling loudly. Kimberley hears the whistle from the bottom of her deep sleep and for a minute or two involves the sound of the whistle with the dream she is having. She floats to the surface and opens her eyes. She sits up. She sees Marcus at the seashore. She quickly fastens her bikini top and ruffles her hair with her hands. She stands up and begins to walk towards the sea. Marcus turns around.

"Hello," he says, "not too toasted, I hope."

"Just right," says Kimberley. "I am getting out of the sun now. I'll buy you a drink in the little hut."

"Okay," says Marcus. "I accept."

They walk together into the hut where the old man is sitting motionless on a wooden chair. He is looking at nothing. He pulls himself together when he sees that he has customers.

"Welcome," he says, "What time is it? Am I late?"

"No," says Marcus, "we have just stepped in to buy cold drinks from you. It is only five forty."

"Five forty," says the old man. "Where is my grandson? He is helping me today."

Marcus and Kimberley each buy a cold bottle of beer, which is sunk into a huge block of ice in the hut, and they walk outside to sit in the shade, which the extra-large palm roof provides.

"These are the easy days," says Marcus. "Once we begin to travel it may be tiring. However, we come back here again at the end of our travels."

"Right here?" asks Kimberley.

144

"No, a different place," says Marcus, "and we have a bungalow to live in right on the beach and a local woman to cook for us and clean and go shopping."

"So if we are tired after our travels we get a good rest," says Kimberley. "We are not going to get tired, Marcus. We are not a couple of very old people. We are going to have fun."

"All right," says Marcus and sips his beer.

"So what is the story about all of your fruit every day? And what about the fireworks and food tonight? What's going on, Marcus?" says Kimberley. "Are you trying to be president of the country? Catching votes with fruit bribes."

"This country has four times more people than the United States," answers Marcus. "Can you imagine the work and the effort required to be president of India? There are eighteen different languages spoken here for a start."

"Okay, maybe just mayor of Mapusa," says Kimberley. "Come on, Marcus – give. What's the plan?"

"No plan really," says Marcus. "Just that everywhere we go we will be followed by children. Just five or six children here but it will be far worse when we get to Bombay. Dozens of children all begging. So I am experimenting with the fruit. It seems to me that if we give little children money they have to take it and give it to somebody older. If we give them something which they can eat, then they may stop begging and sit down and eat. That way we get a break from all of the children following us everywhere like mosquitoes."

"We are going to need a lot of fruit," says Kimberley. "Four times the population of the United States and by the look of it here about a third of those are children. You may need a handcart, Marcus."

"It's just an idea, Kimberley," says Marcus. "I will give it a try in Bombay."

"Okay, what about the fireworks and food?" asks Kimberley.

"I like fireworks and food," says Marcus, smiling. "You are going to give dance lessons to the children. I've put posters up in the village."

"Shut up," says Kimberley.

They sit quietly listening to the old man inside the hut instructing his grandson about what to do for their supper.

"Did you see the crabs?" asks Kimberley.

"Yes, there was a big wooden box of them. All are walking about," answers Marcus. "The old man had a bucket of seawater and he was throwing some of it over them from time to time."

"Okay," says Kimberley, "what time is it?"

"It is six thirty," says Marcus, "just about to get dark."

"I'm going for a swim," says Kimberley. "Come with me and look after me. There are big waves now."

"All right," says Marcus. He tells the old man that they will be swimming and that they will be ready for supper at around seven o'clock.

"Yes sir," says the old man.

Darkness is falling quickly as Marcus and Kimberley walk down to the sea and face the big waves. Marcus tells Kimberley to dive through the wave and then out to sea, twenty or thirty feet beyond the waves to where the water will be calm.

"You'll come with me?" says Kimberley.

"I'll go first," says Marcus, "then you only have to copy me. It will be quite safe."

"There is that word 'quite' again," says Kimberley. "Just tell me that it will be safe without a quite."

"It will be safe, Kimberley," says Marcus, "and you will enjoy it."

"Okay, let's go," says Kimberley and gives Marcus a little push.

Everything works out fine and Marcus stays close to Kimberley as she swims. They come ashore in a rush, riding in on a wave until they feel the sand beneath their feet. It is pitch dark now, only a light in the hut guides them. Kimberley springs up and runs swiftly to her beach towel, dries herself and brushes her hair. She is laughing as Marcus walks up.

"We should dress for dinner, Marcus," says Kimberley, as she wriggles into her dress and then proceeds to take her bikini off underneath it. She slips on some white cotton underwear, standing with her back to Marcus whilst he struggles to change his costume with his towel round his waist. Soon they are both clothed and tidy looking. Marcus has combed his hair and made a play of combing his eyebrows.

Marcus knocks at the open door of the hut. "We have a reservation for dinner," he says.

"Yes sir," says the old man. "Please come inside."

The small room inside the hut has been scrubbed and the central table is now covered with a beautifully embroidered cloth. A paraffin lamp lights the room and there are two lit candles on the table. Knives and forks and glasses and plates are all symmetrically arranged for eight people at the table.

Marcus pulls Kimberley's chair out for her and she sits down. He then sits opposite to her. The old man goes to the big wooden ice chest and takes out a bottle of wine. He shows it to Marcus, who is surprised to see that it is Premier Cru Chablis from a very good chateau.

"Marvellous," says Marcus. The old man opens the bottle and pours a little into Marcus's wineglass. Marcus sips and says, "Excellent."

The old man then fills Kimberley's glass. She takes a gulp, smiles and says, "Better Marcus, much better." She hesitates. "Thank you," she says, cautiously.

The man walks outside and comes back with his grandson and his friends. "Your guests, sir," the man says.

The grandson walks out and then comes staggering in from the outside barbecue. He is carrying a very big oval plate of cooked crabs in a red sauce. He puts it down in the centre of the table and runs outside and returns with a big patterned china bowl containing cooked rice. The boy places big spoons beside both of the dishes and stands back with his arms outstretched. "Eat," he says, "please." He gives a delighted smile.

His friends wait politely for Marcus and Kimberley to help themselves. Afterwards the children spoon rice and crabs and sauce onto their own plates. Marcus and Kimberley begin to tuck in to the exotic but simple crab curry dish. The curry is extra hot and the plain rice makes it bearable to the palate. The crabs are like the Florida soft shell crabs and are delicious to eat. Marcus thinks that maybe the hot curry is designed to aid their digestions in the hot climate. They both drink copious amounts of cold bottled water and the wine is remarkably fine. Altogether the dinner is most delicious. Both Kimberley and Marcus are pleased. The children look happy as well.

"It is nearly time for the fireworks," says Marcus. "Can you tell the children about the fireworks, please?" he asks the man who owns the hut.

"They all know, sir," answers that man. "Village children are already waiting outside, sir."

Marcus walked out onto the beach side. It is dark outside but he can see rows and rows of children sitting quietly on the sand. None of them seem to be more than seven or eight years old. Behind them is a long wooden table, which must have

148

been carried onto the beach, and a long metal trough on long metal legs, which is full of burning charcoal with wire grills fixed above. Four men are working to put pieces of chicken, onion and peppers onto long skewers. The children are all very quiet; there is an atmosphere of excited apprehension in the night air. Two men appear in the distance. They are pushing a handcart along the sandy beach. As they get closer Marcus sees the great quantities of brightly-coloured tubes and boxes and large red rockets on the handcart. The two men are wearing dark blue overalls. Marcus's eyes have become accustomed to the moonlight and the white-tipped waves at the edge of the beach, shining in the grey light, clearly defining the start of the deep sea. The man with the handcart wheels it to a position centrally and fifty feet in front of the rows of children. They begin to push wide short metal pipes into the sand in a deliberate pattern. One of the men then starts to place a variety of fireworks into the tubes. The other man pushes long metal tins into the sand and places rockets into the tins. One man then fills two metal buckets with seawater in case of an accident or a faulty firework. When they are ready one man carefully lights a taper, which is fixed to the end of a broom handle. He hands it to his workmate and lights a second taper fixed to another broom handle.

The older man says some words very loudly in a language which Marcus and Kimberley do not recognise. The children sit up straight and the two men light the four rockets one after another as quickly as possible. After barely three seconds there is a piercing whistling sound, followed by another and another and another as the four rockets fly up into the night sky and, one after the other, explode with deafening bangs and a circle of cascading coloured sparks.

The children look startled and some of them are frightened. They are wondering if something has gone wrong.

One little boy puts his arm protectively around his sister's shoulders. The firework men are rapidly lighting fireworks in the tubes and once again there are only a few moments before the extravagant colours of the flames and the sparks light up the dark sands. The children are more confident now, realising that the colours and the sparks and the flames are not a mistake. The confidence runs through the group and the seated children begin to relax. The men are discarding spent fireworks and replacing them with new ones, which they light. They follow the ground fireworks with more rockets and at this point one of the children lets out a sharp giggle and other children pick up on this and begin to laugh with happiness. The happiness is contagious and the rows of little children are now rocking with delight. Barrages of fireworks and rockets are lit and fizz and explode and spark. The men then light one big box firework, which they have placed down the beach away from the children and closer to the sea. The firework is one of those which changes colour. Marcus remembers that these were called traffic lights when he was very young. The noisy firework has just turned to a bright red when an unexpectedly big wave rushes up the beach and extinguishes it. The children are thrilled and all begin to clap enthusiastically.

Kimberley is standing with Marcus behind the children. She glances at him. He is smiling. He looks younger. He is right, she thinks. This was a great idea. I am getting more out of it than the children are. Why did he do it?

Marcus looks towards her. "Are you having a good time?" he asks.

"A very good time," Kimberley answers.

The two firework men are working very quickly now to create a grand finale. They are pushing two fireworks into each tube and three rockets into each tin. They will have to light them all very rapidly. They are working on the assumption that they will only have to light one of the ground fireworks in each tube and that the ensuing flames and sparks will ignite the others. The rockets however will all have to be lit individually and they are aware that they must do all three of them in a tin and then work backwards to the next tin and the next, moving out of the line of fire as they proceed. The new rockets have special siren type whistles, which will give a softer, and together, a more harmonious sound than the previous whistle rockets. The rockets when they explode are designed to release little parachutes of small white flares, which will float down into the sea. The ground fireworks are a contrasting display of colours with little bangs, which fire different coloured mini fiery teardrops, which fall to the ground. It is important to light everything as nearly simultaneously as is humanly possible. The more coordinated, the better the effect will be.

The children are relaxed now and happy. A few of them are still laughing and some of them are whispering to their neighbours. The fireworks men shout out a word to get their attention and then run from side to side with their flaming broomsticks to create the final effects. Rockets shoot into the sky as the ground fireworks begin firing their little skyward projectiles. By dexterity and good luck the final display is perfectly coordinated. It is noisy, colourful, surprising and lights up the night sky very brightly for a few intense moments.

Then all is silent. The children are stunned and then begin to applaud.

While that the final display has been created, the skewers of food have been put onto the wire grills above the charcoal and are already half-cooked. The four men who are preparing the food shout to Marcus, "Feast is very soon ready, sir, shall we tell the children?"

"Have you got enough?" asks Marcus. "I think that I have counted over forty children."

"We have very extra, sir," says the leading caterer. "We brought extra chicken and vegetables sir. Very, very plenty, sir."

"All right," says Marcus. "Could you try to get the children to line up?"

"Very good children, sir. They will line up, sir."

Marcus catches sight of the taxi driver who had helped so much to create a success of the evening. The driver is standing with three little children, two boys and one girl. All of them are exquisitely dressed in bright colours.

"Good evening," Marcus says, as he walks up to the man. "Thank you for your organization and hard work. I think that it has been a success."

"It is the most wonderful success, sir," says the taxi driver, "and I and all of my children are thanking you, sir."

"Please stand at the front of the lineup for food," says Marcus, "and make sure that your children get plenty to eat."

"There is plenty sir," says the taxi driver pushing his children quickly to the front line.

Soon all of the children are eating. Next the firework men are eating and finally the caterers finish the remaining food between them. The evening is at an end. Marcus does not know what to do, but Kimberley does.

"Three cheers for Marcus," she shouts. "Hip hip, hurrah."

The children look curious because they do not speak English and then five or six of them shout, "Hap, hap, harroo."

The other children follow suit and soon all forty-two children are laughing and shouting, "Hap, hap, harroo," as they slowly depart and begin to walk along the seashore towards their homes in the village, hap, hap, harroo sounds in the distance. Soon they have all gone. The caterers are packing up and so are the fireworks men. The surprise party is over. Marcus and Kimberley are left standing alone. All lights have been taken away and the beach is dark.

"Well, it's just you and me," says Kimberley. "Let's walk back."

They collect their beach things and slowly start to walk down the beach towards the entrance path. There is nobody else on the sand. Kimberley says, "I've got a torch. I bought a torch in the market. One minute." She reaches into the bag which Marcus is carrying and pulls out a red metal torch.

She strides out in front of Marcus and turns the torch on and shines the light into the sand. The sand is moving. Kimberley gives a little shriek and shines the torch more carefully at the sand. The wet seashore of the beach is covered with crabs. Crawling and slithering around each other and over the top of each other. Their claws held out high in front of their bodies as they strive for personal space.

Kimberley gives a shout. "Look out, Marcus. Brace yourself. I'm jumping onto you." She takes two big strides and with the third she jumps gracefully onto Marcus's shoulders.

For a moment Marcus experiences the warm sharp sweet tang of Kimberley and then she pushes her hands down onto his head and shuffles herself round until she is facing forwards with her thighs over his shoulders and her calves tucked under his arms.

"You have to carry me," she orders.

Marcus keeps his back straight and walks steadily forward across the sand. Kimberley has dropped her torch but Marcus senses as well as hears the crabs scuttling sideways out of the pathway of Marcus's heavy footfall on the sand. The crabs must feel a slight tremble through the sand and self-

153

preservation causes them to move out of the way. They must have done it last night, thinks Marcus, when we had no torch. He strides purposefully and strongly along the beach, keeping his back stiff and straight, and he is acutely aware of Kimberley's upper thighs on either side of his neck. They reach the pathway to the village road and Marcus walks up the path. At the road he stops.

"Bend your knees, not your back, Marcus," shouts Kimberley.

Marcus crouches only slightly and Kimberley slips off him and lands lightly onto the road.

"Thanks for the ride,' she says.

They walk to the hotel and because it is late they go straight up to their respective beds.

14
Bombay

In the morning after the usual breakfast routines they spend the next few days at the beach. No crab curry, no fireworks and they walk back to the hotel each afternoon before it is dark in order to have a drink on the terrace and a vegetable dinner at the hotel.

"We are leaving for Bombay soon," says Marcus, "and from there we will go to three other big places. We will not take a lot of luggage with us. I have arranged for our things to be stored in the hotel here until we get back. Just take a single bag."

"I didn't think we were coming back here?" says Kimberley.

"The bungalow we are going to stay in before we start back for England is only three or four miles down the beach," answers Marcus, "and it is owned by the people who own this hotel. So they will cooperate by storing things here for us until we return. When we go to the bungalow our luggage will be waiting for us. I will arrange for us to have some clothes made in Bombay and we can travel in those."

"Okay, Marcus," says Kimberley, "but we take our own walking shoes, yes?"

"Yes, that's right," says Marcus, "particularly if you want me to carry you again."

When they are rested, exercised and tanned, Kimberley having sunbathed somewhere secluded every day and skipped and done her stretches every day and Marcus having swum up and down, up and down every day, they are ready to depart for the big cities.

Both Marcus and Kimberley have packed one hand luggage bag each.

A coach arrives at the hotel to take them to Bombay.

"Quick Marcus, get the front seat," says Kimberley, pushing Marcus ahead because he was just about to step aside for an elderly couple to get onto the coach first. "Be gallant back home," says Kimberley. "I want to get a good view."

Kimberley seizes the front seats ahead of any other possible contenders and sits down in the window with a little shout of triumph.

"Ready, Marcus," she says. "Let's go."

Other passengers are still boarding the coach ponderously, however, and it is half an hour later before the driver starts the engine and pulls away from the hotel.

Kimberley stares out at the ever-changing variety of scenery and people and animals the whole way to Bombay. She almost has her nose pressed against the glass window. After sidling through the city suburbs, which are thronged with people, and driving down a vast curved road fronting a promenade and a bay of spectacular size and innumerable crowds of seagulls, the coach arrives at a luxurious ornate waterfront hotel. There are cargo boats moored at the quayside and ferry boats and fishing boats and pleasure craft. An enormous expanse of sea stretches into the distance in front of the hotel.

Once inside Marcus plays his trick of simultaneously flattering and bribing the hotel manager and they are shown upstairs to two splendid and spacious rooms.

"That was a dusty and tiring journey," says Kimberley, "but I saw a lot of things that I would never see in the United States. Boy, this is a great room, Marcus. What are we going to do now?"

"Okay, well because we are a bit travel worn I thought that we should get a horse and carriage to take us on a little tour of this part of the city. It will be comfortable, we will move at a faster pace than walking and we will be higher up than walking. We can look around and then if we like something we can come back to see it more closely another day. I also thought that we should eat in the hotel restaurant tonight. It is said to be one of the best restaurants in the city," says Marcus.

"I agree with everything, Marcus," says Kimberley, "and when are we getting a load of clothes made?"

"I thought that we could order them tomorrow morning," says Marcus, "and then they should be ready the same day."

"Great," says Kimberley. "How long do you want to get ready? I am ready now."

"I will meet you downstairs in fifteen minutes," says Marcus. He walks down the stairs to arrange for a tailor and dressmaker to visit them at the hotel in the morning and he asks the concierge to hold a horse and carriage for them. He tells them that they will be ready in ten minutes.

Marcus then books a table at the hotel restaurant for dinner. Kimberley comes bouncing down the stairs. She is wearing her safari outfit and looks cool and relaxed.

"Your carriage awaits," says Marcus, and takes her hand to lead her to the waiting horse driver and carriage. Marcus helped her up into the carriage

"Just like New York," says Kimberley. "You can ride in a carriage through New York. Different language, of course."

The driver has been told by the hotel concierge about the route and the timing and the horse pulls the carriage at a slow trot. It is a wonderful height from which to sightsee and the speed of the carriage is comfortable. Kimberley is smiling and so is Marcus.

"I feel as if I am in India now," says Marcus. "Bombay."

"Sure," says Kimberley. "Do we have plans?"

"We do," answers Marcus, "three distinct destinations over the next couple of days, before we move on."

"Good," says Kimberley.

The carriage is moving slowly now because the traffic has slowed. A small boy is running alongside the carriage with one hand stretched out. "Rupees, rupees," he shouts. The driver tries to whip him away.

"Where is your fruit now, Marcus?" asks Kimberley.

"None," says Marcus. "I am not prepared."

"Okay then," says Kimberley. She opens the little door of the carriage, leans out and picks the boy up and puts him into the carriage.

The driver looks around. More crazy foreign people, he thinks. I will have to wash the inside of the carriage.

The boy is about six or seven years old. He is not frightened. He looks curious.

Kimberley looks inside her bag and finds some chocolate, which she gives to the boy. She helps him to unwrap the silver paper and indicates by pointing to the boy's mouth that he should eat the chocolate. The boy does, making a grim face as he chews the soft chocolate.

"Do you think he likes it?" asks Kimberley.

"It is different for him," says Marcus, "so he is not sure."

The little boy is frowning and then slowly he begins to smile. He sits up and looks around. He seems very pleased to be in the carriage with two crazy foreigners.

Kimberley and Marcus are watching the crowds of swiftly moving people on the pavements. Some obstruction to the traffic causes the carriage to stop. Whilst it is stationary the little boy scrambles over the side of the carriage and drops down onto the road. He looks around quickly and then runs away along the edge of the pavement.

"I think I have been snubbed," says Kimberley. "There is a young man who doesn't want a girl like me."

"He is one in a million," says Marcus.

Kimberley smiles.

They are passing a building which is covered by bamboo scaffolding, all tied together with thick string. It looks random but it must be a tested method. There are dozens of workers on the scaffolding and Marcus wonders how the bamboo can carry their combined weight. They all appear to be working very hard. The horse and carriage pass by the building and the next sight is an elephant with a piano roped to his back. The elephant does not appear to be distressed and is lolloping along with quiet footsteps. There is an elephant keeper walking along with him and talking softly to him. The elephant's back is very high and the piano looks precariously tied.

"Marcus, this is the hell of a place," says Kimberley. "There is a motor scooter with two adults and two children on it and over there is a bicycle with two people on it."

"And there are crowds of people walking," says Marcus. "It is not like America."

"It certainly is not," says Kimberley. "Nobody walks in America. Even the poorest people have cars."

"Do you want to stop and get out anywhere?" asked Marcus.

"No," says Kimberley. "I'm cool right here. I like this movement and I'm not mixed up with all of those people on the pavements. We can do all that tomorrow. Today, luxury."

"We are in the best hotel in Bombay," says Marcus. "My guess is that the menu in the restaurant tonight will be international. The standard should be very high."

"Good," says Kimberley. "I snuck my smallest dress into my bag so I can look like a lady tonight."

The coach and the horse are trotting quickly along amidst all of the traffic.

"Shall we go back?" says Marcus. "I would like to take a long soak in the bath."

"You speak as if there is only one bath," says Kimberley. "The bath. What about my bath? Do we have to share a bath?"

"Regrettably, no," says Marcus. "Your room has a luxurious bathroom."

"Okay," says Kimberley. "Let's head back there."

Marcus speaks to the driver, who nods his head and turns right at the next turning, bringing them around a huge block until they are facing back to the hotel.

At the hotel entrance the doorman helps them both out of their coach. Marcus pays the driver generously and they walk inside.

"I'll see you in the restaurant bar at eight o'clock," says Marcus.

"Sure thing," answers Kimberley.

Marcus is there first, wearing a blue blazer, white shirt and grey trousers. The bar is very ornate. Like an over-decorated, exaggerated version of the Ritz, thinks Marcus. Huge, with intricately carved panelling and elegant tables and chairs arranged to create little intimate areas separated from

160

one another by exotic plants or statues or folding screens. Each table gives the illusion of isolation – a tranquil little island for private meetings between couples or foursomes. The tables are topped with white marble, inlaid with coloured patterns. There are rugs on the floor and the ceilings are high like an English church, concave and with decorated support beams.

A waiter comes up to the table where Marcus has chosen to sit. He is wearing white gloves and a white uniform. He also has a white turban on his head. Marcus is not sure whether that is an indication of his religion or simply the preferred style of the bar or the hotel.

"Good evening, sir," says the waiter. "May I fetch something for you?"

Marcus answers, "I am waiting for my guest. We are dining in your restaurant. When my guest arrives I will order drinks for us both. Thank you."

"Thank you, sir," replies the waiter and glides away.

Marcus sits, still mildly disorientated by the atmosphere of calm and luxury. How do they clean this place? he thinks. It must be a lot of work. He sits and begins to relax. Bombay, he thinks. Well, it is different.

At this moment Kimberley walks into the bar. She does not immediately see Marcus and she stands for a few moments, staring at the grandeur of the place.

Marcus observes her. His first thought is that she is a very healthy specimen, but that makes her sound like a horse. She is not. She is a very beautiful girl; fresh, strong, optimistic. Looking at her, Marcus feels the onslaught of a heavy sadness. Something deep inside him. A feeling of loss. As if he has missed the last train to paradise and there will not be another one. He is aching with loss and almost overwhelming sadness. What did she say? A man has to know that he deserves a cheerleader. Has to know that he is good enough for her, better yet that he is too good for her.

Marcus feels none of these things. He does not even understand the rules or the culture or the values surrounding Kimberley's life. He does not fit with her. He is an outsider. She is a prize who will go to the man who knows all the rules. A winner. A man completely unlike Marcus. A man who takes his success seriously. Whereas Marcus does not take material success seriously. He finds it very hard to take seriously. Financially successful men in Marcus's expertise have always seemed one-dimensional, sort of shallow, as if the inability to see the other person's point of view is what strengthens them. It's what drives them on. Marcus finds other people's points of view interesting. Not convincing but not wrong, just an interesting angle to his own. He has no doubt that he could legally take money from the other people around him, but if he did that he would need to suppress any interest in them altogether and see them as numbers. Steps on his way to the top. Marcus, however, does not really believe that there is a top. That is his problem. That is what puts a gulf between him and Kimberley. A gulf as big as the Grand Canyon and tonight it makes him ache with loss and wanting and knowing that it is impossible. Pull yourself together, Marcus, he tells himself. What you are feeling is lust, nothing more. Could you really be happy on a day-to-day basis with this girl? She is so determined to progress onwards and upwards. Could you live with that? Possibly you don't even like her? I like her, thinks Marcus. She is a challenge to my way of thinking. And she has fabulous legs.

Kimberley sees him and walks over to his table. She is dressed to attract attention; a small dress indeed. And it fits everywhere and emphasises her physical perfection. Her perfect curves. Her height and elegance. Her dynamic energy.

162

Her gymnastic body. Her irrepressible, overwhelming sex appeal.

Marcus feels suddenly lonely. What the hell is a homecoming queen, is the first thought which pops into his head. And what is a prom dance? A different world, he thinks. Buck up, Marcus, and find out about it all. Get to know her better.

"Good evening, Miss Jacksonville," Marcus says. "May I arrange a drink for you?"

"Yes, sir," says Kimberley. "I am ready for a drink and I am ready to eat. Boy, we had a different day today."

"Different again tomorrow, I think," says Marcus. "We are joining some kind of walking tour to see certain parts of the city. Safety in numbers and we will have a guide. We leave right after we have ordered our travelling clothes."

"After we get our breakfast, I hope," says Kimberley.

"Of course, we are here for pleasure," says Marcus. "Now what would you like to drink?"

The waiter glides up to their little table. He has two dinner menus and enquires what drinks they would like.

Marcus and Kimberley order cocktails, wine and an extravagant dinner.

"I am having a good time here, Marcus," says Kimberley.

"Okay, but now you have to keep your side of the bargain," says Marcus.

"Ooooh, Marcus, what is it that you want?" says Kimberley. "You're not suggesting that we break the rules?"

"Certainly not," answers Marcus. "I want answers to some questions which I asked you before. You would not talk in England. You told me to wait until we got to India. We are in India now so I would like some answers."

"Marcus, you sound like the FBI," says Kimberley.

"Tell me what you want quickly. I'm getting frightened. Oh and Marcus," she says, with her eyes dancing, "make it exciting, okay?"

"Education," says Marcus. "I don't know how exciting that is in the United States but I would like to know about it."

"Well, some parts of it can be exciting," says Kimberley, "but they are not on the curriculum. Ask away, Marcus, but don't go so fast that I can't eat my roast beef."

"We will take it slowly," says Marcus.

"A boy said that to me before," says Kimberley, "but he soon speeded up."

"Behave yourself," says Marcus. "I want to understand the United States education system."

"You are masterful, Marcus," says Kimberley, smiling and pretending to bat her eyelids at him. "Go ahead."

"Well, you have state schools, don't you?"

"Not all state schools, Marcus," says Kimberley. "And we call them public schools. We have some private schools as well, but they are generally no better for education than the public schools. Private schools just have uniforms and decorum and traditions. Mostly to do with established rich people wanting their children to be educated alongside other rich children. For real education you get it all at the public schools and you get a lot of traditions and pageants and so forth at public schools as well."

"Pageants?" asks Marcus.

"I don't know what you would call them. There is a lot of effort made to create a kind of team spirit in the schools, sort of competition with friendships. And a lot is done to make you feel as if you are part of something. Your school yearbook. Your photograph and all that stuff. A little writing about what you were good at, at school. So I guess you grow up knowing that you are going to be good at something and knowing that

164

everyone's going to read about it in the yearbook. I mean, you don't get any entries which say, 'Here is Sally Springfield and she was no good at a damn thing'. No, they will give her some praise for dressmaking or something. So that she leaves school kinda knowing who she is. These yearbooks last forever, you know. I mean you can go in thirty years' time, more even, and read about the classmates of your year. Of course it's much better to have entries that say that you won things, that you were champion at something. And there's a whole lot of things you can be champion at. All kinds of things. Better if you are popular. You've got your homecoming Queen and King, that kind of thing. Your classmates have to nominate you because maybe you have done a lot to contribute to the school. And then all the students have to vote to see who gets to be the winner, the homecoming Queen. This is a big public ceremony just before the football game. Usually last year's king and queen show up to crown the new guys. It all takes place around late September, early October. Then it all gets put into your school yearbook. Can be a real bummer if later in your life you only manage to run a burger bar or something and it says right there in your school yearbook that you were going to be a real life success."

"Would it say that?" asks Marcus.

"Why sure," says Kimberley. "There you are in your yearbook. The most popular guy in the school. Top at a number of important school activities. It is obvious from that that you are going to be a success. And then somehow you just fuck up and don't make it. Means all your best times are behind you then. You're busted. You didn't get anywhere. No, the whole education system is designed to get the best out of you so that after you leave school you have a good idea about who you are and what you're gonna do. The whole system kinda gives you a push."

165

"What about education itself?" asks Marcus.

"I reckon we've got a good education system," says Kimberley. "I mean we've got people into space, onto the moon and all that. We have a helluva defence system. We are leaders in computer systems and back up and we also study all your old literature, Shakespeare, Thomas Hardy and all that, as well as all of our own American literature. We have a top class science education and really good physical coaching as well. We have some great TV shows. Real good scriptwriters. We have Hollywood. Films, which we sell all over the world. By the time we leave our education system we have had a good start for life. 'Course we don't do much about languages but then we don't need languages unless we are leaving the country. Only six percent of Americans have a passport, do you know that? They can go north if they want snow, south if they want sunshine. They don't have to leave America. And what good would languages be? Look at it here. Eighteen separate languages here and I bet you couldn't learn one of them in Britain."

I bet you could, thinks Marcus.

"No, Americans are educated for America. They are educated to love their country and to know all about their history. American kids know all of the names of the American presidents and all the dates of the main things which have happened in the country. I am proud of my country, Marcus. Proud to be an American. Ask me something else."

"What about recreation?" asks Marcus.

"Recreation?" asks Kimberley.

"You know, sport. That kind of thing," answers Marcus.

"We get sports coaching," says Kimberley. "We get taught how to do it properly; netball, baseball, running, jumping, swimming. Whatever. We have coaches."

"Swimming?" asks Marcus.

"Yeah, I missed out on swimming," says Kimberley. "I wanted dancing more."

"Dancing?" says Marcus. "You get taught dancing?"

"Sure thing," says Kimberley. "Competitive dancing. You just don't go out to dance. You go out to win dance contests. So you train and you learn and you practise so that you can win a dance contest. Kids don't just jig about in the States. They dance."

"So when you are young you enter dance contests?" asks Marcus.

"So do you," says Kimberley. "I've seen it on TV. British dancing."

"Not quite the same," says Marcus, "but tell me more. Tell me about after school. About college and about your first job."

"Okay, that's enough for today, Marcus. I gotta eat my food, to keep my strength up for adventures in India. I will answer more questions tomorrow or the next few days. Right?"

"Of course," says Marcus. "Are you comfortable in your room?"

Kimberley swallows some food and looks up and smiles. "I sure am," she says, "but we are only staying a couple of days, right? Then we are travelling across the country, wearing new clothes. What will mine be like?"

"They will cover you up more," says Marcus. "We will want to visit temples and other holy places. And we will be in towns where you cannot show all of your arms and legs."

"Okay," says Kimberley. "Do I get to wear a balaclava as well?"

"No," says Marcus. "That is an all over hat for cold weather. You don't need one of those. You are thinking of a burka; some Indian women wear those but not many do."

"So I can wear my great straw hat? My lady's Panama hat?"

"Of course, you can," answers Marcus.

"It is gonna be great," says Kimberley. "Just great."

Kimberley carries on eating and then looks at Marcus who, because he had not been talking, has already finished his main course.

"So what about the British education, Marcus?" she says. "Tell me all about that."

"Well, all right then, but briefly," says Marcus, "otherwise we will be here all night. The British system has three types of schools: state schools, which are supervised by the county local authority, private schools, which are called public schools because of their history and the special arrangements surrounding their being started in the first place, and then the smallest sector is private schools which are simply privately owned schools that parents pay to send their children to."

"So what is special about these public schools then, Marcus?" asks Kimberley.

"I could give you a lot of answers to that, Kimberley," says Marcus. "I would guess that there is almost nothing like it anywhere else in the world. First off you can't just go to one you have chosen unless you first go to a preparatory school – a prep school to get you ready for the public school. You have to go to the prep school at the age of about eight and usually you go as a boarder, so you leave home to stay at the school. And certain prep schools line you up for certain public schools so your parents have to choose the right one. And all of these schools, the prep schools and the public schools, are single sex schools. That is almost always for boys only."

"Go on, Marcus, I'm fascinated. So these guys don't get educated with girls. They get educated just with other guys.

Wow. That is a handicap for life. And they got to live with all the other boys all the time."

"They don't think it's a handicap," says Marcus. "Public schools have tremendous status in Britain. If you go to one you are almost certain to get a top job."

"What? Just because of your school?" asks Kimberley. "Not because of your talent?"

"I think we are beginning to open up the whole complexity of British society here," says Marcus. "Shall we order a dessert?"

"I'll order for both of us. You carry on telling me. This is like some crazy fairy story. Don't stop now, Marcus," says Kimberley. "And we haven't even started on the other types of school you've got."

"All right, but I don't want to get too caught up in all of this. I'm just trying to explain it without really commenting on it," says Marcus. "I'm keeping my opinions to myself. I am trying to be fair."

"Oh, okay Marcus," says Kimberley. "That's not fair. Now I want to know what you think about it all. These boys all leaving home to live with other boys and then all of them ending up with all the top jobs. Sinister, eh? Like a kind of secret club?"

"I will just try to explain the whole British education system and then you can make your mind up about it," says Marcus.

"So I started with the public school system because it is the oldest form of education in Britain and I explained about the prep schools because that is how you get into the public schools. Of course, there are exceptions. A lot of rich foreign parents with influence can get their boys into public schools without the prep school bit but I am simply explaining the usual."

"Usual. Oh boy," says Kimberley. "So what do they teach at these usual schools?"

"Well, I did not go to a public school," says Marcus. "So I don't have real first-hand experience, but from what I can make out the education is carefully structured to reach a certain end point. For instance, a public school education teaches the classics but also Latin and Greek. So that a child gets a foundation into what life may have been all about two or three thousand years ago. Therefore he gets an idea of what life may be really all about now, in spite of all modernity. He learns about rule. He learns about power. Then, of course, there is a lot of sport. All involved with the school. And the boys are broken up into four different groups. The groups have names and they are called Something House. You know, Ashton House or Turner House or something. And every boy belongs to one of these houses and has to be loyal to his house."

"I was right," says Kimberley. "This is really sinister. Go on, tell me more."

"The different houses have different sports teams. Rugby, cricket and so on. Not much football though. It is not really a public school game. So all of these different houses play against each other. And every house has a house master and the boys in each house all sleep together."

"They all sleep together?" says Kimberley. "That is pretty kinky, Marcus."

"No, I mean that the different houses all have their own separate boarding rooms."

"I'm beginning to get it," says Kimberley. "All these little boys being educated to believe that they are going to get all of the top jobs, but the only competition they get is against boys just the same as them. In the same school, but with some little trick about different houses in the same school. So they never meet any other kids from any other place."

"They do get to play sports against other schools when they get older," says Marcus, "but, of course, they are other public schools so you are right. They only ever meet and mix with and compete with other boys who are the same as they are."

"And then when they get these top jobs I guess that the guys who give them the jobs are just a lot of older men who all went to public schools like the younger men who they are giving the jobs to."

"I suppose that to some extent you may be right," says Marcus.

"So none of them knows whether they are any good at all," says Kimberley. "They are just passing the parcel to the same people all of the time. Untested people. Never faced any real competition. Everything fixed from the outset. That is dead wood, Marcus. That is real sterile. Not tried and tested talent at all. So what are all of these top jobs?"

"I think mostly that they are established wealthy companies. Public schoolboys don't want to start anything. They latch onto something which was started long ago and is now a big success. Lots of money," says Marcus. "Established British industries. Insurance. Banking at the top and, of course, government jobs. The top end of the civil service. One of the leading public schools, named Eton, considered by many to be one of the best public schools, almost entirely dominated the British Foreign office for decades. British ambassadors all over the world had been educated at Eton. So, I suppose, they all made the same decisions."

"Maybe that is how you lost your British trading empire, Marcus," says Kimberley.

"None of those guys had any real judgement. They just believed what they were taught to believe and they were taught by a bunch of jailers who all believed the same things. Boy, what a system. Tragic. What about your Queen? She could not have been to a boy's school. So how did she get the job?"

"It's not a job really," says Marcus. "It's an inheritance. Her father died. He was the King and so she became the Queen because she was the oldest."

"So where did she go to school?" asks Kimberley.

Marcus laughs. "She did not go to school. She got taught at home."

"What did she get taught?" ask Kimberley. "How does she know if she is any good or not? But she is already the Queen. No job interview. No election or anything. Her dad dies and then, bam, she is the queen, but none of the British people know if she is clever or stupid. Who were her teachers, Marcus?"

"I don't think anybody ever told us," says Marcus.

"The teacher is probably locked away now," says Kimberley. "So that the British can't talk to her and ask her if the Queen was bright or dull. So now we will never know. Maybe they put the teacher on one of those British islands in the middle of nowhere. You know like where you guys put Napoleon. So the teacher can't talk. What a country, Marcus. Go on, tell me about your other education. For the poor saps who are not going to get the top jobs. Go on, Marcus, tell me about your state schools run by your county."

"Have you ordered dessert yet, Kimberley?" asks Marcus.

"I'm doing it, I'm doing it," says Kimberley, waving a hand at the waiter. "Go on talking, Marcus."

"So state schools are the ordinary schools that really almost all the boys and girls go to," says Marcus. "And they

172

are run according to government policy. In the government the education department decides on the policy for education. I must say that I don't really know what motivates the education department. It seems very political, left wing. I don't know what it is that they are trying to teach. I don't want to be unfair."

"Oh Marcus, be unfair," says Kimberley.

"I'm trying to be accurate," says Marcus. "Okay, British schooling is broken into two halves. I'm talking about before university. The first half is infant school, little children from about four or five years old up to eleven years. Then there is senior school, which is eleven years old until seventeen or eighteen. Children take state exams at sixteen and another lot at eighteen and then they apply to go to university."

"So do all the boys and girls go to the same schools?" asks Kimberley.

"Mostly they do up to the age of eleven and then in senior schools the boys and girls are separated."

"What a tease," says Kimberley. "So the boys and girls in senior school can't play with each other. So what do they do when they grow up, Marcus? Boys play with boys and girls play with girls. That's unhealthy. That is going to lead to trouble."

"Education, Kimberley," says Marcus.

"That is education," says Kimberley, "learning how to get along with each other, how to get along with the kids in the neighbourhood. That's education, Marcus. That's education for life."

"Perhaps not for British life," says Marcus. "British life is full of contradictions. Schools in better neighbourhoods, you know where there are expensive houses, tend to be better schools than those in poor neighbourhoods."

173

"Why split up the boys and girls?" asks Kimberley. "It is estimated that girls study better without boys around," answers Marcus.

"So what about the boys? Do they study less?"

"I don't really know," says Marcus.

"And do the older kids get to live at home or do they have to live at the school?"

"No, they don't live at the school," says Marcus.

"Great, so after the schools have messed them up with all of this boy girl rubbish, the parents at home can put them straight again. Better than your public schools, but no top jobs. That's a bummer, Marcus."

The waiter brings a dish to the table. It is kulfi, frozen milk with mango and nuts. Kimberley has asked for two spoons and the waiter puts them onto the table.

"Stop for a while, Marcus, and try some of this," says Kimberley, "and tell me something funny. This education stuff is kinda dull."

"All right. Well, I don't know if this is funny but it is distinctive," says Marcus. "A number of grown up men who went to public school have speech defects."

"Defects?" says Kimberley. "What you mean they miss words out or something?"

"No, my theory is that they were so terrified of being torn away and shut up in a big school with a lot of bullies…"

"Bullies?" says Kimberley.

"Oh yes, public schooling is famous for its bullying," answers Marcus. "So I think that when they were little they were so frightened that they developed a stutter. Then when they are grown up they still speak like that. Their manner is very distinctive. They expect people to listen to what they say. People lower down the social scale develop short witty sharp ways of speaking because they know that nobody is going to

174

listen to them for long. The upper crust, that is the public school lot, are confident but a small number of them still speak oddly. Sort of, 'ah ah ah I don't want any tea. Ah ah thank you.' That sort of thing. It takes a variety of forms. Strangulated speech. Awkward speech."

"I don't think that is funny at all, Marcus," says Kimberley. "Just sad is all."

"The thing is," says Marcus, "that now this odd way of speaking has become a status symbol. A mark of the man's superiority. Actors copy it when they get a part where they have to play a top man."

"Holy cow," says Kimberley.

"Okay then, here is something else," says Marcus. "At English state schools now, government schools, there is a new idea coming through that children should not win or lose at sports. All of them should feel that they have won. So competition is being discouraged. Prizes for winning are discouraged."

"Get out," says Kimberley. "You're kidding. No winners or losers? How are you gonna live? A little country like Britain is taking from loser countries to feed the British people. Competition in all of the world markets. Only the winners get to eat. What are they gonna say? That the fast lion gets to eat the slow wildebeest? And then what? You gonna rescue the wildebeest and punish the lion? Education in your country, Marcus, has nothing to do with life, unless maybe your private schools are the only other ones to make sense."

"I don't know about that," says Marcus. "Private schools are all different. All individual. Run on different lines; as long as they stick to that British education curriculum they can do as they like. They are really a third choice. Eccentric. Unique. Nonconformist."

"Sounds great," says Kimberley. "May save Britain after all. What do you think of this desert, Marcus?"

"It's a bit sloppy," says Marcus, "a bit too sweet."

"Sounds like my first boyfriend," says Kimberley. "So what kind of school did you go to, Marcus? Come on, own up."

"I was sent to a private school," says Marcus. "It was owned and run by a very rich old man who had survived a Japanese prisoner of war camp. He was eccentric, strong and kind. He had a wife and two sons. One of the sons made a fortune in the USA. My father didn't help much. He kept telling me that teachers knew nothing about life. Never cared about my report cards. Thought that education was a waste of time."

"He sounds great," says Kimberley, "judging from the bad choices you all got at your British education. A real mess. The USA educates you to be good at living in the USA. What is the deal with the British?"

"I think that we are educated to advance ourselves without the education," says Marcus. "I've never really thought about it until now. There are a lot of people in Britain. All competing for space to live in. All trying to get a good life. I think that it is true that the education system does not help any of them, in fact it does, as you say, mess them up a lot but after a struggle a lot of British people succeed."

"Succeed, Marcus?" says Kimberley. "I guess that I would believe that to succeed would have to mean that you got out. Otherwise, your children have to go through all the mess of an education all over again. Unless a kid has a father like your father, who tells him that all education is rubbish, the kid could get stuck. At the bottom or, worse yet, stuck halfway up. Not up and not down, just stuck in the middle, exactly where your education system wants to keep him. A wage slave.

Paying taxes to pay for your Queen who cannot know what life is, Marcus. She cannot. I mean she has sat there. Top dog and watched quietly whilst her politicians gave her British Empire away. I never read anywhere that she objected. Maybe she is so uneducated that she did not notice. Or maybe she does not care. But Marcus, she's got five palaces. I mean that's got to cost a lot. If you've got Canada, Australia, India, Africa and all the rest then you can pay for five palaces, but if you've ended up with a little country like Britain then how are you gonna pay for all of those palaces and golden carriages and soldiers in red with funny hats on? That's a hell of a cost, Marcus. Maybe she doesn't know. I read in the States that your Queen never carries any money. So I guess she doesn't know what anything costs, but she's got to know that all of her people are not going around in golden carriages. Do you think that she notices that the people can't afford it? That she is the only person who can? It all seems very financially dangerous to me, Marcus. Ignorance is bliss. Do you think that that is what all of those top people in your country thought when they decided that your Queen was not going to school? And it must have been all of your top people, all of your public school guys, who decided that a little island like Britain, the size of a postage stamp, was going to give a load of people who lived in countries as big as six baseball pitches, British passports. An invitation to come in and live but, and here is the real fuck up, Marcus, they forgot, your English top educated guys, forgot to give the British special passports to be allowed to go and live in all of those baseball pitches around the world. They blocked British access to all of those raw materials. Your top guys, your foreign office guys, were ruling everything. They messed up big time, Marcus and nobody explained it all to your Queen. What a country. From the top to the bottom in one generation. Oh boy. And what about all of those baseball pitch

177

countries? No Brits can live there. So no Brits are going to invest there. Start businesses there. Run anything there. So they are all left to themselves. Inexperienced. The inexperienced leading the inexperienced. So their leaders start taking all the money to Swiss bank accounts and their people start killing each other. Your top guys really fucked up the world, Marcus."

"Stop, Kimberley, stop!" says Marcus. "You are priceless. I do enjoy your point of view. So original. I have to say that I don't know. I don't know what the Queen notices and I don't know what the Queen knows about the old British Empire and passports and investments. She does not know me, that is for sure, but the taxes I pay have got her name on them. Her Majesty's Revenue and Customs. I have never thought about it until now and now I am exhausted by thinking about it. Let's quit. I'll tell you a joke before we go to our rooms."

"Okay," says Kimberley, "if you want to quit then we can. What is the joke?"

"Cannibals don't eat divorced women," says Marcus. "Too bitter."

"Marcus, that is bad," says Kimberley. "Not your worst one, but bad. Let's leave."

Marcus signs the bill and they get up and make their way upstairs.

"Breakfast at eight, Marcus?" asks Kimberley.

"What about your skipping and stretching?" asks Marcus.

"I'll do that at seven o'clock," says Kimberley. "They have a pool here and a lot of space around it for me."

"Okay. Good night," says Marcus. "Sleep well. Don't worry about the British Queen."

"She is not my Queen. Good night, Marcus," says Kimberley, and they turn away from each other.

15
Ruby

Marcus and Kimberley wake up to a bright hot day. The close proximity of the sea brings a small breeze but Marcus remembers the advice given to him to drink a lot of water every day in India. When he goes down to breakfast he asks the waiter to deliver two litre bottles of spring water to his room.

"Please make sure that the bottles are still sealed," adds Marcus.

"Yes sir," says the waiter, smiling as if he is very pleased to have been asked to carry out such a special task.

Kimberley is already sitting at the breakfast table, which overlooks the gardens and the swimming pool. The pool is unlike European or USA pools in so far as it is not one of those blue lined or blue tiled pools with white edges. The pool here in India is brilliant white in colour and made of marble. This is ornately patterned at the edges and has marble benches set spaced apart on the edge of the pool terrace, which abuts the garden lawns. The white marble benches are for swimmers to sit on when they remove their towelling gowns just before they enter the water. They are also a resting place for the swimmers who leave their shoes or their slippers beneath the bench where they have left their gowns. It all looks very elegant and rather old-fashioned. An Edwardian feel to it all, but for no definite architectural reason.

Kimberley is, as usual, drinking orange juice. "I saw that guy working some kind of handheld orange squeezer," she says, "so I had to have some. Delicious. Hi, Marcus. How are you doing?"

"I'm fine and you look fine," says Marcus.

"Sure am," says Kimberley, "all exercised and stretched and showered and fresh, Marcus. Ready for anything."

"Well, after breakfast we are seeing a dressmaker and a tailor. Then we launch ourselves into Bombay."

"What should I have for breakfast, Marcus?" says Kimberley. "They have a lot of yoghurt and fruit, but I want eggs. Where do you think the hens live, Marcus? Do you think the eggs will be okay?"

"I'll have eggs if you are having eggs," says Marcus. "That way we will either both be fine or we will both be ill. I think it will be fine. This is a good hotel so let's order eggs. Strengthen us for the day. If the egg yolks are bright yellow it means that the eggs are fresh."

They give their order to the waiter. Both of them also ordered coffee and Marcus asked for an orange juice. They both see two or three early risers who are swimming in the pool. Almost all of the guests in the hotel are Indians. The swimmers are Indians too and as usual the girl in the swimming pool is wearing a light cotton dress. The swimmers are unselfconsciously enjoying themselves. Laughing and calling to each other.

Kimberley and Marcus enjoy their breakfast, the fragrant scents of the garden blowing towards them on the soft breeze. They are relaxed in each other's company.

"Kimberley, you look so delicious that we are going to have to cover you up, so that we are not followed everywhere we go," says Marcus.

Kimberley smiles and says, "Oh Marcus, you can cover me up, but I'll be the same girl underneath."

"You have finished?" says Marcus. "Come on then, let's go and find the dressmaker and tailor."

They walk inside the hotel, where the concierge points out four Indians who are waiting in reception, a man and a boy, and two women.

"Good morning," says Marcus. "This is my companion, Kimberley. I believe that you have come to see us."

"Very pleased indeed, sir," said the Indian man. "My name is Ramesh. This is my son Arjun. We are here to prepare for you most suitable, most comfortable clothes sir. And…" he turns towards the two women. "This is my friend, Gagana, and her esteemed associate, Deeba. They will look after your wife sir. Very much, sir. You are travelling and your wife is now wearing something for the sun tanning, I think. Gagana and Deeba will make something suitable for your wife's journeys, sir, comfortable, long at the arms and legs and very good, sir."

"Thank you," says Marcus. "Perhaps it would be better for you if you came upstairs to our rooms?"

"Indeed, sir," says Ramesh, smiling. He nudges his son who starts smiling at once. The four Indians gather the rolls of different cloths which they have brought with them.

Marcus walked ahead followed by Kimberley, and then Ramesh and his son Arjun, followed by the two Indian women, Gagana and Deeba. Marcus ushers them into the lift. They stop at Marcus's and Kimberley's rooms and Marcus shows the women Kimberley's door while she unlocks the room. The three women walk in; Marcus then unlocks his own bedroom door and welcomes the Indian tailor and his son.

"Have you told your wife what she will order, sir?" ask Ramesh. "She knows what you would like her to wear?"

"She knows what she likes," says Marcus.

"Ahh, you have trained her well, sir," says Ramesh. "Now your life will be exceedingly more easy. I admire your strength, sir."

Arjun takes a linen tape measure out of a leather bag, which he has carried into the room. The boy and his father proceed to measure Marcus in detail.

"You are a large man, sir," says Ramesh, "a healthy strong man, sir, and with legs and arms of a very good length, sir. It will take much material to clothe you, sir."

After a lot of examination of cloth and much discussion, Marcus chooses two colours to be made into baggy linen African safari suits with ample patch pockets on the shirt coat and four tailored inner pockets on the trousers. Marcus asks that the trousers should be wide and that the shirt jacket should be loose and the shirt pockets six inches by four and a half inches.

"Especially so, sir," says Ramesh. "Everything will be ready for you today, sir."

"Thank you," says Marcus. "I will go and see my, err, my wife now."

He leaves the father and son in his room and knocks on the adjoining door. Kimberley opens it, looking delighted.

"Marcus," she says, "I am having a great time. Gagana and Deeba are making me great outfits, Marcus. One in yellow and one in red. They are also making me an Indian wedding dress in pale sky-blue silk with pearl buttons and silver thread running through it. I will look exotic in the States, Marcus."

"We can't carry it around with us on our travels," says Marcus.

"I know that," says Kimberley. "Gagana is going to post it to my mother in the States after I have tried it on and checked it out tomorrow. What did you get, Marcus?"

"I have ordered two comfortable linen safari suits, one in the dark grey and one in dark blue; lots of pockets and a loose fit."

"Marcus, you will look too old for me," says Kimberley. "And I will love that feeling. Are you having anything posted home?"

"No," says Marcus. "I did not think of it and anyway I would not have known what to order. I am happy."

"I am so glad you are happy, Marcus," says Kimberley. "Have you left those two guys ransacking your room? We had better go and check them out. I will say goodbye to my dressmakers. Ladies, I will see you tomorrow morning."

She opens the door. The two Indian ladies walk out and she leaves, with Marcus taking care to lock the door behind her. "Don't want to lose my skipping rope," she says.

They walk into Marcus's room. Ramesh and his son are sitting quietly on two bedroom chairs, not speaking at all. Ramesh jumps up when Marcus walks in and pulls his son Arjun to his feet. "We are very ready to begin our esteemed task, sir. We shall work most diligently and are already looking forward to our meeting tonight, sir."

Marcus stretches out his right hand to shake hands with Ramesh and his son. Both Indians bow their heads whilst shaking hands. Marcus shows them both out whilst thanking them again.

"Okay," says Kimberley. "What's next?"

"We have a trip late this morning and another one before lunch," says Marcus, "but before all of that and for the next hour or more I have a surprise for you. Get yourself ready and I will meet you in reception."

"I'm ready. I'm ready," says Kimberley. "What is the surprise, Marcus? Tell me. What is it?"

"Then it would not be a surprise," says Marcus. "If you have everything you need we can go now."

"Go, Marcus? Go where?" asks Kimberley.

Marcus leads her to the lift and when they reach the lobby Marcus asks for a taxi. "You have arranged everything for me?" he asks the dignified concierge.

"Indeed, sir," answers the concierge. "Simply ask for Turner's Field, sir."

Marcus opens the taxi door for Kimberley and gets in the other side. "Good morning," says Marcus. "Please take us to Turner's Field."

"Yes sir, at once, sir," says the driver and pulls out into the traffic.

All around Bombay throbs with active life. People are moving about in every direction and every different kind of vehicle, animals in the streets and boats on the sea are making journeys to important rendezvous. There is no shouting but cars sound their horns to warn of their close proximity to animals and there are hundreds of little children moving in small groups and dressed in the sort of simple clothing which children in the 1950s wore in England, with the exception of the fact that many children in India are barefoot.

The driver weaves his way through all of the life on the streets and they drive along a huge seafront like an enormous version of England's Brighton. There is a wide promenade and views are interrupted by the clouds of small brown birds flying in perfect formation over the promenade, out to sea, and back over the promenade again over tower blocks of flats and shop premises on the other side of the road. There are busy people everywhere. The driver proceeds until they are in a separate area of the city, which appears to be quieter and residential.

Unexpectedly he stops in front of two high solid wooden gates.

"We are here, sir," he says.

"We will be an hour," says Marcus. "Would you please wait for us and then take us back to the hotel?" He pays the driver generously.

"Yes, certainly, sir. Of course, sir," says the driver, looking pleased. "You must knock on the gates, sir. Bharat will be opening the gates, sir."

Marcus and Kimberley alight from the taxi and Marcus walks up to the gates. Kimberley hangs back, looking nervous.

"This is like that King Kong movie, Marcus," she says. "What is behind those big gates?"

"Your special treat, Kimberley," says Marcus.

He raps hard on the gates with his knuckles and he hears a chain being pulled through metal. Slowly the gates are open only to reveal another set of metal gates inside. Beyond the metal gates is a field, which looks to be about twenty acres in size. In the field, moving calmly and slowly, there are about fifteen fully-grown elephants.

"Mr Bharat?" asked Marcus.

"At your service, sir," answers Bharat. "What would you like, sir?"

"We would like to hire an elephant," says Marcus.

Kimberley is standing with her mouth slightly open.

"An elephant for what purpose, sir?" asks Bharat. "For moving furniture, sir? Or for roadworks, sir? Or for agricultural purposes? Or to pull machinery?"

"We would like to ride an elephant around Bombay," answers Marcus.

"Marcus," says Kimberley, and then says nothing else.

"You will be wanting to hire Ruby the elephant, sir," says Bharat. "And you will be wanting Shaurya to lead you, sir. He is a brave boy, sir."

"All right then," says Marcus. "We are ready. Are you ready, Kimberley?"

"Marcus," says Kimberley. "Oh, Marcus."

Ten minutes later a tall Indian boy aged about twelve leads a very big elephant towards them. The elephant's face and ears have been painted with poster paints and flower petals have been painted around her eyes. The elephant has large wicker seats on her back strapped securely in two places under her body and arranged so that there is one seat on either side of her prominent spine. The seats are very high above the ground.

Shaurya is speaking quietly to the elephant in an affectionate manner and with coaxing sounds. The elephant kneels down alongside a high brick built mounting block.

"Here please," says the boy. "Get on now, please."

"You're the gymnast," says Marcus to Kimberley. "Get on."

Kimberley springs up the steps of the mounting block and steps carefully onto the first seat and then crosses the elephant's back to the seat on the other side. Marcus follows her and sits himself carefully into the first seat.

Shaurya looks at the two of them carefully. "Hold onto the hand rails," he says.

Marcus notices the rail in front of him and guides Kimberley's hands onto the handrail which is in front of her seat. Shaurya watches them carefully.

"Harrup," he shouts, "harrup."

Ruby the elephant stands up, taking Marcus and Kimberley high into the sky on her back. Shaurya walks along next to Ruby and Bharat opens the metal gates for Ruby to

187

walk through and then closes them afterwards. He moves forwards and opens the high solid wooden gates.

Ruby lollops through and with the boy Shaurya at the side of her she walks steadily along the road.

Marcus and Kimberley are up very high and Kimberley has not yet said a word.

Kimberley is so high up and yet she does not feel unsafe. The elephant's walking is steady and does not undulate from side to side. The elephant's feet are big, almost two feet across, and they are placed one after the other, carefully on the ground with each step. A horse moves its front legs and then its back legs when it runs at speed and when it is trotting or walking its hooves still hit the ground unevenly. The elephant walks with great care and to ride on top of it is a comfortable experience. Yet Kimberley notices that because of the sheer size of the elephant they are moving forward comparatively quickly and the boy, Shaurya, is running lightly alongside.

"Ruby," says Kimberley. "Hello, Ruby." I'm riding on top of a prehistoric monster, she thinks.

What am I doing here? There are so many people here and they all look poor. Maybe the rich people don't come out of their houses. Don't walk in the streets. There must be rich Indian people, thinks Kimberley, surely the whole country isn't like this. Bombay is teaming with people, children, animals and every imaginable kind of vehicle. But, thinks Kimberley, we are staying in a fabulously luxurious, calm, quiet, efficient, spacious hotel in the middle of all this swirling humanity. The contrast is unbelievable. Oh, shut up, Kimberley, she thinks, stop all of this analysis. You wanted to see an elephant and Marcus has arranged it for you. My God, is he one of those men who wants to please you? Buy you things and try to do things that he thinks you would like? One of those men who fiddles about with you in bed to get you in the mood? A man who takes a long time because he has read somewhere that it is better for the woman? Kimberley looks across the elephant's back at Marcus. He doesn't look as if he gives a damn, she thinks. I guess that he is a selfish man who is excessively polite and generous with money; he does not care to conceal the fact that he is a doggedly selfish man. He is good-looking, though. I would like to grapple with him some day. Use up all of his energy, just for me. It's not going to happen, though. He gives me these charming little compliments, smiling at me like an uncle, and then he doesn't look at me at all. I dressed to attract him at dinner; wore a short, tight-fitting dress and no underwear. He didn't take his eyes off my face. Not once, and I was watching out for it. Not a flicker of interest and he didn't make a pass at me when we got to my room. Okay sure, I told him that it was a no sex holiday, but you'd think that he would make a try for it. He can't be gay. There is nothing gay about him. He is masculine and tough and selfish underneath all of this charm and evasive answers to everything. What does he want, then?

"What do you want, Kimberley?" asks Marcus, suddenly.

"Oh pretty rough, really," says Kimberley, "selfish and demanding. A lot of energy." She looks confused and a bit warm in the face. "The elephant. Ruby the elephant."

"Are you comfortable?" asks Marcus.

"Well, are you?" snaps Kimberley, blushing.

"We can go back now if you like," says Marcus.

Considerate bastard, she thinks. Perhaps I hate him. No, I don't hate him. I want him.

"I'm okay, Marcus," she says, "let's go on a little bit further. Try to get Ruby to trample over a bus or something."

"You are bored, Kimberley," says Marcus. "We will go back." He shouts to the boy, "Shaurya, we can go back now."

189

"Oh no, sir," says Shaurya. "We have to give Ruby her bath, sir. We are nearly there now. Very close."

"All right then," shouts Marcus, "not too long, please."

"Not long, sir," says Shaurya.

You could almost believe that Ruby recognised the word 'bath' because she is walking much more quickly now and Kimberley and Marcus are bouncing on her back. The boy, Shaurya, is running hard. The elephant turns a right-hand corner.

"No signal," says Marcus. "We might have trampled a bus."

Kimberley looks startled. "Where is she going?" she asks.

"For a bath," says Marcus.

"What about us?" asks Kimberley.

"I suppose we will have to get off," says Marcus. "You can jump down and then I'll walk onto your head, shoulders and back until I get to the ground."

"The hell with that," says Kimberley.

At that moment they both see a large ornamental lake surrounded by grass and large trees. Ruby sees it at the same time and hurries her speed.

"No Ruby, no," shouts Shaurya. "Slowly, Ruby, slowly. Stop now. Kneel down, Ruby."

Ruby carefully kneels down, bending her front legs.

"Please get off now," says Shaurya to Marcus and Kimberley.

Kimberley immediately begins to walk across Ruby's back and down her neck, leaning forward to hold one of the elephant's ears as she stepped lightly onto one of her knees and then onto the ground. Marcus has watched her closely but he is certainly not going to risk walking down the elephant's back without holding on to something. He grips with his left hand one of the straps which holds the seats in place and hands himself downwards until his feet are on Ruby's back and his right hand is gripping her ear. The elephant does not move. She does not seem to mind. Marcus then walks onto her knee and then jumps down. He feels relieved to be on the ground.

Shaurya says, "Hup, hup," and Ruby stands. Shaurya unbuckles the two thick straps which hold the wicker seats in place, and then shouts, "Kneel down, Ruby." The elephant moves calmly. "Please to help me please, sir," asks Shaurya. "I must take off the seats, sir."

Marcus helps the boy and they carefully remove the seats and the red and blue blanket beneath the seats and place it all on the grass next to the ornamental lake. Ruby moves her whole head sideways and looks down at the seats and the blanket. Then she shakes her head and waggles her ears before walking into the middle of the lake. The water is about six feet deep. Ruby stands happily for about a minute and then sucks water into her trunk and, throwing her trunk backwards, she sprays the water across her back. She gives out a little cry. A happy noise and then does the same thing with the water again.

"Harrumph." Ruby then fills her trunk for the third time and accurately and deliberately drenches Kimberley with the spray. Ruby then shakes her head from side to side with her mouth open, "Harrumph."

"Pretty rough, Kimberley," says Marcus. "Selfish and demanding."

"If I had a bucket I'd get her back," says Kimberley.

"Use my hat." Marcus takes off his straw hat and hands it to her. "Have to be quick before the water runs through the hat."

Kimberley launches into the lake and then finds that it is too deep for her. "Marcus," she shouts before her head goes under. Marcus is beside her in a moment. He lifts her up.

"I'll walk you out," he says. "Put your head on my shoulder quietly now." He holds her at the waist and keeps her head out of the water whilst his own face goes under the water for the few steps he takes to reach the edge. He pushes her to the edge, bobs up and takes a breath.

Shaurya hands Marcus his hat. "The lady is all right, sir, I think."

"Yes, she is fine," says Marcus. "She was cross with Ruby."

"Ruby is happy to play games with the water," says Shaurya. "She knows her strength, sir. She is gentle with the water."

"We are both wet," says Marcus.

"Marcus, I am okay. It is warm weather. And tomorrow I get my new clothes, right? Maybe the hotel can launder our clothes tonight?" says Kimberley.

"Your most excellent hotel can do anything you wish, lady," says Shaurya.

Kimberley looks around to see where they are. "Marcus, I am going over the road to buy something from that shop," she points. "I'll be five minutes."

Sure enough exactly five minutes later Kimberley walked back across the road. She is wearing a sari of purple cloth expertly wrapped around her slender body. She is carrying a hessian bag which contains her boots and her white socks, her shorts, her underwear and her shirt. Marcus notices that Kimberley is wearing simple flat leather sandals. She smiles at him. "I am comfortable now," she says. "All of my wet clothes are in this bag, even my underwear." She tells Marcus that just to put the idea into his head and unsettle him during the journey back to the hotel. Marcus has to travel in his wet clothes.

Ruby is standing on the grass and is being brushed by Shaurya. Somehow he has managed on his own to put a blanket onto Ruby and to strap the wicker seats back onto her back. Marcus suspects that Ruby must have helped him somehow.

Shaurya tells Ruby to kneel down and she does so quietly. Marcus and Kimberley scramble back to their seats. Well, Marcus scrambles and Kimberley moves slightly and gracefully, managing the movements comfortably in her new sari.

Ruby starts the walk back to her field with Shaurya trotting alongside.

"She doesn't smell clean," says Kimberley. "She doesn't smell any different."

"Shaurya did not use bath salts," says Marcus, "or shampoo. So Ruby is not spoiled by chemical scents."

"I am happy," says Kimberley. "I guess an elephant should smell like an elephant or there is no point in being an elephant."

"She doesn't paint her toenails red either," says Marcus.

"What are you talking about, Marcus?"

"You know the old school joke about elephants painting their toenails red so that they can hide in the cherry trees without being detected. The next line is to say that you have never seen an elephant hiding in a cherry tree so that just proves that their disguise works."

"Get outta here," says Kimberley.

Shaurya starts to laugh and laugh. "Oh, that is very funny, sir," he says. "An elephant hiding in a cherry tree. Elephants do not need to hide from other animals, sir. Elephants are not afraid of anything, sir. Only humans are their enemies."

"Well, that kills your story, Marcus," says Kimberley. "I can see the field where Ruby lives."

"You are wearing a big diver's watch, Kimberley," says Marcus, "but you do not go diving."

"Looks pretty sporty though, don't it?" answers Kimberley. "Waterproof, so I didn't damage it today."

They all stop at the big wooden gates of Turner's Field.

"Time to give King Kong back," says Kimberley.

"Queen Kong, I suppose," says Marcus.

They climb down onto the mounting block and Marcus walks off to pay Bharat, who is the manager and keeper of the elephants. Kimberley walks round to Ruby's head to say goodbye. Kimberley pats the side of her head and pulls at her ear. "You be a good elephant now, you hear? Don't forget me."

Kimberley walks back to Marcus.

The taxi driver who Marcus had asked to wait is asleep inside his car. Marcus walks up to Kimberley and whispers to her.

"Sure," she says. "Why not?"

The two of them thank Shaurya, and Kimberley gives him a kiss, which shocks and pleases him very much.

Marcus and Kimberley open the rear doors quietly and then carefully get into the taxi and close the doors extra carefully and silently.

"Are we nearly there yet, driver?" Marcus calls out in a loud and clear voice.

"Eeeh," the driver sits up so quickly that he bangs his head on the roof of his taxi. "You are playing a game on me, sir," he says. "We are at Turner's Field, sir. I have been asleep, sir. You have seen your elephant?"

"Yes, thank you, we have seen our elephant and we have been swimming with her," says Kimberley. "Does your head hurt?"

194

"Not as much as it could do, madam," says the taxi driver. "The head hurts hardly at all, madam. Thank you for asking."

"Please drive slowly back to our hotel," says Marcus.

"Thank you, Mr. Taxi Driver," says Kimberley.

The man drives them back. Marcus pays him well because of the wet seat where he has sat and the man's bruised head and then Marcus and Kimberley walk inside the lobby. Kimberley asks the concierge if they can have some laundry done quickly. "We fell into a lake," she explains.

"Two hours is the quickest we can arrange, please," says the concierge.

"That will be great," says Kimberley. "Here." She handed in her hessian bag. "My clothes are here. Marcus will give you his in a few minutes."

"Thank you," says the concierge.

"So what now, Marcus?" asks Kimberley.

"Look at your diver's watch and tell me the time," says Marcus.

"You got a watch, Marcus. What's up?"

"We are going out in ten minutes to have a guided tour of the cities laundries," says Marcus.

"You gotta be kidding," says Kimberley.

"It is said to be something special," says Marcus. "Do you need anything in your room? I am going up to change my clothes."

"You mean I need to put on some underwear, Marcus?" says Kimberley. "I had forgotten and you have reminded me, I guess I will. Five minutes okay?"

She bounds away, laughing.

Sex, sex, sex, thinks Marcus. She creates sexual fantasies at every opportunity. I will be glad to see her covered from head to foot in her travelling clothes. He walks up to his room to put on dry clothes and shoes whilst he carries on thinking about Kimberley. I will still think about her body and her hair and her skin. There is only one way to put an end to this fantasy. Stop it from being a fantasy. Make it a reality. I've never been on holiday with a girl without romance and sex before. And then what happens afterwards? Would she be satisfied with a romantic sexual holiday? Would I be satisfied with that? Would I want her forever? What are you contemplating, Marcus? Just sex? Is it your ego? The ego which Kimberley says is so big? You had better stick to the rules, Marcus. This is a no sex holiday, but she seems to want more. Is it simply her natural vanity? She has a right to it. She is spectacular, beautiful and strong. But she has a complete formula for her life. She has it all worked out. I like her. That is the damnable thing. I like being with her. We are together every day and I never get bored with her. What is going to happen between us? Nothing, thinks Marcus. We will see India and then we will both go back to our very different lives. And miss each other? No, I don't think so. Not when we're back in our own lives. We will slowly forget each other, won't we?

16
Laundry and Slums

Marcus goes downstairs and hands the concierge his wet clothes and his boots.

"Can you please dry these boots?" he asks. "And then oil them well, and please do the same for my companion's boots. They are inside the bag which she gave to you."

"Certainly, sir. All will be ready for you after lunch," says the man, smiling at Marcus.

"Thank you very much," says Marcus and turns to greet Kimberley who is wearing different clothes and chunky-looking trainers on her feet.

"I'm all ready, Marcus, ready for our next adventure," she smiles at him.

"We are joining a small group of other people," says Marcus, "and a guide. They should all be waiting outside. Come on."

"I'm coming," says Kimberley.

They walk out to the front of the hotel. There are seven people waiting there, three couples and a female Indian guide.

"You are late," says a bitter-faced haughty Englishwoman aged around sixty. "It is now 11.10. What have you been doing?"

"Having sex, of course," says Kimberley, "lost track of time." She takes Marcus affectionately by the arm. "Isn't he just wonderful?" she asks the Englishwoman.

The woman turns to her tired-looking white-haired husband. "Do something, Desmond," she says.

"What?" asks Desmond.

The other four people in the group look at them, smiling.

"Everything is all right now," says a man in his forties who sounds like a Canadian. "Guess we can leave now?"

"Finally," says the bitter woman whose name is Daphne. "I just hope we have not missed anything."

"Ladies and gentlemen, here is our minibus," says the guide. "My name is Bavishni. I am most honoured to be your guide. We will not have missed anything, madam. Please get onto the bus."

"Get a good seat, Desmond," says Daphne. "We don't want to miss any views."

"All seats have splendid views," says Bavishni.

"Hardly likely," says Daphne.

They all get onto the bus. Kimberley and Marcus are shown into the front two seats by the Canadian.

"My name is Ken," he says. "Glad to meet the two of you." He winks at Kimberley, who smiles at him.

Daphne is furious. When everybody is seated the bus starts up. The guide, Bavishni, takes a seat next to the driver. Her seat is fixed so that it faces backwards towards the passengers.

"We are proceeding to one of the unique industries of Bombay," Bavishni says. "We are now passing through the busiest shopping district of the city. One hundred and seventy-eight shops are here to sell clothing and shoes. These shops are open for twelve hours every day from eight a.m. to eight p.m. Very good shops indeed."

"Stuff and nonsense," says Daphne. "The clothes all fall to pieces in six weeks. All rubbish."

Bavishni takes no notice of Daphne at all, because she is experienced and has met many frightened, hot and angry tourists over the years. She enjoys her work.

"There is the Coca-Cola factory," she says. "India does not allow the importation of US Coca-Cola so the US Department of Trade negotiated with the Indian government to allow Coca-Cola to be made here in India under a license from Coca-Cola and there is the place, ladies and gentlemen."

She waves her hand to the left and the passengers on the bus look at the building as the bus drives by. Kimberley does not look because she has noticed on the other side a stern-looking Indian man with a magnificent moustache riding a horse. Over his shoulder is a wide gauge single-barrelled shotgun and across his chest is a cartridge belt, almost full. He looks like Wyatt Earp, thinks Kimberley. Except that he does not have a Stetson hat on. I have not seen any Indian men with hats on, thinks Kimberley. Not any Indian women either. Hats don't seem to be popular here. I wonder if there are any gun restrictions here, thinks Kimberley. Maybe not. He is riding through busy streets with his gun all ready to be fired. What a country of contrasts this is. I wonder what Indian Coca-Cola tastes like.

The minibus trundles on into an area with more and more people. Unexpectedly they come into a huge open area seemingly crisscrossed with washing lines. Almost all have an astonishingly large assortment of clean washing flapping freely in the warm air.

"We are now at the Bombay city laundry," says Bavishni. "We are stopping here for a few minutes so that I can show it to you. Please to get out of the bus now."

The passengers file off the bus in an orderly fashion. Desmond and Daphne from England, Ken and his wife Sheila from Canada, and a happy fresh-faced couple called Barry and Caroline, who are newlyweds from Norfolk in England. Barry wants to buy some Indian tea. They all introduce themselves whilst standing by the bus.

Barry explains. "I want to go right up into the tea plantations," he says. Caroline looks admiringly at him.

Daphne looks at Kimberley. "So you are an American?" she says. "Strictly speaking there are no American names. Your name would have been brought over from England."

Kimberley looks at Daphne steadily. Marcus steps forward. "You are ill-informed and rude," he says to Daphne. "You may be an unhappy person but none of the rest of us is. So please keep your bad opinions to yourself."

"Desmond, this man said that I was ill-informed and rude. Desmond?"

"Well dear," says Desmond, "I suggest that we do not talk to them again."

"Desmond," says Daphne, angrily.

Desmond leads Daphne to one side. "Why not take some of your wonderful photographs of the laundry?" he says.

"What? A photograph of a lot of other people's washing? I should think not," snaps Daphne.

"Thank you, Marcus," says Kimberley.

"Of course," says Marcus.

Bavishni claps her hands together. "Guests," she says, "please walk behind me whilst I show you the washing area." She starts to walk. "Here you will see are hundreds of concrete troughs, some with soapy water, and next in line are many with clean water. There are wooden washboards and mangles to squeeze moisture from the clean laundry before it is hung out to dry. All of the laundry workers are dressed in white cotton uniforms."

"How do the workers identify the washing?" asks Caroline. "I mean, don't they get it all muddled up?"

"Never is it muddled up," says Bavishni. "It is identified by a very small mark on each item. The mark is recorded in the laundry book, next to the name and address of the customer. Many of the customers send washing to the laundry every day. Most of the people who live in Bombay use this laundry. Its efficiency and the accuracy of its records are essential. All clothing, sheets, towels, everything are packed into cotton bags when they are clean and dry and ironed." She points at a neat pile of snow-white bags. "When the customer's washing is washed, dried and ironed, it is immediately delivered back to his house or apartment or shop or restaurant or hotel. Immediately, and there are never any mistakes made. Oh no, never."

Kimberley and Marcus are walking in front of Barry and Caroline and the Canadians, Ken and Sheila, are at the side of them. Daphne and Desmond are in front of Kimberley.

Suddenly Kimberley shouts out, "Oh look, Marcus, there is my underwear." She points to some small scraps of erotic black lacy underwear flapping provocatively on a line set apart from other clothing being dried.

Marcus picks up the joke and says, "Oh no, Kimberley. Those are too big to be yours, I am sure."

"Well, you must be right, Marcus," says Kimberley. "You sure do know my underwear very well."

Daphne, who is immediately in front of them, gives a gasp. She punches Desmond on the arm. "Desmond," she says. "Do something."

The rest of the party have enjoyed the little play-acting. None of them believes that Kimberley has any washing at the

201

laundry but they all appreciate the joke quietly and without comment.

"Many companies have made great efforts to sell washing machines to the people of Bombay," says Bavishni, "but not one washing machine has been purchased. The laundry here collects dirty washing and delivers it clean and ironed and all of this is done within three hours, and the price for this excellent work is most cheap indeed. No person in Bombay would buy an electric machine to carry out this task. So the laundry is a very successful part of Bombay life."

"I think that is pretty cool, Marcus," says Kimberley. "Nothing like that for speed and efficiency at laundries in Florida."

"Nothing like it in Canada," says Ken. "The washing would freeze itself stiff as iron on an outside line where we live. We have to use a big tumble dryer in the basement. Do it all ourselves."

"I do it all," says Sheila. "Ken would not know how."

"Best woman in the world," says Ken, as he gives his wife a squeeze.

"We have seen the laundry," says Bavishni. "We shall now walk back and get onto the bus again. We shall visit another wonder of Bombay."

Daphne pushes to be first on the bus and sits with Desmond in the front seats which Marcus and Kimberley had previously occupied. Daphne stares straight ahead of her with a little triumphant smile on her face as Marcus and Kimberley pass down the bus. Daphne glances back over her shoulder to see Marcus and Kimberley sit in the middle of the bus. Daphne stares forward again, rapt with success. Her husband feels a momentary sense of relief. The bus proceeds once more through the crowded roads and streets and approaches an area of very dense population. They are in the biggest slum district of Bombay, where the people live on bare hard packed land under whatever shelter they can make from recycled materials. It could not accurately be described as a shantytown; it is more like a temporary refugee camp occupied by tens of thousands of people of all ages.

"Please to get off the bus now," says Bavishni.

The tourist party all start to get out. "You know how to show a girl a good time, Marcus," says Kimberley, as she steps off the bus.

"Stay close together, please," says Bavishni. "We will walk a little into the area. People live in every place here. Families live inside the city drains here and in every shelter they can make or find left empty by somebody who has died. All life is here, ladies and gentlemen."

"This is goddamn awful," says Kimberley. "Why don't they riot and break into big buildings of the city for their shelter? Why are they here? They are so quiet, dignified in their deprivation."

Barry speaks up. "It is in the Indian culture for the people to accept their fate, and the caste system of India is one of the oldest systems in the world to enforce social divisions. The tradition is believed to be over three thousand years old. The people of India do not fight against their circumstances. Their philosophy is to accept the position they are in and to enjoy happiness where they may find it. There is no ambition to be catered for here. No upward social mobility. Education is treasured but I doubt if children here in this area have access to formal education. Some families may attempt to pass on the knowledge which they have, but in a slum area that knowledge may be very small, parents and grandparents having had no formal education or structures of learning to pass on. No books here either." Barry stops talking. Caroline takes his arm.

"Barry is always studying," she says. "Read everything he could about India for weeks before our trip. Now he is seeing the real thing."

"The real thing," says Kimberley. "Holy cow."

Animals in a zoo do not like to acknowledge or even to look at the many visitors who pay to come and see them in their cages or restricted fields. It is the same with the people who live in the slums of Bombay. They cannot leave. They cannot travel with the tourists back to hotels where they will get a bath and a meal. So the slum dwellers of Bombay do not look at the visitors. They go on with their daily tasks. Only the children turn the tables on the tourists. They stand and stare at the visitors as if it is the visitors who are freaks. Their looks are ones of curiosity, mystification and hostility. What are these people doing here? What do they want to take from us?

Marcus has walked a few yards ahead and has discovered a most surprising thing. An Indian man of middle age is working on the last of six chairs which he has made. He is using old tools, probably two hundred and fifty years old in their design, and he has glued the pieces of the chairs together most skilfully using the same natural-based glue as would have been used in England in the eighteenth century. The six chairs which the man has made are dark rich mahogany wood, undoubtedly from the Caribbean. Not mahogany from Brazil, which is redder in colour. The chairs are highly polished and yet with an aged patina. The chairs are absolute replicas of Georgian English Hepplewhite chairs, identical in every detail, including the seat coverings in the pink and cream silk. The chairs are fake antiques. Their value in a London antique shop might be three thousand pounds a chair or twenty thousand for a matched set of six chairs. Yet they were being made in a slum area of Bombay by a skilled Indian craftsman. Fake antiques. Marcus guessed that they must have been commissioned and paid for by an English antiques dealer, but how did he find the Indian workman? And how are the chairs kept safe here? And what happens if it rains? Marcus is very surprised and he is impressed. He waves a hand in greeting to the workman and walks back to Kimberley.

"The oddest thing," he says. "That man," he points towards the furniture maker, "has just finished making twenty thousand pounds' worth of fake antique English chairs. Accurate copies of Hepplewhite, a famous English furniture maker."

"He has wasted his time then," says Kimberley. "He is not going to find a buyer here. He would have been better to make little shelters for the people, but I guess that nobody would pay him for that either. Don't see that anybody has any money here. Maybe the guy is just crazy. Did he look dangerous?"

"No, he did not look dangerous," answers Marcus. "He looks serious."

"He must be serious," says Kimberley, "making fancy chairs in an area where all the residents sit on the ground." She grins at Marcus. "Okay, I give up," she says. "What is the scam? What is he doing?"

"Obviously somebody is paying him to make these fake chairs. Then they must get shipped back to England; sold as antiques in the London market. Big profits. Not big profits for the man though, but he must get paid well enough for him to do it. Whoever has planned all this must have supplied the Indian here with the mahogany wood and from the right place. Also the pink and cream silk. Everything is a perfect match. Somebody is making money here."

"It is not any of these guys," says Kimberley. "They don't have a thing. Wonder what they eat?"

"They scavenge in the waste of other areas," says Bavishni, who has walked up behind them, "and of course, they beg."

"I have not seen any horribly crippled people in this slum area, Barry," says Caroline.

"Their family or somebody will carry them into a rich area of the city where they are more successful at begging. They would not get food here," explains Barry. "Nobody here has food to spare."

"It is their parents or relatives who break their arms and legs when they are babies and bend them to heal together in a distorted way," says Bavishni. "Relatives know that these children are not going to win scholarships to Oxford," she laughs delightedly, "and so some of them help their babies to be successful beggars by crippling them when they are young. Then from the age of around eight years they are left in a favoured area of the city."

"One week's income from our hotel would feed these people for a year," says Kimberley. "People never get the balance right." Unusually for Kimberley she looks sad. She pushes Marcus. "What did you bring me here for? I may never be able to forget about all this and I don't figure on being sad all my life. It's your fault, Marcus."

"Quarrelling now," says Daphne as she walks past. "Love didn't last long, did it? It never does in my experience."

"Mine too," says Desmond quietly, as he walks along behind.

"She has cheered me up," says Kimberley.

"You are forgiven, Marcus, but think up a better trip for me tomorrow, please. I gotta get this out of my head. It's not that I don't care, it is that I can't help. Haven't even got any fruit today. Or chocolate. I just can't stand it, Marcus. Spoil me with something different, please."

"I will," says Marcus. "India is not my creation. It is what happens when a billion people all live in one place. Only a small number of them prosper. The others just help those who do prosper, but Barry says that they all enjoy such happiness as they can find."

"Well, okay," says Kimberley, "but I want to get out of here. Crushing my optimism. I want to find some new happiness of my own."

"Are we ready, ladies and gentlemen?" asks Bavishni. "We should get back onto the bus now, please."

They all obediently get back onto the bus. For some reason guests sit at the back of the bus, leaving Daphne and Desmond separated by six empty rows of seats between their two seats at the front and everybody else who is sitting at the back.

"Cruel," says Marcus.

"She started it," says Kimberley.

"Yes, but it is her own limited personal ability," says Marcus. "She cannot change herself. She is a confused and angry person. So it is cruel to punish her."

"I didn't ask everybody to sit at the back," says Kimberley. "They wanted to avoid her angry confused personality. It is Desmond I feel sorry for. No, I don't. It is his choice. Anyway maybe it is just an accident. Everyone wanted to sit at the back of the bus." The bus starts off and the driver steers back towards their hotel. The occupants of the bus are quiet. Coming as they do from affluent societies in the Western world they are each affected differently by what they have seen. Only Barry seems satisfied as he writes carefully in his little notebook. Caroline is smiling at him contentedly.

Bavishni points to the right hand side of the bus. "You can see there, the towers of the Silence," she says. "These towers are wide and hollow and are inside filled with deep shelves.

The tops of the towers are open. The Jainism religion guides its people to place the dead bodies of the newly departed onto the shelves on the inside of the towers. Then vultures fly down and slowly and thoroughly pick the bodies clean. Look, there is one now."

A large sinister-looking vulture is flying out of one of the towers with a large piece of flesh hanging from its mouth.

"There he goes," says Bavishni. "Cleaning the bodies of the departed Jains. It is most efficient. Later the clean bones are collected and placed in a sarcophagus for all eternity." Bavishni smiles at her tourist party, who are silent with horror.

After a comfortable journey through the busy city the bus pulls up outside their hotel. Everybody gets off and they all go their separate ways.

"Your laundry is here, sir," says the concierge, "and your boots have been dried and treated.'

"Thank you," says Marcus. "How much is the cost?"

"It will be added to your bill, sir," says the concierge. "Your items have been placed in your separate rooms, sir, madam."

"It was your underwear on the line after all," says Marcus.

"No, it was not," answers Kimberley. "I did not bring any black underwear with me. It was Bavishni, she is a small size."

Marcus smiles. "She was a very efficient guide, I thought. I liked her."

17
Indian Lunch Companions

"We have nothing else arranged for today and tomorrow morning we have to leave at five a.m. to catch a train," says Marcus.

"A train?" says Kimberley. "Five a.m.?"

"Yes, we have seats reserved on the early morning train to New Delhi," says Marcus. "Now we can have lunch and if you like we can just lie by the swimming pool this afternoon."

"Can I wear a bikini?" asks Kimberley.

"Of course," says Marcus. "The pool area is not a public place. It is private for the guests of the hotel, but wear something over your bikini when you walk through the hotel."

"Oh hell," says Kimberley, "I was going to walk naked through the hotel then put my bikini on at the pool."

Marcus looks at her. "Our new clothes should be ready," he says. "They are probably in our rooms."

"I want lunch first," says Kimberley. "I am hungry."

They enter the restaurant and are shown to a table in the window overlooking the hotel gardens, which are rich with flowers.

"Must avoid anything dirty," says Kimberley, "so what shall I have?"

At a table nearby to Marcus and Kimberley is a handsome Indian man wearing an expensive-looking cream coloured suit in material which might be alpaca. He is accompanied by a boy of about eight years old, who is also expensively dressed but casually so. The boy has big brown eyes and very shiny dark hair. The boy stares at Kimberley with admiration.

"Hi there," says Kimberley to the boy. "How are you doing?"

The boy is surprised and looks at his father. "Papa?" he says.

"Yes, Rajesh. You may answer the lady," says the boy's father.

"I am doing well, thank you very much," says Rajesh, "and how, please, are you yourself doing, madam?"

"I'm fine," answers Kimberley. "But I cannot decide what to eat for my lunch."

"My father will know," says Rajesh. The father smiles at his son.

"My name is Mr. Choudhry," he says. "I have stayed in this hotel many times. I would be pleased to be of assistance."

"If you have not started your lunch then please come and sit with us," says Kimberley. "My name is Kimberley. I am an American and my friend here is called Marcus and he is from Britain. We are pleased to meet you both. We have not met any Indian people socially and it would be a real pleasure to talk to you, and get your opinion about lunch."

Kimberley smiles at the Indian gentleman and his son in such an open, honest and welcoming way as to make her invitation almost irresistible to Mr. Choudhry.

"Your companion, Mr. Marcus, would not be disturbed by our presence at your table?" Mr. Choudhry enquires.

Marcus gets to his feet and walks a few paces over to Mr. Choudhry's table. Marcus holds out his hand. "Delighted to meet you," he says. "Please join us."

Mr. Choudhry does not wish to cause offence by refusing the invitation. Nor does he want to leave himself open to claims by what he calls a middle ranking Englishman that India was better run under the British Raj and that the country has suffered since the British left.

India, thinks Mr. Choudhry, is a country where people lived in palaces many hundreds of years ago when the British were living in caves and holes in the ground. A country where superior Vedic medicine was trampled into reduced status by the British and many other cultural atrocities committed irretrievably. Mr. Choudhry wants his son to have broad experience and a fine cultured and scientific education. The woman is American. Perhaps Rajesh would benefit slightly by dining with her.

"Thank you on behalf on my son, Rajesh, and myself," says Mr. Choudhry. "My friends call me Raahithya."

Raahithya and Rajesh move to the large window table occupied by Marcus and Kimberley. Raahithya sits down.

"Sit next to me," Kimberley says to Rajesh, who looks at her in wonder with his big brown eyes.

"Yes, I will," he says. "I have a very nice room in this hotel. Do you and your husband have a nice room?"

"We have two rooms, Rajesh," says Kimberley, "because Marcus is not my husband. He is my friend."

"Your friend?" says Rajesh. "You do not have a husband?" His eyes are wide with delight.

"Rajesh, do not ask questions," says his father, Raahithya. "We have just met and we must not be curious."

"Oh, it's fine," says Kimberley. "Anyway I want to ask Rajesh what I should have for lunch."

"You should have fresh cooked lamb with hot chilli peppers, garlic, green pepper, turmeric and rice," says Rajesh. "The chilli peppers are for your digestion because it is very hot in India."

"Somebody else told us that," says Kimberley.

"Oh dear," says Rajesh. "I wanted to be the first person to tell you about it."

"Well, tell me what to drink," says Kimberley.

"Lots of water," says Rajesh, "but not cold water. Cold water is bad for the stomach."

"Thank you, my son," says Raahithya. "Let us consider now what you and I will have for lunch. It is your holiday so you may have anything you wish for."

"Thank you, Papa," says Rajesh. "I would like a lot of vegetables, please."

"You may have them," says Raahithya, "and I will have the same but I will also have some lamb with the young lady."

"Papa," says Rajesh.

Marcus says, "I will have the same as you, sir. Thank you for your recommendation."

Raahithya turns to the waiter and translates their order, including the addition of several side dishes.

"You are on holiday here in Bombay?" Raahithya asks Marcus, breaking his own rule about being curious.

"We are on a sort of tour," says Marcus. "We started in the south and tomorrow we go to Agra to see the Taj Mahal and then New Delhi and then on to Udaipur to stay at the Lake Palace Hotel. Then we come back to the south again for a rest on the beach. Then we go home."

"So you will see some different views," says Raahithya. "India is a very large country with much life in it."

"We have tigers and elephants," says Rajesh. "You can talk to an elephant if he is tame but no tigers are ever tame so you cannot talk to them." He looks excited.

"Whose idea was it to undertake such a long and tiring journey, may I ask, if the question is not impolite?" says Raahithya.

"It was Marcus's idea and I have come along to look after him," says Kimberley.

"Admirable," says Raahithya.

"I had forgotten that there are tigers in India," says Marcus.

"None in this hotel, I think," says Raahithya, "but yes, there are many tigers in India. Some workers in the cornfields are eaten every year."

"Holy cow," says Kimberley. "How does that happen?"

At this moment four waiters appear and lay out the food onto the table together with large glass jugs of water.

"Is the water…?" starts Marcus.

"Yes, my dear sir, the water has been decanted from sealed bottles," says Raahithya.

The waiters begin to serve the food carefully to each of the guests. They also pour water into everyone's glass.

"Please tell me about the workers in the cornfields," says Kimberley. "I have just decided that working in cornfields is the wrong job for me."

Raahithya looks at Kimberley seriously. "In America you have machines for your cornfields," he says. "The problem does not arise."

"We don't have tigers either," says Kimberley. "How do those guys get eaten?"

Rajesh is looking very happy.

"It may take over twenty men and women to scythe a corn field when the crop is ripened," says Raahithya. "There are always one or two workers who are naturally slower than the others. These are the ones who are eaten. It happens with unexpected rapidity and deadly efficiency on the part of the tigers. They wait at the edges of the fields. They know when the harvest is due and they feed themselves accordingly. One could say that the tigers were here first and did not invite the humans to grow corn."

"Wow," says Kimberley. "I've only ever seen a tiger in a zoo. The notice said that he was four hundred and twenty pounds of muscle."

"A most secure zoo is the only place to look at a tiger with safety," says Raahithya. "They are a most effective machine of nature."

"You are an effective machine of nature yourself, Kimberley," says Marcus, "but in a different area of expertise."

"What do you do, madam?" asks Rajesh.

"Rajesh, please," says his father.

"It's okay," says Kimberley. "Rajesh wants to know about the world he is going to live in. Let me answer."

"Of course," says Raahithya.

"I work at a law firm. I am a kind of lawyer," says Kimberley, "and I am a special kind of outside dancer as well."

"Serious law and happy dancing," says Rajesh. "That is a very good combination of work from which to be paid."

"Yes it is," says Kimberley.

"My father is a very important man," says Rajesh. "He is a top executive with an Indian oil company. I have learnt how to say that." Rajesh sits up in his chair and looks very pleased. "Did I say it right, papa?"

"Yes, my son," answers Raahithya, "but possibly Miss Kimberley is not interested to hear about it."

"Oh but I am," says Kimberley. "Please. An oil company. I have not associated India with oil."

"If I may be permitted to say, that could be because you come from the great country of America. India perhaps is not a country whose economics are taught to you in the USA."

"I guess not," says Kimberley.

"India has no economic need to export or to import anything," says Raahithya. "It is a country which can exist on its own. This is the reason why you see no European influence here. Nor any United States nor Russian nor Japanese influence. India is its own country. We have our own film industry, our own lives and our own languages, little known outside of India."

"Some of your languages are spoken in England," says Marcus.

"Yes, that is because of your own country's immigration policy, not ours," says Raahithya, "and I have heard that some British people call the Indians who reside in Britain, Pakis. That is, of course, a mistake. Although it has to be conceded or observed that no Indian gentleman of middle ranking social position or even lower social and economic position would ever contemplate leaving the country of India to live in the tiny cold country of Britain, pleasant though it may be for yourself. Here there are many services available day and night for an Indian gentleman. There are many luxuries. There is fresh food available every day and not grown with chemical pesticides. Animals are eaten here without the taste of antibiotics in their flesh. There are no processed foods here.

The people are thin. The hospitals in India are spotlessly clean. The medical standards here are very high, doctors and nurses most well taught and trained to deal with unhealthiness. India does not have the communist system of medicine which is enforced in your country of Britain; ignorance and many

215

restrictions and rationing of medical attention masquerading as the best in the world. Freedom of choice of medical care is here. Responsibility, accountability, unlike your British system, which is administered by more people than the medical staff it employs and no one is answerable for its many faults and tragic errors. Indian advantages are not available in Britain. You notice that I say Indian gentlemen. It is the men in India who have the responsibility for and the authority over the women and the family. It is the men who make a big decision to leave their own country. It is frequently, indeed always, the lower orders of Indian society who travel to improve their financial positions in Britain. The men decide. The men in your country do not have this authority over your women, I think. You have feminism and so your criminals are cosseted, sympathised with, protected; the poor boy, not the evil man. So your society is weakened. Punishments are not feared by your criminals. Nobody accepts his or her guilt. It is all the fault of society. Your celebrities indulge themselves in public confessions. 'I ate too much, I drank too much, I was a drug addict' and your feminine society is forgiving, supporting, continuously supporting the belief of there being no blame. You have crime in your towns and cities. Did you see crime here? Were you threatened? Were you attacked?* Perhaps I have spoken too much"

"No, it is most interesting to hear you," says Marcus. "It is flattering to us that you confide in us by telling us your opinions."

"I do not confide in you nor do I tell you my opinions. I am explaining what Indian people know and think about your country. If, in fact, they ever think about it," says Raahithya. "It is a matter of perspective."

"Thank you," says Marcus, who has perceived a world of criticism in what Raahithya has said. It is, as the gentleman

216

has told him, a matter of perspective. Marcus decides to tread carefully.

"What are you going to do on your holiday, Rajesh?" Marcus asks.

"Father?" Rajesh looks at Raahithya.

"Yes, Rajesh. I am sure that Marcus and Kimberley are interested in your holiday," answers Raahithya, somewhat ambiguously.

"We are visiting an island this afternoon where there are big caves and inside there are statues of the gods," says Rajesh. "We shall go by boat, of course, and on the island we may see hundreds of most colourful and beautiful birds. India, my country, has many beautiful birds. Later I will go fishing with my father. I have a new fishing rod. It was present for my holiday. I shall catch a big fish. Oh, I hope that the line does not break."

Kimberley thinks about going fishing with her brother's family and remembers how important it is for a little boy to catch a fish soon or he becomes disheartened by the idea of fishing. Rajesh is convinced that he will catch a fish so big that it might break his fishing line. Kimberley decides that she likes Rajesh.

The food which they are all eating is excellent and Raahithya and his son have delicate table manners. Only Kimberley eats with a fork in her right hand, identifying herself clearly as an American.

"I am sure that you will see what you expect to see in your travels around my country," says Raahithya.

Marcus moves in his seat and appears to be about to speak.

"Would you like to see me dance?" Kimberley suddenly asks Rajesh. "Of course you would, honey."

Rajesh is astonished to be called after the product of bees but before anyone can protest Kimberley has leapt up, grabbed two linen napkins from an adjoining table and is prancing up and down in an exaggerated march on the spot. She shouts out Rajesh's name letter by letter, waving the napkins as she does so.

"R.A.J.E.S.H."

She moves quickly and lightly out of the reach of Marcus, drops the napkins and after glancing at the wide gap between the tables begins to somersault over and over until she is on the other side of the room. She then jumps high in the air, flinging her legs and arms out to form the shape of a star. Without stopping for a second she begins to cartwheel silently across the restaurant towards Raahithya and his son Rajesh. Raahithya's face is a mask of fury. He dare not leave for fear of the embarrassment of bumping into Kimberley but he is fidgeting with impatience. Rajesh is captivated and excited and speechless. He does not look at his father but he has noticed Kimberley's sky blue underwear at the top of her long brown legs. He has never seen these parts of a woman before.

Kimberley arrives at their table and throws herself down into the splits.

Raahithya has risen to his feet. He takes his son firmly by the arm.

"We must not keep you from each other's company for a moment longer," he says, and stalks out, pulling Rajesh with him. Rajesh looks back at Kimberley.

Kimberley springs to her feet. The two restaurant waiters have stood frozen throughout the performance, staring in front of them and not looking at Kimberley or at her dining companions for a second. They are now visibly relieved.

"Well, that got rid of them," says Kimberley. "I couldn't stand it a minute longer, Marcus. He was being deliberately rude to you."

"He has gone now," says Marcus. "His little boy was okay, though."

"The boy was a sweetheart," says Kimberley.

"It's a good thing you are wearing underwear," says Marcus.

"Am I?" says Kimberley. "I couldn't remember."

Kimberley is still standing up. Marcus gets up from the table and stands in front of her.

"You are a treasure," he says and kisses her on the lips briefly but gently and softly.

He walks away towards the two waiters. "May I pay for our lunch?" Marcus asks.

Kimberley is standing very still.

"The gentleman who was with you has paid for everybody," says the waiter.

"Good," says Marcus.

Kimberley now moves, walks up and stands close to him. "Marcus," she says, "you, you…"

"Would you like to go to the Statue of Gods, Kimberley?" asks Marcus. "I feel too restless now to relax by the swimming pool."

"I feel all stirred up now, Marcus. Yes, let's go and see some caves and statues of gods."

"I'll ask the hotel about it,' says Marcus. "I'll meet you in the lobby."

Kimberley meets Marcus barely ten minutes later.

"We are fortunate," says Marcus. "A boat is leaving in a few minutes. The doorman has pointed it out to me and told me what to ask for.'

"Ask for return tickets, I hope,' says Kimberley. "There might be wild animals on the island, Marcus."

"I don't think so," says Marcus. "Some of the other hotel guests are coming as well."

"Okay, let's go," says Kimberley. They walk carefully across the road to the harbour front and join a short queue to get onto a big ferry boat.

On board the ferry they recognise Barry and his new wife, Caroline, who waves to them. There are a lot of other passengers, including six rather incongruous-looking transvestites, long-faced men with poorly concealed four o'clock shadows and unmistakeably large hands. They are all dressed colourfully as glamorous women.

Kimberley is by this time chewing bubble-gum, and stares openly at the men dressed as women as she blows pink bubbles and then pops them around her lips, before licking them into her mouth again to begin to chew and prepare another bubble.

Marcus walks to the side of the ferry and looks at a boat sailing past. It is heavily laden with barley, barely four inches out of the water, and moving along with the aid of one little straight sail. Surely it must sink, thinks Marcus. He turns and is horrified to see Daphne and Desmond sitting in the middle aisle seat of the ferry. Marcus glances around for concealment, steps behind the wheelhouse and comes out on the other side. Daphne and Desmond are looking westward so Marcus is not noticed.

He looks towards Kimberley who is now orchestrating all of the men in women's clothes to chew bubble gum and then all together, at a countdown and a hand clap from Kimberley, they blow and then burst bubbles all at the same time. They are successful and Kimberley claps her hands. Marcus joins in.

The group are now starting to chew again. They all look very happy.

The ferry begins to approach the island. Marcus can see the quayside. One of the ferry workers leans out with a boat hook in his hand as the ferry boat captain slows down and throws the engines of the ferry into reverse so that it drifts slowly towards the quay. The boat hook is used to grapple an iron hook set into the stone quay. Ropes are thrown and the ferry secured.

Two men stand and lightly guide the passengers off by offering each of them a hand onto the firm quay.

"Dry land," says Kimberley, smiling. "What now?"

Barry and Caroline are behind them. "We walk in this direction," he indicates. The walk is for about one hundred yards until they reach an enormous set of stone steps. "One hundred and sixty-five steps to the top," says Barry.

Waiting for them are Indians with sedan chairs, ready to carry passengers up the steps. Barry and Caroline each step into a different chair and are carried steadily upwards. Kimberley steps lightly into a blue and red chair and two Indian men pick it up and begin the long walk up the stone steps. Marcus, who is tall, muscular, strong and consequently heavy, approaches a waiting sedan chair. The two Indians in charge of it look at him, begin to talk excitedly, let go of the long handles of the chair and run away.

"You'll have to walk, Marcus," calls Kimberley happily. "Don't worry, I'll wait for you at the top." She laughs cheerfully.

Marcus without hesitation begins the long walk upwards. The two runaway Indians come back and start to carry an old lady who is small and light. Marcus treks onwards and upwards, trying not to count the steps as he progresses. It would be discouraging, he thinks. He breathes in and out and keeps up a fast pace.

Kimberley is waiting for him at the top. She is underneath the shade of the tree.

"Marcus, sit down," she says.

Perspiration is pouring out of him and the back and sides of his shirt are wet. Kimberley opens a bottle of water and pours it over the back of his head.

"Your brain will boil, Marcus," she says.

"Please do it again," says Marcus.

They sit quietly in the shade for a few minutes whilst Marcus's heartbeat slows down.

"Here, eat some chocolate,' says Kimberley, "raise your blood sugar.'

The chocolate is soft in the heat but Marcus eats three squares of it slowly. Kimberley puts her hand firmly onto Marcus's right thigh. "Strong legs," she says.

"I'm okay now," he says. "Let's go and look at the caves."

He gets up and stretches his legs.

"Up there," says Kimberley, pointing.

They enter a huge stone cave. Its entrance is probably about thirty feet high and the cave is large, about three thousand square feet, and branches off into three different directions. There are flaming torches on brackets on the wall.

Barry is standing just inside with Caroline.

"The statues of the gods are extra-large," he says. "Normally statues of human figures are life-sized but when creating images of the gods the sculptor decided to make each of them twelve feet tall. It is intimidating when you see them. Impressive, I mean."

Barry is happy with his wife and says to Marcus and Kimberley, "Come on, I'll show you."

They walk into the interior and, after a few yards of walking between the patches of yellow light thrown out by the flaming torches, they approach the first statue. It is the figure of a man, handsome and with those eyes that statues often have; no irises or pupils, just a blank stare into the distance.

"Who is he?" asks Kimberley.

"I don't speak the language," says Barry, "but I think that he is the god of war."

"I don't like him," says Kimberley.

"Don't say that," says Caroline. "He will hear you. There may be trouble."

"Let's go and find the god of gymnastics," says Kimberley, "or the god of love."

As they drift away Marcus is setting the light aperture and the shutter speed on his camera and, just at the moment that he presses the shutter, Daphne walks in front of him between his camera and the statue. Click, the photograph is now one of Daphne with a statue behind her.

Marcus hurries to catch up with the others.

"Get a picture?" asks Barry.

"No, Daphne walked into the frame," says Marcus.

"Bad luck," says Barry cheerfully. "There is another statue here. The god of fertility."

A bosomed female statue looks into the distance. Marcus prepares his camera and there is Daphne again. She moves in front of Marcus, right in the way. She is staring at the statue.

"Rather rude, don't you think?" she says to nobody in particular.

"That is what Marcus is looking for," says Kimberley, "photographs of women, all ages and all types. I think he has two photos of you already. Marcus runs a kind of dating agency in London. Really more of an escort service business. He is going to decorate his offices with the photographs he is taking today. He is real pleased to have got two great shots of you. You are going to put them in your reception area, right?" Kimberley looks at Marcus.

"Well, Daphne certainly has a dominatrix look about her," says Marcus, "coupled with a sort of erotic mumsy look. Perfect for my offices."

"I forbid it," shouts Daphne. "Desmond, come here. My image has been stolen from me."

"Your image, dear?" asks Desmond.

"To be used for a filthy escort service in London," says Daphne. "Dominatrix, indeed."

"Dominatrix, dear?" says Desmond.

"Do something, Desmond," shrieks Daphne.

"Let us walk further away, dear, and look at other things," says Desmond placidly.

"They cannot use my photograph, surely?" says Daphne.

"I'm not sure of the copyright laws," says Desmond. "Perhaps you just wandered into the picture, dear. You know you do not notice other people's activities, dear, their priorities."

"Damn their priorities," says Daphne. "They have no right to use me for pornography."

"Perhaps they won't, dear," says Desmond.

Caroline has got the giggles and finds it difficult to stop. She is holding onto Kimberley's arm.

"You are naughty," she says. "Poor lady. She is worried now."

"There are another four statues to look at," says Barry. "Follow me."

Kimberley is certainly impressed by the towering figures, silent and menacing, carved from light grey coloured stone, different from the walls of the cave.

"How did they get in here?" says Marcus. "Different stone and it is too dark to have created them here. So somebody or a lot of people must have moved them here."

"You would think that if they could move twelve foot statues all the way up the hill and into the caves that some guys could manage to carry Marcus in a sedan chair," says Kimberley.

"Marcus, did you walk up one hundred and sixty-five steps in this heat?" asks Barry.

"I didn't want to let Kimberley get away from me," answers Marcus.

"That is so romantic," says Caroline, "but Barry, surely we could arrange for four men instead of two to carry Marcus down the steps again."

"I'm sure we can," says Barry, smiling. "Save your strength, Marcus."

"Yeah, save it for me," says Kimberley, deliberately wanting to create another false impression.

"Honey," she says and flaps her eyelashes at Marcus.

"What are you two doing tomorrow?" asks Barry.

"We are catching a goddamn train at five o'clock in the morning," answers Kimberley. "I don't know why we can't get a later train."

"All public transportation in India is full up," says Barry. "You have to book two or three weeks in advance if you want to go anywhere. Marcus has undoubtedly looked after you by booking in advance. You can't travel anywhere if you just turn up at the bus or railway station or the airport. The train will be full of passengers anyway. Every seat occupied and people hanging onto the sides and travelling on the roof of the train. Did you reserve your seats?"

"We did," says Marcus, "reserved them weeks ago and I have the receipts and all of the booking documentation."

"You will be all right then," says Barry. "You can sleep on the train."

"I'm not going to sleep," says Kimberley. "I want to see everything."

"Very good," says Barry, and Caroline takes his arm warmly. "Let's look at the rest of these statues."

The four of them stroll around the caves. Daphne stays well away from them and Desmond looks tranquil and vacant.

They leave the caves and Barry manages, using sign language, to persuade four men to share the weight of carrying Marcus down the steps.

Marcus is relieved and thanks Barry.

"Nothing at all," says Barry. "Glad to help. Hope we see you again."

"India is a big place," says Marcus. "I think we had better say goodbye when we get back to the hotel."

After another ferry ride they arrive at the jetty opposite their hotel.

"I drank two litres of water while we were out today," says Kimberley. "Apart from the constant heat this is such a dry country, dusty everywhere."

"We can cross this road, go into the hotel and have cold showers to get rid of today's dust," says Marcus. "I'll meet you in the gardens around the swimming pool."

"Okay," says Kimberley.

18
Train Journey

Thirty minutes later Kimberley walks out to meet Marcus, wearing a thin cotton trouser suit in bright yellow.

"I feel like Calamity Jane," she says. "These are my travelling clothes. They are comfortable, light, lots of pockets and I am as respectable as a nun in them. What do you think?"

Marcus is wearing equally thin cotton in slate grey colour and made into a safari suit.

"You look comfortable, Kimberley," says Marcus.

"You look like some kind of 1950s mad film director, Marcus," answers Kimberley, "but I guess it is a good idea for us because it is so hot and dusty here everywhere. I've drunk two litres of water every day and not needed the restroom. I had a good day today, Marcus. Did you?"

"I did," says Marcus, "but I've had enough now. I just want a light dinner and a heavy sleep."

"You said that we have to get up early tomorrow," says Kimberley. "How do we get to the station?"

"We will take a taxi," says Marcus, "and if you don't mind I would like us to get out of the taxi just before we get to the station and then walk the last few yards."

"Well okay, Marcus," says Kimberley, "but what is the reason?"

"It won't mean much to you," says Marcus, "but the road to the station looks exactly like Regent Street in London. That is a big famous London street full of shops. The Queen owns Regent Street, as a matter of fact."

"As a matter of fact, I know a toyshop in Regent Street," says Kimberley, "called Hamleys toyshop."

"Well, the reason I want to walk a few yards down the street tomorrow is that two million people walk down the street every day. So that if a person sets up a little stall selling shoelaces or hair combs, then with the amount of people who walk by he is certain to make a living. I want to have a quick look at it before we leave," says Marcus.

The two of them enjoy an early dinner together and then go to their rooms to pack for their next journey.

"Five thirty tomorrow, Marcus," says Kimberley. "I will be ready in reception."

They go to bed.

In the morning they get a taxi from outside the hotel and Marcus gives the driver instructions. They drive along quietly in the early morning light and the driver drops them about one hundred yards from the station, so that they can walk. Marcus is right. There are hundreds of street vendors setting up little stands selling every possible kind of everyday purchase. There are more ambitious vendors selling shoes and shirts and saris. There is a man with a barrel organ and a monkey. There is a clairvoyant. There is a barber. People selling bottles of water. Some people selling nuts.

As they walk by they see two men, one old and one young, sitting on the pavement cross-legged and eating their breakfast, which looks like some kind of red kidney beans wrapped in a big leaf. In front of them are two hessian sacks. Marcus and Kimberley stop to look and in a flash a mongoose escapes from one sack and begins to attack the other sack, from which emerges an angry cobra snake. Its neck is fanned out and it hisses aggressively. The two men drop their breakfast and the young man reaches out to grab hold of the mongoose. He is too late. In a lightning strike, the mongoose has bitten the snake fatally behind its vicious head. The snake lies dead on the pavement. The mongoose is wrestled back into its sack and the neck of the sack is tied with string. The snake lays flat on the stone pavement. The threat is gone. The two men are now squabbling furiously, each blaming the other for the calamity.

Marcus and Kimberley walk on.

"That was something," says Kimberley.

"The mongoose and the snake were trained to play a game for the crowds to watch," says Marcus. "The snake attacks the mongoose and then the mongoose catches the snake without killing it. It went wrong today. The two men were not watching vigilantly enough and the mongoose got out and decided not to play anymore. Just killed the snake."

"So the two guys have not got any business for today," says Kimberley. "They have got to find themselves another cobra."

"Yes," says Marcus, "and take its fangs out before they start to train it."

"Oh boy," says Kimberley. "Sounds like a six week job before they can get any money."

The two of them walk along the street past an attractive young woman who is selling spectacles and then pass a boy who is setting up a shoeshine stand. Another person is selling umbrellas and another selling small fold up mirrors.

"Do you think it's going to rain?" Marcus asks Kimberley.

"I guess there are some kind of people who are happy to buy an umbrella on a sunny day," says Kimberley. "Insurance."

They have reached the railway station.

"The world must be empty," says Kimberley. "Everybody is here."

After a lot of struggling and attending at the wrong ticket offices they are finally not only directed but escorted to the correct ticket office. Marcus shows the man in the office his tickets. The man makes a careful note of the ticket number using a big old fountain pen. They are directed to the next opening, where another man clips their tickets and hands them back to them. They next move to a third position where a porter is allocated to them. He takes hold of their light bags and puts them onto a trolley.

"Please to follow me, sir," he says and walks a long way onto a big platform where an enormous train is waiting.

Its huge diesel engines pant softly. The porter walks alongside the train counting the carriages, until he stops.

"This is for you sir, madam," he says. "Seat number 126 and 127."

He gets onto the train, finds the seats and places their bags above their heads in a luggage rack.

"The train will leave in fifteen minutes, sir," says the porter. "Do not move. Do not get off the train until you arrive at Agra, sir. You will become lost if you move."

"All right," says Marcus. "Thank you."

He tips the porter generously.

"Thank you, sir. You can have a fresh breakfast cooked for you on the train, sir. I will tell the steward to look for you when the train commences."

The porter walks away down the long platform.

"Would you like the window seat?" Marcus asks Kimberley.

"I surely would, Marcus," answers Kimberley, and shuffles across the first seat into the seat by the window.

"Five thirty in the morning I got up today," Kimberley says, "to see a big animal kill a snake. How do they get the fangs out of a cobra, Marcus? Do they have like snake dentists here in India?"

"I've never seen it," says Marcus. "I guess they hold the snake just behind his head and pull the fangs out with pliers. Dangerous job. You wouldn't want to slip or make a mistake."

"Holy cow," says Kimberley. "These are pretty good seats, Marcus. I think that they are leather."

"We are in the first class seats," says Marcus. "They have second class seats and third class seats. Then some people ride on the roof of the carriages and some people hold onto the sides."

"What class are they?" asks Kimberley.

Marcus smiles. They sit for a few minutes listening to the footsteps above their heads and watching people climbing up the sides of the train to get to the roof. Eventually there is a lot of shouting and the noise of the doors being slammed closed. Then they hear a whistle and the train begins to move, slowly at first and then faster and faster as it leaves the station.

"How do those people on the roof stay up there?" asks Kimberley.

"There are brass railings at the edges of the roof," says Marcus. "Perhaps they simply tied themselves on."

"The people holding onto the sides are in the most danger," says Kimberley. "If they don't stay close to the train they could be knocked off and killed by a train coming the other way. They must really want to get to another place. Holy cow."

There is a lot of rattling and shouting as a train steward pushes a big cart through the carriage.

"Breakfast. Breakfast," he shouts. "Who wants breakfast?"

231

"I'll have it," shouts Kimberley.

"Be careful what you eat," says Marcus.

"I'll watch what he gives me," says Kimberley.

This steward stops his cart next to where Marcus is sitting. Kimberley is sitting on the inside, next to the window.

"Bacon and eggs," the steward shouts. "Bacon and eggs."

Kimberley says, "Yes."

The steward without hesitation lights a large paraffin Primus stove, which flares and produces a big flame which reaches up to the wooden roof of the carriage. The steward bangs a big frying pan on top of the flame just before the paint on the inside of the carriage roof begins to blister. The steward is very cheerful as he knifes a lump of lard into the frying pan, and as it melts he places three rashers of bacon on top of it. The flame beneath the frying pan is so fierce that nothing can cook slowly and after a few moments the bacon begins to sizzle and spit.

"I'm glad I'm wearing these cotton clothes," says Marcus. "They have bacon fat all over them now. I am sacrificing my sartorial elegance for your stomach, Kimberley."

The steward turns the bacon over.

"A sacrifice worth making," says Kimberley. "Keep a sharp look out for what he is cooking me, Marcus."

The steward is now deftly breaking two eggs into the pan with the bacon. He breaks the eggs with one hand, one after the other quickly and discards the shells into a metal bin at the lower level of his trolley.

The breakfast certainly smells appetising, thinks Marcus, who has brought some bread and fruit from the hotel for his own breakfast. I don't think I would risk it though.

The steward produces a large white plate from under the Primus stove and carefully moves the eggs and bacon onto the plate. He adds a large slice of white bread and then pours the fat from the frying pan all over the bread.

"A breakfast for a princess," he exclaims and hands Kimberley a knife and fork wrapped in a cotton napkin before leaning over Marcus to give Kimberley the plate of bacon and eggs.

Kimberley looks at it thoughtfully. "Okay," she says.

Marcus pays the steward and watches as the steward pushes his trolley further up the carriage. Marcus notices that the Primus stove is not fixed to the trolley and wobbles as the trolley moves along. The steward has left the Primus stove flaming until he gets another customer.

Marcus looks up and down the carriage and sees no fire extinguishers anywhere.

Kimberley is eating her breakfast and shows every sign of enjoying it.

"I wish he had some of those curried potatoes I like so much," she says.

"You will have to skip for a long time to get rid of all of that fat," says Marcus.

"I am not fat," answers Kimberley.

"Not you. The fatty breakfast you are eating," says Marcus.

"Ahh, he is gone now and you are sorry that you did not get a breakfast like mine," says Kimberley. "Too late, Marcus." She finishes her meal.

The train is passing through the countryside. Trees, bushes, grass with animals on it. Large fields full of crops and people working in the fields. Mostly women, Marcus notes. All working very hard with old-fashioned hand-held tools. Hoes, rakes, forks and spades. Some crops are being pulled up and collected in sacks at the sides of the fields.

"There is a lot of work for women here, Kimberley," says Marcus.

"Sure is," says Kimberley. "We should get a lot of those New York ladies out here. The women's libbers. Plenty of liberty for them to work here in the fields."

The train goes rattling on and as it reaches a slight incline it slows down a little. Kimberley is looking out of the window at an area of woodland which is passing her window. Suddenly it is replaced by an enormous wheat field. The wheat is ripe and heavy on the stems. The train begins to turn a corner. There is a shout and the figure of a man rolls off the train roof and into the wheat field. Somebody on the roof throws the man's suitcase down to him. Kimberley stares out of the window, which she has now opened. She sees a speedy movement of something black and yellow before hearing a desperate scream, which turns into a howl of agony which goes on and on without stopping.

"Marcus," cries Kimberley, who puts her hands over her ears but still looks out of the window to see legs and arms flailing as a tiger eats the man who has fallen off the train roof.

"Why isn't the man dead?" asks Kimberley in distress. "Why does he keep on crying?"

Marcus leans over Kimberley to watch the scene, which is diminishing into the distance. He does not want to tell Kimberley that lions and tigers eat their prey whilst it is still alive. They do not kill it first but eat it hot with the blood coursing through the body. David Attenborough doesn't show that on the television.

Marcus feels very sobered by what he has witnessed. He instinctively puts an arm round Kimberley's shoulders and hugs her to him.

"The man is dead now," he says. "It was very quick for him."

Kimberley has tears in her eyes and is shaking slightly under Marcus's arm. She tries to cheer herself up.

"You didn't even get a photograph," she says quietly and nervously.

"Your breasts were in the way," says Marcus, trying to move her thoughts away from the horror. He continues to hug her as the train moves away from the tragedy. Marcus wonders where the man was going and who will now tell the people he was visiting that he will not arrive. The Indian people on the roof are beginning to chatter and laugh again. The journey goes on with one passenger less and Marcus knows nothing about him. He squeezes Kimberley's shoulder.

"Don't lean out of the window," he says. "I don't want to lose you."

"Don't you, Marcus?" says Kimberley in a small voice.

"My brother and I used to travel to school every day by train," says Marcus. "In those days the trains had little notices over the two carriage doors which said, 'Do Not Lean Out Of The Window. Penalty £5'. My brother used to carry miniature tins of enamel paint in two colours. He also carried two of his artist's brushes. He would work carefully to change the signs from 'lean' to 'leer'. Day after day he would work on the journey to school and the journey home again. We were on the London train but got off after only twenty minutes. It took him weeks to complete every carriage. He was a very serious boy."

"How very odd, Marcus. Did he ever get caught?"

"No, he was very vigilant and it was not a very noticeable crime. It was only a slight amendment. I don't suppose the guard on the train ever looked," answers Marcus.

"What a strange family you have, Marcus," says Kimberley. " 'Do not leer out of the window'. Who would be the judge of whether somebody's expression was a leer or a smile?"

"We never thought of that," says Marcus.

"Do you make up these stories just to cheer me up?" says Kimberley.

"They are all true," says Marcus, "and I tell them to cheer myself up. You are tougher than me, Kimberley. You are a brave girl."

"Not today, Marcus, and I like it that you say that the stories are true," says Kimberley. "Even if they are not true they are good stories. Where are we going?"

"This train is taking us to Agra," says Marcus.

"Why are we going there?" asks Kimberley.

"Because the Taj Mahal is at Agra, Kimberley, and we are going to see it. I would like you to do something for me if you would be so kind."

"I would be so kind to you, Marcus," says Kimberley. "What would you like?"

"The Taj Mahal is covered with white marble and people say that it is white during the daytime and blue at night and pink at dawn. I would like to see it at all of those times," says Marcus.

"So see it,' says Kimberley. "You don't need my permission." She smiles mischievously at him. "Oh, I get it," she says. "You want to drag me along with you at midnight and dawn and then in the daytime." She looks at him. "The answer is yes," she says.

The train moves on, moving rapidly again. The steward rattles back with his trolley and collects Kimberley's plate, napkin and cutlery, which she had put under her seat. The Primus stove is not burning now and Marcus is glad.

"Thirty-five minutes to Agra," says the steward. "Thirty-five minutes."

There is a cheer from the people on the roof. The people at the sides of the train are too tired to make a noise. Their arms are aching and becoming cramped from holding on to the railings at the sides of the carriages. So close to their journey's end and they do not want to fall off now.

19
Taj Mahal

The train arrives in Agra thirty-five minutes later. The city lacks the pizzazz of Bombay. Its atmosphere is immediately different. Marcus and Kimberley walk out of the station to the taxi rank and Kimberley says, "It is quieter here."

Marcus answers, "There are not so many people for a start, but I agree. I feel as if everyone is moving more slowly."

A lot of the people are simply standing in small groups staring at the passers-by. There are tourists here who have come to see the Taj Mahal but most of the tourists are Indians who have journeyed from other parts of the country to see one of the Wonders of the World. Marcus finds a taxi which looks clean inside, and opens the door for Kimberley.

The taxi drives them to their hotel. The hotel is large without being grand and whilst it is the best hotel in Agra it lacks style. The staff of the hotel lack a pride in what they do. They look as if they have all been beaten with a stick and shouted at. The manager succumbs to Marcus's trick of bribing him for better rooms, but lacks discretion, openly pocketing the money Marcus gives him but first looking at it carefully so that the receptionist, the concierge and the two hotel porters all witness the transaction. They exhibit mixed feelings and there is certainly resentment. The resentment, however, is not directed at Marcus and Kimberley but seems to be reserved for the hotel manager himself, who is undoubtedly a tyrant to his staff.

Marcus and Kimberley are allocated big rooms with a distant view of the top towers of the Taj Mahal. The rooms are clean. The furnishings are not ornate or rich but rather plain. The bathrooms are clean and adequate. Marcus and Kimberley decide to go for a walk.

Outside on the streets they encounter the usual rush of children begging. Today they are determined to ignore them and carry on walking. They encounter a children's orchestra on a street corner. There are four children aged about five or six years old and they each have a wind instrument; a trumpet, a flugel, a trombone and a saxophone. The instruments are all child-sized. The children begin to play a classical melody and after about thirty seconds they all freeze motionless and stop playing.

"Rupees, rupees," the oldest boy calls out.

Kimberley gives him ten rupees and he looks at it carefully before they start to play again exactly where they left off. After another thirty seconds they stop again and the oldest boy asks for payment. Two minutes later Kimberley has given them forty rupees and after a final ten rupees she says goodbye.

"At least they have some enterprise," Kimberley says. "I get tired of all the children walking alongside and behind us all calling out for money. They do not offer to work or to do anything, just rupees, rupees, rupees. At the start when we were in Goa, I felt sympathetic, but I guess I can't keep it up. Now I am tired of them. There are too many. If I gave away a thousand dollars a day I would not make any difference."

"You would probably create a traffic jam and a riot," says Marcus. "So it is a good thing that you are not doing it."

They walk on a little further and around the next corner is a man sitting cross-legged on a small mat on the pavement. In front of him is a big earthenware pot. The man is playing a flute and a black cobra rises out of the pot and starts to sway backwards and forwards in time with the music.

Kimberley takes a small pink camera out of one of her pockets and takes a photograph of the vase, the cobra and the man with the flute. She puts the camera back into her pocket.

"Rupees, rupees," shouts the man.

Kimberley ignores him. She has her photograph now anyway.

"Rupees, rupees," shouts the man.

Marcus is watching but Kimberley begins to walk on.

"You pay, you pay," shouts the man with great anger.

He deftly snatches the cobra snake from the pot holding it tightly by the back of its neck. He begins to run after Kimberley, waving the snake. He is running barefoot. Kimberley hears his feet slapping on the pavement stones, looks around at him and seeing the snake she begins to run. She is taller, longer-legged, stronger and fitter than the little snake charmer and she outruns him easily, dodging in and out of the crowd until she is out of sight.

Marcus crosses the road to avoid the snake charmer. He did not take a photograph after all but he still wishes to avoid an encounter with the cobra, whether it has teeth or not. Marcus finds Kimberley in the next square, looking at six hens which are pecking the ground.

"Holy cow," says Kimberley. "He nearly got me."

"He was never anywhere near you," says Marcus. "You went off down the road like Zola Budd."

"Who the hell is Zola Budd?" asks Kimberley.

"She used to be an Olympic champion runner," says Marcus. "She was from South Africa. White girl. Very young. She used to run barefoot."

"Well, okay then," says Kimberley. "This is not a country where we can get a coffee in a pavement café in the mornings. They don't have places like 'The News Café' in Miami, North Beach. The Indians do not seem to drink coffee at all and the two cups of coffee we had in the hotel were horrible."

"I suppose they drink tea," says Marcus. "They grow a lot of tea here. Do you want to try to drink tea?"

"Why not?" says Kimberley "But I don't see a café around here.'

"Let's walk back to the hotel," says Marcus.

"When are we going to see the Taj Mahal?" asks Kimberley.

"Two thirty this afternoon," says Marcus. "I have arranged for a guide."

"Okay, let's try the tea in the hotel," says Kimberley, "but I'm not eating cucumber sandwiches. That is what you British like with your tea, right?"

They order a pot of tea in the gardens of the hotel. The gardens are unexpectedly exotic and in contrast to the drab interior of the hotel. Marcus and Kimberley sit on ornate white painted metal chairs at a circular ornate white painted metal table.

"This tea tastes weird," says Marcus, as he takes a sip.

Kimberley calls the waiter back. "There is something strange about the tea," she says.

"It is very hot here, madam," says the waiter. "So the tea is brewed with peppercorns in it. Both green and black. It assists the stomach in the heat, madam. It is very good." He walks away.

"There you are, Marcus," says Kimberley. "It is medicine. Drink it up like a good tourist. It will help your stomach."

"You should drink it then," says Marcus, "after that risky breakfast you had at six thirty this morning."

"I'm drinking it," says Kimberley. "Tastes good to me. Better than that pale mud-coloured tea you get in Britain. This peppercorn tea is exciting," she smiles warmly at Marcus. "We are a long way from home, right? Are you nervous?"

"I've got you to look after me," says Marcus.

After a light lunch they take a taxi to the Taj Mahal. The guide is waiting for them outside two big wooden gates. The guide has gathered an extra four people during the period he has been waiting. He is tall and thin with dark hair and a long face. He is wearing a pale grey lightweight suit and sandals. He speaks in an exaggeratedly plummy voice, sounding like a character from a PG Wodehouse novel.

The Taj Mahal is surrounded by thirty-metre high, red sandstone walls. Two tall solid wooden doors in the walls open to reveal a wide gap and then another set of high walls. Set in these walls is another set of solid doors, which cannot be opened until the outside doors are closed. When the inner doors are opened Kimberley and Marcus get their first view of the Taj Mahal. It is a controlled view because of the security of the walls. The distance from which you first view the Taj Mahal is carefully measured. You see the whole building immediately but from over two hundred and seventy-five metres away. There is a long stretch of water, creating by its measurements a diminished perspective. The Taj Mahal itself seems to be standing on a sort of plinth. At first it appears comparatively small until you realise that the ant-like figures walking alongside the plinth do not measure more than a third of the height of plinth itself, let alone the giant mausoleum which is the Taj Mahal.

Marcus and Kimberley walk into the grounds, which are arranged and planted as gardens to highlight the beauty of the mausoleum. They are divided into four parts by two canals. At the intersection of the canals there is a wide ornamental lake, which mirrors a complete reflection of the Taj Mahal and the tall cypress trees, which contribute to the symmetry of the whole. There are fountains and the noise of the falling water together with the double sandstone walls surrounding serve to eliminate the sounds of the city outside. Here it is tranquil.

Marcus continues to stare at the building.

The guide starts to speak. "The architect of this wonder endeavoured to create perfect symmetry," he says, "but to do this he had to adjust things which you see. The four towers are wider at the top than they appear. They gradually increase in width because if they did not then they would appear to the human eye to be narrowing from the base to the top. As it is the fine thin lower towers appear to be in perfect proportion and positioned on the four corners of the base. There are prayers written into the marble columns and these are of increasing size as they approach the highest points, so as to increase the illusion of perfect symmetry. From whatever angle you look at the Taj Mahal it is always symmetrical.

The dome which you can see is actually two domes, and pear-shaped, one inside the other, with a gap in between to create a vacuum. The vacuum modulates the temperature inside the structure, keeping it cool in the daytime and warm at night.

The mausoleum was built to keep the body of Mumtaz Mahal, who was the second wife of the Mughal Emperor Shah Jahan. She died giving birth to his fourteenth child in 1631. The mausoleum took twelve years to build and the body of the empress was placed in a crypt surrounded by gold railings in the deep basement of the building. The cenotaph of white marble has gems and semi-precious stones inset into the marble and in the intricate patterns. The marble is extensively carved with decorative patterns of plants and flowers."

"The building is effeminate, don't you think, Marcus?" says Kimberley. "There is nothing aggressive or even defensive about it. It is pure beauty."

At this point the guide speaks unexpectedly. "By the by," he says, "does anybody have a fag?"

He is given a cigarette and furnished with a match and he breaks off from his lecture to smoke luxuriously in the most contented way until the cigarette is completely finished, whereupon he carefully extinguishes it and puts the remnants into his coat pocket. He then proceeds to conduct the tour by leading the group up the steps until they are on a level with the building and able to look closely at the big panels of marble, the inlays of gemstones and the skilful patterns of carving in the marble.

"Please notice," says the guide, "that the carvings on every panel are of the same size, depth and pattern of design. Whoever arranged for this work ensured that it appears to be the result of the sculpture of only one man. There are no variations here."

The small party walk slowly around the outside of the building, observing what the guide has pointed out to them.

"There is an awful lot of work here," says Marcus. "Every detail, every feature is elaborate and the workmen would have to have been top craftsmen."

"Twelve years is a long time to build a building," says Kimberley. "I wonder where they put the body whilst they were waiting. No deep-freezes then. She must have been a volcano in the sack to have had this place built for her."

"Not necessarily," says Marcus. "She might have been a good cook."

"Get out of here," says Kimberley. "They had fourteen children, don't forget. They must have been at each other all the time. She didn't cook."

"Well, they are both gone now," says Marcus, who is rather disturbed by Kimberley's enthusiastic description of the love life of the Emperor Shah Jahan and his wife Mumtaz Mahal.

"We can't see a picture of them, I guess," says Kimberley. "No photography then and with all of that physical activity to produce fourteen children they can't have stayed still for long enough for portraits to be done. What do you think, Marcus?"

"I think that if you are a very good girl, Kimberley, then somebody someday might build something like this for you."

"Hell, you don't get a monument like this by being a good girl," says Kimberley. "Anyway I don't think you could get the zoning to build something like this in the States. It is pretty big; would look out of place in the local cemetery."

The guide has hesitated again to enquire identically, "By the by, has anyone got a fag?"

Once again he is supplied with his immediate requirements and breaks the tour briefly to indulge in another luxurious smoke. When he has finished he tells his little group, "We are privileged to be here today. It is one of the rare years and the one day in that year that the mausoleum is open and small numbers of the public are allowed inside. I have made an application and today now we are to be allowed inside the tomb of the great lady. Come this way, please."

They all have to take their shoes off and wear thick slippers, which are provided to them.

The guide leads them inside the building, which Kimberley feels is about the size of the White House, and they are hushed by the tranquillity, vast emptiness and beauty of the interior. Two guards stand at the top of a wide flight of marble steps, which descends towards a big decorated door. At the door are two more guards. The guide shows the first two men his paperwork and the permits to enter the tomb. The two guards then permit the little group to pass down the marble staircase to where the second pair of guards open the huge doors. They all have shuffled inside to find the inner sanctum to be dark, although there are myriad strips of light entering from the carved ceiling and the carved tops of the walls. Their eyes adjust to the light. A deafening clatter is heard and hundreds of bats fly over the heads of the group and then round and round the room.

Centrally there is a heavily decorated marble platform and in the exact centre of the Taj Mahal is the decorated marble tomb of the emperor's wife. Discordantly there is another platform to the right and another tomb, completely wrecking the symmetry of the room. The second tomb is that of Shah Jahan, who died many years after his wife.

"He couldn't leave her alone," whispers Kimberley. "Not even in her grave. He had to come in next to her."

The bats are still fluttering around.

"How did they get in here?" says Kimberley.

"Through those patterns in the marble panels," says Marcus. "I've heard it said that a bat can fly through an electric fan, but I've never seen it."

"Just one of those exaggerations that people repeat," says Kimberley. "Like the idea that if you shoot a gun at a plane after it has taken off then you'll never hit it. Another myth."

She looks around carefully.

"Death here," she says. "Two deaths. Do you want to get out of here and walk up into the gardens? Get some clean air?"

"Of course," says Marcus.

He tells the guide that they are going outside.

"Okay cokey," says the guide, who is himself looking forward to getting outside and cadging another cigarette.

Marcus and Kimberley go outside. Kimberley finds a sign on the grass which says, 'No photographs. No walking on the grass.'

Marcus takes Kimberley's photograph standing on the grass leaning against the sign. Afterwards they go and sit on the bench at the beginning of the ornamental water. Marcus asks Kimberley to photograph him, adjusts his camera and hands it to her. Whilst she is walking a short distance from him he unravels a sheet of white paper and holds it across his chest. 'Hello Mum', the notice says.

Kimberley takes his photograph and says, "Okay Marcus, let me use that, please."

He then takes her photograph with the paper sign.

By this time the guide and the rest of the party are outside as well and the guide is cadging another cigarette. Marcus discreetly pays the guide for his tour and gives him a little extra.

"Buy yourself some cigarettes," Marcus says.

"Oh no, my dear sir, I will not," says the guide. "I wish to stop smoking, sir, so I will never buy cigarettes."

Marcus and Kimberley thank him and walk away towards the big gates.

"Did you know that his name is Leonard?" says Kimberley. "I have just asked him."

"It can't be Leonard," says Marcus. "He must have adopted a name which he thinks sounds English. Leonard is an old-fashioned name."

"He is an old-fashioned man," says Kimberley. "Shall we go back to the hotel and sit in those wonderful gardens?"

"Okay," says Marcus, and they get into a taxi.

Back at the hotel they order more peppercorn tea and sit as before in the exotic garden.

There is an Indian man and his wife there, both elegantly dressed. Kimberley immediately begins to talk to them, telling them of their intention to visit the Taj Mahal at midnight and again at dawn.

"Most necessary visits," says the man, "to appreciate the grandeur of the structure at all hours."

Kimberley introduces herself and Marcus and the man says, "My name is Manish Balan, this is my wife." He does not give her name.

"The creation of the Taj Mahal bankrupted the entire region," says Manish. "The cost of it was very great and Shah Jahan ransacked his people for the money. Later his son imprisoned him because of it. The emperor intended to build a second Taj Mahal in black marble for his own burial, but his son prevented it and imprisoned him in such a place as to prevent him being able to see his treasured Taj Mahal ever again."

"Puts you off having children," says Kimberley. "You have a hobby and then your son stops you."

"Shah Jahan died and was then put inside the Taj Mahal next to his wife," says Manish, "but that was never his wish. He had created the mausoleum for his wife alone. Not for two."

"Goodness me," says Marcus.

"Goodness you?" says Kimberley. "I've never heard anybody say that before."

She leans to Manish. "What authority did the Shah have over the people?" she asks.

"They were his people," says Manish. "It was six hundred years ago. In previous days one hundred million Indian people were ruled by the maharajas. Over seventy years ago five hundred and sixty two princes owned over half of India and India is a country as wide as from London to Athens and bigger than that from north to south. Twenty-two princely states were absorbed into the new Republic when India changed after 1947. Rajputana became Rajasthan. Jaipur was the capital with all of its ancient glory and extravagant poverty."

"Tell us about the maharajas, please," says Kimberley. "I am most interested."

"Maharajas possessed unimaginable riches," says Manish. "They had the power of life and death over their people. They believed themselves to be maharajas because of a divine right, descended from God, and the people believed that also. After independence was created for India in 1947 the maharajas were compelled by the new parliament to join the world's biggest democracy. They were granted privy purses, that is, government allowances to continue with their ancient pomp and ceremony."

"Sounds like your Queen, Marcus," says Kimberley.

"However," says Manish, "in 1971 Mrs Gandhi took away their privileges and turned them into ordinary citizens. They were given over to the hands of the new tax collectors. The maharajas' families had ruled for centuries and the people still believe in them. Some of the proudest maharajas came from Rajasthan, Jaipur, Jodhpur, Udaipur, Bikaner and Gwalior. Jaipur resisted change. From the Palace of the Winds the ladies of the maharaja's harem watched the passing crowds from lookout positions concealed from prying eyes. The maharaja's main palace covered one seventh of the entire city and he had another nineteen palaces and forts besides."

"Not like your queen at all then," says Kimberley. "She has only got five."

"One of the late maharajas of Jaipur was a famous player of polo and in 1970 he died whilst playing polo in England in a place called the Cotswolds. He was leading an Indian team called the Lavender Tigers. After that the next maharaja became known as mister, a great reduction of status. Polo was in their richest years played with elephants. Later they were reduced to playing on bicycles."

"It didn't occur to them to stop playing and go to work?" asked Kimberley. "Polo on bicycles sounds like you have no money."

"It was their lifestyle," answers Manish. "The people still expected the maharajas to rule. Some of them previously had between five thousand and seven thousand servants, before death duty ravaged their wealth. How do you value a palace for the death duties, which nobody else could afford to buy?

The new government were trying to belittle the princes to damage their natural pride. Their influence was halved during each generation and wealth was taken from them but Indians are a simple people and without obvious natural leaders they were confused. Democracy confused them a lot. During the socialist period of the 1960s tax inspectors investigated Jaipur's riches and invaded only one of the prince's palaces from which they took a ton of gold and half a ton of jewels and silver.

Ruling families were jailed for several years alongside prostitutes and thieves. Mrs Gandhi accused them of currency offenses. Palaces were taken and turned into hotels. When the country's royalty was released from prison much of their wealth was gone. It was not, however, accounted for by those who took it away. It had disappeared. The Indian people are now lost."

"What was that expression you used, Marcus?" says Kimberley. "My goodness. That is hell of a big story, Manish, much bigger than cowboys and Indians. What a country. Oh boy."

"We had better have a rest, Kimberley," says Marcus. "We are going back to the Taj Mahal at midnight."

"And then again at dawn," says Kimberley, "and I agreed to it!"

The two of them thank Manish and say goodbye to him and his wife, who has not spoken a word. They walk back into the hotel.

"What time do you want to meet, Marcus?" asks Kimberley, "and are we not going to eat something first?"

"Of course," says Marcus. "Shall I arrange a supper for us at about ten o'clock and then afterwards we will get a taxi to the Taj Mahal? We have had a long day so far and a siesta will perk us up."

"Perk us up?" says Kimberley. "I don't think I've been perked up before. Will I like it?"

"See you later," says Marcus, smiling.

20
Midnight and Dawn

The Taj Mahal at one o'clock was blue under the moonlight.

"I never knew that moonlight really was blue," says Kimberley.

She and Marcus are sitting on the lonely bench at the end of the ornamental water looking at the building. It can be seen clearly in all of its details but the marble is no longer shining white in the sunshine, it is now shining a magical blue colour underneath a full moon.

"This is romantic," says Kimberley, "sitting in the moonlight in front of the Taj Mahal."

Marcus stands up and walks towards the building on the pathway next to the water. Kimberley follows him. There are only five or six other people in the gardens and they are all absolutely quiet. The only person to have spoken at all was Kimberley and she used a very quiet tone of voice. There are small wispy brilliant white clouds moving over the dome of the Taj Mahal.

If you're going die then this is a special place to be laid to rest, thinks Kimberley. They must have had a real big love, the two of them, and six hundred years ago. People are still hearing about it and still visiting. Hollywood has got nothing on this.

"This place is truly wonderful, Marcus," says Kimberley quietly. "Thank you for bringing me here. It is awe inspiring."

She has walked up to him. They stand in the warm night and look at the most decorative extravagant mausoleum in the world created for one woman.

"Marilyn Monroe has got nothing like this," says Kimberley.

"No man ever loved Marilyn Monroe," says Marcus.

"A lot of men thought that they did," says Kimberley.

"That is not the same thing," says Marcus. "The woman on the cinema screen and the woman in real life were different. The woman resting here was in real life all the time."

"You may be right," says Kimberley. "Anyway she has got the Taj Mahal."

"Shall we go back for a few hours and lie down until dawn?" suggests Marcus.

"I don't want to miss the changeover, Marcus," says Kimberley. "Let's get back here before dawn, while it is still dark."

"We could sleep here for four hours if you like," says Marcus.

"No, we'll go back for a short time," says Kimberley, "but let's arrange a taxi back here and get the hotel to wake us up in time."

"All right," says Marcus.

Four and a half hours later, sitting on the same bench, they watch as the blue marble turns slowly pink as the dawn light comes up. The colour change is gradual; it is almost like trying to watch a flower unfolding with the morning sunshine. If you glance away you miss it.

Eventually the Taj Mahal is glowing in an almost fairy tale pink colour, which changes again as they watch the sun fully emerge. The pink turns to pale yellow, and then slowly brilliant white.

"Okay, I've seen it," says Kimberley. "I don't believe it but I have seen it. Now we can go someplace else, Marcus. There is nothing else to stay in Agra for."

"Maybe breakfast at least," says Marcus. "Then I agree we can move on. The taxi is still waiting."

In the afternoon and with their bags they get onto a bus. It is more of a luxury coach but it is about half-sized. Kimberley sits in a window seat at the front with Marcus beside her. The bus driver looks around and counts everyone. Most passengers are English or European.

"The bus is leaving," he says in a loud voice. "Delhi, next stop."

The driver speaks in English to pander to the requirements of his passengers.

"You were right about breakfast," says Kimberley. "Did you get any water? It is really hot already."

"I got two one litre bottles from the hotel," says Marcus, "one for you and one for me. Ration yourself. We won't get any more until we arrive."

There are children running alongside the bus offering miniature carved chess sets for sale. A boy is pushing a boxed set into Kimberley's hands.

"I don't want it," she says.

"Only twenty-five rupees," shouts the boy.

The bus is gathering speed and the boy is running fast to keep up. Marcus leans over and gives the boy ten rupees and takes the chess set.

"Goodbye, sir, happiness sir," shouts the boy, who is delighted to have got ten rupees.

"Don't look at me," says Kimberley. "I don't play chess."

They both settle down in their seats to try to make up for their lost sleep. The bus is comfortably air-conditioned.

They are woken, as the bus approaches the outskirts of Delhi, by the bus driver pushing his horn over and over again. Marcus and Kimberley sit up and look out of the front window.

There is a tall, sinister and shabby-looking man holding tightly to a long thick pole. On the other end of the pole is an iron collar round the neck of a black bear. The man has a whip in his right hand and is pushing with his left hand to keep the bear out of reach of him. The bear has sharp claws and a big jaw with strong teeth.

"Dancing bear," shouts the sinister man. "Stop to see the dancing bear."

The bus driver has no intention of stopping and the man has no intention of moving. It is a stalemate and the bus driver has not even slowed down but keeps going, aiming directly at the man and the bear.

"We are going to hit them," says Kimberley.

With ten feet to go the man suddenly jumps aside, pulling the bear with him. He puts out his arm to break his fall and drops his whip. As he scrambles to his feet he momentarily lets go of the pole.

The bus driver has now stopped the bus and urges his passengers to watch. Marcus and Kimberley stand up to see over the other passengers to the view out of the rear window.

The bear is attacking the man, clawing at him and biting him savagely as the pole swings around his neck freely. The man on the ground is crying out loudly and the bear bites him again before putting his front two paws onto the pole and biting it before breaking it up on the roadside, breaking it by jumping on it with his front paws. The bear turns back to the man, who is now limping away shouting for help. The bear

255

evidently has no goodwill towards the man and does not wish to go near him again. The bear simply growls with frightening anger as the man hurries away with his terrible wounds bleeding onto the road as he progresses slowly towards the city. The bear snarls and starts to run in the opposite direction, away from the city and towards the woodland, with part of the pole still attached.

"How will he ever get that collar off?" says Marcus.

The bus driver sits down again and shouts, "This show is over, next stop Delhi, twenty minutes."

Delhi is a city of wide streets, almost as wide as the main streets of Paris. In Marcus's opinion the large, slightly Dutch-looking, gable ended, white rendered buildings with red edges look different. Un-Indian, almost but not accurately art deco. The streets were certainly clean but that is not unusual in India because everything is recycled. If you drop a biro it will be picked up and every part of it used to make something else. Discarded newspapers are made into papier mache, which makes toys and souvenirs. Cloth is recycled. All waste is recycled so the streets have no litter except for people everywhere. This city has less street people than Bombay or Agra.

"I believe that this place was designed by Lutyens, the architect," says Marcus.

"What a job to get," says Kimberley. "Imagine being commissioned to design a city. Think of the fees."

"It is called New Delhi," says Marcus, "to distinguish it from the original Delhi, which was a slum."

"How do you know?" asks Kimberley. "When was this place built?"

"I don't know," says Marcus, "possibly in the 1920s."

"Do you think that this coach is going to stop at our hotel?" asks Kimberley, "because I am hot and dusty and tired of travelling."

"The coach will stop at the hotel," says Marcus. "Then we can both freshen up. I hope to have a swim if the hotel has a pool."

"If not you can float in your bath," says Kimberley.

The coach arrives slowly towards the centre of the city and stops outside a hotel of modern appearance, although it is eighty years old. They all get out.

"Looks like everybody is staying here," says Kimberley.

At the desk the manager smiles at Marcus in a wax-like way and explains that all of the rooms are superior unless Marcus would like a suite.

"Do we want a suite, Kimberley?" asks Marcus.

"A suite for two?" says Kimberley. "Sure, if you can stand it. You may have to wait for the bathroom."

"No madam," says the hotel manager. "Our suite has two bathrooms, a sitting room with a balcony, and a bed which is nine feet square in a room of large proportions."

"Okay," says Kimberley. "Let's go for it, Marcus."

They are shown to the top floor of the hotel by the porter who carries their luggage. The porter opens the door of the suite and steps back to let them walk in first.

The rooms are stunning; a small hallway with a cloakroom and a toilet off it, then a sitting room about thirty feet by twenty feet, furnished opulently in Indian style and with its own wide balcony. A bedroom with two red velvet sofas, a large ornate balcony with two chairs and a table, and of course the enormous bed covered with cream silk bedspreads and a dozen silk cushions.

"I think we can camp here, Marcus," says Kimberley.

Marcus tips the porter and thanks him. The porter puts their two small bags onto a luggage stand and formally hands each of them a key to the suite.

"Marcus, we have been tourists every day. Travel and special things to look at and trips all of the time. Can we have a day off?" asks Kimberley.

"Kimberley, I did not know that you were finding it difficult. You should have told me before," says Marcus.

"Marcus, I am having the most wonderful time," says Kimberley. "I want a day of relaxation just so that I can think about it."

"We have nothing arranged here today or tomorrow," says Marcus. "So we can just relax. I will go down and have a swim then I'll come back up here and we can play backgammon. I see that they have a set on that table. Do you play?"

"Can I play? Okay, yes," says Kimberley.

"I'll have a bath whilst you are swimming. See you later."

When Marcus comes back an hour later Kimberley is outside on the balcony wearing a big white cotton dressing gown embroidered with flowers and elephants. The backgammon set is all ready.

"Give me a minute," says Marcus. "Where did you get that dressing gown?"

"There may be one in your bathroom," says Kimberley.

Marcus goes to see and takes off his bathing shorts, dries himself and puts on the cotton dressing gown. His is decorated with embroidered pictures of tea plantations with women picking tea and mountains with snowy tops.

Marcus walks onto the balcony and notices that it overlooks the gardens and the swimming pool and hills in the distance.

"This is lovely," says Marcus. "Shall we have a drink? It is our day off."

"Of course we should have drinks," says Kimberley. "You decide."

Marcus walks back into the sitting room and telephones hotel reception. He gives them a comprehensive order, asks advice and then continues his order. He walks back outside. Kimberley is sitting at the table with her legs up on the balustrading of the terrace. She has no shoes on, her dressing gown reveals her thighs and her toes are gripping the stonework.

"Can I take a photograph of you?" asks Marcus.

"Of course," says Kimberley.

When Marcus comes back with his camera, Kimberley has slipped the cotton dressing gown off her shoulders, showing the tops of her tanned arms and her impressive cleavage. Marcus takes three pictures in silence. There is a knock at the door. It is the Indian man from room service. He is pushing a trolley.

"The canapés will be another thirty minutes, sir," he says. "May I serve the alcohol, sir?"

"Certainly," says Marcus. "We are sitting outside."

Kimberley has pulled her gown tightly around herself and has taken her legs down. Marcus is mildly disappointed.

The waiter pushes the trolley onto the balcony. There is an ice bucket containing two bottles of French wine and a large bottle of water. There are various liquor bottles, limes, oranges, nectarines and tonic water.

"What time is it?" asks Kimberley.

"You have your diver's watch," says Marcus.

"I've got nothing on underneath this dressing gown. I left the diver's watch inside," says Kimberley.

"It is 12.45," says Marcus.

"Okay then. Please make me some kind of fruit cocktail with vodka," Kimberley asks the waiter.

"I'll have the same," says Marcus.

The waiter chops fruit into two large glasses and brings out ice in a vacuum flask.

"Is that ice clean?" asks Marcus.

"Evian water, sir," says the waiter, and places several cubes into a silver-plated cocktail shaker. He adds vodka, Cointreau, a small amount of dark syrup and lemonade. He shakes the mixture vigorously and then pours the drink over the fruit in the two glasses. "I will put the shaker here, sir." He indicates a shelf under the trolley. "There are perhaps two more drinks, sir," he says.

The waiter then opens both bottles of the white French burgundy and opens the water.

"The canapés will arrive shortly," he says and backs out of the suite.

"Cocktails, wine, canapés. We are having a day off," says Kimberley.

"I may have been a bit thoughtless," says Marcus, "pushing us along everywhere. We are on holiday."

"Marcus," says Kimberley. "Every day has been special. Now today can be special too." She looks him in the eyes for a second. "Let's try these Indian drinks."

They both sip their cocktails.

"Oh boy," says Kimberley. "That is special as well."

The backgammon board is all set up and Marcus offers Kimberley the choice of coloured pieces.

"I'll have black," says Kimberley, "the colour for a bad girl. You can have white because you are a good guy."

Marcus plays an aggressive game, pushing Kimberley to make defensive moves. She is unlucky with the dice and Marcus wins the first game just as they finish their cocktail drinks. Marcus pours out second drinks for them and there is a knock at the door. It is room service again and a trolley of sumptuous canapés and fruit is wheeled into the sitting room. The waiter whisks a large white cloth over it and leaves the room.

"I can't believe you beat me, Marcus. I am good at this game," says Kimberley.

"Well, let's play for a bet," says Marcus. "Something you want against something I want. We can each write the bet down and if you lose you have to keep to your side of the bargain."

"And if you lose, so do you," says Kimberley. "I'll get the paper."

She gathers hotel stationery, two pens and two envelopes and brings them onto the balcony.

"Okay then," she says and writes something onto her paper.

Marcus is writing too. An atmosphere of excitement has crept into the game. They exchange envelopes and start the game again. Kimberley is thoughtful and careful and Marcus cannot hurry her along. The dice rattles and falls and the game after half an hour is still even. They have finished their drinks. Marcus places wineglasses onto the table and pours the cold French burgundy. They throw the dice and continue. Slowly and slightly, Kimberley begins to lose and then pulls herself up and gains an advantage. She looks at Marcus. He is concentrating. He must want to win his bet, thinks Kimberley.

They are both drinking more wine and Marcus pours each of them a glass of water from the ice bucket. Kimberley wins another throw. Kimberley is gaining the upper hand. The game slows down.

"You are a tough player, Marcus. You just can't take it easy, can you?"

261

"I want to win," says Marcus.

Marcus refills the glasses, this time from the second bottle of wine, and they start to play again. Kimberley must have a head like rock, thinks Marcus, as his game slips a little more. Kimberley looks determined as she presses home her advantage. There is a crucial throw of the dice ahead of them. Marcus loses again and Kimberley romps home and wins the game. She looks fiercely at Marcus and snatches up both envelopes.

"We don't have to keep those bets," says Marcus.

"Oh yes we do," answers Kimberley, and tears open her envelope.

She also opens Marcus's envelope and reads it as well. Kimberley is flushed with success and her nakedness under her thin cotton dressing gown, together with the alcohol, makes her feel wanton and adventurous.

"Let's do both," she says, "both bets."

Kimberley has written 'kisses' and Marcus has written 'dancing'.

"Your bet first, Marcus."

Marcus uses the radio in the room to find some dance music. Eventually he locates a station playing swing music. He takes Kimberley by her left hand and puts his right arm around her waist. The beat of the music moves their feet and they start to float around the room. Marcus lowers his right arm until his hand is resting at the base of Kimberley's spine. He moves her closer to him with the next manoeuvre. They are perfectly in step with each other and moving easily. Marcus turns Kimberley, swinging her through the double doors into the big bedroom. Still they dance on without speaking.

Boldly Marcus brings his lips down onto Kimberley's and they begin a kiss, which goes deeper and longer than either of them expected. They move their lips apart and Kimberley pulls Marcus's head down to hers again; her hands are caressing his hair. Marcus pulls her body close to his, holding her firmly at the small of her back. Kimberley is surprised to find herself losing her usual logic as her senses take over. I am on holiday, she thinks, as she moves her hands to Marcus's shoulders. Marcus begins to kiss her neck. His lips slide downwards. She puts her arms around his back and he holds her by the waist and lifts her off her feet. Decisively Kimberley slips the dressing down off her shoulders and lets it fall to the ground. To hell with the rules, she thinks. Marcus's lips move downwards. She is muscular but her skin is warm and as smooth as satin. He is tasting her skin as he moves. Her feet are still not touching the ground and she feels out of control of her sensations. Marcus bends and slips one arm under her knees. He picks her up whilst her arms are still around his shoulders. He carries her smooth, naked young body to the bed and lays her down sideways across it so that her head and neck are hanging suspended over the edge of the bed. Blood is rushing to her brain and she feels as if she has been given an anaesthetic, which means she can feel but cannot move. She can feel Marcus's hands and lips as he kisses and stimulates the skin across and down the front of her body until he gets to her thighs. Kimberley regains her awareness to find that she has her bare feet on Marcus's chest and his head then moves downwards, with his mouth and tongue working in a relentless persuasion. He pulls Kimberley's legs over his shoulders and he stretches her arms out wide, holding her hands tightly. She cannot lift her head and the centre of her body is raised. She begins to wriggle until Marcus takes control and drives her resolution from her. She throws her head right back. Her legs are in the air; Marcus is driving with impressive relentless stamina on and on and on. Kimberley sees colours under her eyelids. She feels dizzy and thoughtless. Her stomach begins to flutter and her legs are shaking. She hears a voice crying out in a long lost voice. It sounds like a very young girl who does not know where she is. She is falling and falling and there is no end to it until she forgets herself and lands softly onto the large bed, panting as if she has been running. She cannot say anything, she just breathes hard to catch her breath.

Marcus thinks that he must take responsibility for the encounter and take any doubts away.

"You are a wonderful girl, Kimberley," he says and strokes her hair softly as her breathing slows down. "A wonderful girl."

Kimberley lays there and hears music playing in the sitting room. Her body is fizzing. Her legs feel as if she is running. Marcus strokes her slowly and her body slows down into a sort of restful ecstasy.

"We have canapés to eat," says Marcus. "They are still warm. Here is your dressing gown." Marcus hands it to her.

"I am not ashamed of my body," says Kimberley. "It took me ten years of working out to get it. Does it embarrass you? You seemed to like it before. Shall we eat on the balcony?"

She walks outside naked.

"Yes," says Marcus.

He places six canapés onto a plate and brings them out onto the balcony. Kimberley is sitting there with her feet back on the balustrade. She looks magnificent. Suntanned. Smooth. Beautiful.

"You are a great guy, Marcus," she says. "Is there any wine left?"

He pours her a glass and pours himself water. She begins to eat slowly.

"You are pretty good, you know?" she says. "I am having a great trip. What shall we do next?"

"There is a temple of erotica here," says Marcus. "Do you want to see it tomorrow?"

"Maybe we should have seen it before," says Kimberley, "but let's see it tomorrow. We are here for one more day, right?"

"Right, okay," says Marcus. "We will see it tomorrow. Then we're going to Udaipur."

"The day off is over then?" says Kimberley, beginning to eat the fruit.

"If you don't mind?" says Marcus.

"I am your travelling companion," says Kimberley, "a happy travelling companion."

She smiles at him. Beautiful, thinks Marcus. He looks at her candidly. She must be 36, 24, 36, he thinks, with tennis players' or dancers' legs. She has a perfect body and he remembers her smooth skin with pleasure. I really like her a lot. What is going to happen to us now, he thinks.

Kimberley carries on eating the fruit and drinks the wine and some water.

"I need a rest," she says. "You have tired me out."

"All right," says Marcus. "You take the big bed."

Kimberley moves inside and walks slowly to the bed. She lifts the covers and settles herself comfortably under the covers. She falls asleep.

Marcus drinks the rest of the water and walks inside. He takes off his cotton gown and joins her in bed. They both fall asleep.

21
Erotica

The next day they have a breakfast of fruit and soft spicy Indian bread and tea.

Marcus has arranged a taxi and when they are both ready they travel to the outskirts of the town to visit an area overgrown with what seem to be jungle plants and a temple inside, in which there are many stone statues of above human size. Marcus and Kimberley have to take their shoes off to enter the temple and they then see that the statues are of men and women having sexual intercourse in a surprising number of positions. The women statues are curvaceous with big breasts and bottoms and curvy legs. The male statues have extra big sexual organs. All of the connections are completely uninhibited and some of them look very difficult to achieve. They both walk around slowly and find themselves shocked by the graphic displays.

"This would be a criminal offence in Florida," says Kimberley.

"You mean that position?" asks Marcus.

"No, I mean the statues," answers Kimberley.

"It is rather different to normal pornography in so far as all of the statues are smiling," says Marcus.

"Normal pornography?" asks Kimberley. "I have never seen any."

"I mean that magazine stuff that has everyone looking either aggressive or very serious whilst they are doing happy things. Here, the statues are demonstratively happy about what they are doing. It is pleasing."

"Okay. Which is your favourite?" asks Kimberley.

"Oh, I don't know," answers Marcus.

"Oh come on, Marcus. Which position here do you like the best?"

"The third one inside the doors," says Marcus.

"I like the seventh," says Kimberley. "They both look very happy doing it. Come on, Marcus. Let's have a closer look. There is a lot of work in the statues. I wonder who modelled for them?"

They walk slowly around the temple again, taking in the detailed sculptures, the fingers and toes and limbs. There is a young Indian couple inside the temple and they are laughing together and hugging each other as they walk around. The girl is radiantly lovely and the boy obviously adores her.

"I think they are newlyweds," says Kimberley. "Come here for instruction. This country is a different place, Marcus. Not Europe and not the Far East and sure as hell not the United States. Different."

The young boy and girl are standing side by side in front of the seventh statue. They have their arms around each other's waist. The girl has dark brown eyes and rich and long dark hair which comes down to her waist. She is wearing a pink sari and is barefoot. The boy has dark hair neatly cut and brown eyes. He has well-shaped hands. He is wearing smart black trousers with a knife edge crease and a newly pressed white shirt. They make a handsome couple. The girl is giggling and whispering to the boy, who is smiling at her with love in his eyes.

"This sure is a horny place," says Kimberley. "Were you planning to bring me here before we went dancing last night?"

"Well, it was always on the agenda," says Marcus. "I did expect the temple aspect of it to be rather more prominent."

"Speaking of prominent," says Kimberley, "take a look at this."

"My God," says Marcus.

"It certainly looks as if he is her god at the moment," says Kimberley and then starts laughing a lot. "This is a happy place, Marcus," she says, "graphic but happy."

"These statues are hundreds of years old," says Marcus.

"I hope I look this good when I am hundreds of years old," says Kimberley.

"Get a statue of yourself made now," says Marcus.

"Oh no," says Kimberley, "every year afterwards I will be fighting to look like my own statue and I would lose the fight."

"I have a photograph of you," says Marcus. "You can keep it in the attic at home and look at it when you are eighty years old."

"Let's be happy now, Marcus," says Kimberley. "Let us live for today, live in the present."

"I'm trying to," says Marcus, "but I am distracted by the statues."

"You are not distracted," says Kimberley. "You are living now. The statues are exciting. Look at the young newlyweds."

The newlyweds are leaving the temple hand in hand.

"I bet they don't do a jigsaw puzzle tonight," says Marcus. "This place has a special atmosphere, do you think so?"

"Sure does," says Kimberley, "a sexy atmosphere."

"Let's leave now," says Marcus, "and take a walk through the city. We will get a taxi to take us back to the centre."

They get out close to the city centre and begin to walk. There are some monstrous complicated buildings with huge archways and there are fortresses, which seemed to be the Indian equivalent of castles. The roads are so big that the traffic is light, but it is difficult as a pedestrian to cross a road which is one hundred yards wide. The pavements are mosaic patterns of small stones.

"There is not a place like this in England," says Marcus, "but I can't help thinking that people should dress with more formality and style. This city is so rich and the people look scruffy."

"They are not scruffy," says Kimberley. "They are not British or European. They are dressed very well in their own Indian clothes. The women are attractive. The men are handsome and everybody is dignified. This is India, Marcus."

"You are right," says Marcus. "I was being conventionally English. This is their country, not ours. They are dressed to suit the climate and their own standards of modesty."

"They are also kind of stylish in their own way," says Kimberley. "I like them. Are we going to get some lunch here?" she asks.

"Let's start to look for a place," says Marcus.

"Nothing looks like a restaurant here," says Kimberley. "They don't have Ted's Diner written about the door. Well, they might have but I can't read the language."

"Let's ask the richest looking man we see," says Marcus.

"There is no Pierre Cardin or Versace here. No Rolex watches or Cartier, so it is difficult for a girl from the States to recognise wealth," says Kimberley.

"I'll try," says Marcus.

After walking up to three different men on the pavement, the last one speaks English with an educated accent, and gives them clear directions to a restaurant which he says is first class.

They thank him profusely and follow his directions along the pavement.

They come to a building with a golden façade and large windows shielded from onlookers by muslin curtains.

"I think this is the place," says Marcus. "It is either a restaurant or an undertaker's."

"Don't say that, Marcus," says Kimberley. "It is either a restaurant or a dance hall. A much happier thing. Let's go inside and find out."

It is the restaurant that the stranger in the street had recommended as being 'first class'. There are a few people inside and they are greeted warmly by the manager, who shows them to a comfortable corner table. A waiter brings them menus and Marcus asks for bottled water to be brought.

As usual when they are uncertain of the food they order vegetables. This time as a spicy curry with pilau rice and spicy naan bread. Spicy because of the advice they have been given about its good effects on their stomachs.

Kimberley smiles at the room, which is richly decorated in the Indian style. She turns and punches Marcus on the upper arm.

"I am having a great time," she says.

"So am I," says Marcus.

The water arrives and then the spicy naan bread and then the spicy curry.

The food is delicious, freshly cooked, hot, elegantly served and very tasty. Whilst they are eating, a five-piece band is playing. The music is screechy, loud and discordant. The sound of it pierces into their brains, making enjoyment of the food impossible.

Marcus waves to the manager, who comes to their table.

"Do the musicians play requests?" asks Marcus.

"Oh yes sir, they do," says the manager. "They will be pleased sir, to attend to your request, providing of course, sir, that they know the melody, sir."

Marcus gives a large tip to the manager.

"This is for you," he says.

He then gives the manager a bundle of Indian currency.

"And this is for the five men in the band," he says. "Ask them as my request to stop playing for one hour."

The manager maintains perfect dignity and walks over to the band and talks to them quietly. At the end of his conversation he hands to the bandleader Marcus's bundle of money. Silence prevails and Marcus and Kimberley eat slowly and in comfort.

The band members have expressions of sorry indignation and dented pride to have been asked not to play, mixed with great happiness at the large amount of money each one of them has received. The bandleader took the biggest share.

"Marcus, you are always walking around with a whole lot of cash. Like a Mississippi steamboat gambler. Where do you get it all, Marcus?"

"I change traveller's cheques every day at our hotels," says Marcus. "For the largest sums which the hotels will agree to. India is a challenging place. Bed bugs in a lot of the hotels. Bad sanitation. Dirty water. Contaminated food. By travelling first class and paying attention to details and, I admit, basically bribing hotel officials for our comfort every day, I am trying to buy our way out of the worst problems. Just money I know, but it is what I am trying to do."

"Marcus, just because I don't say anything doesn't mean I don't notice and doesn't mean that I don't really value it. I just don't say anything, is all."

She kisses him quickly on the lips. "Thank you," she says.

"You are welcome," says Marcus.

He turns her face towards him and gives Kimberley a long warm passionate kiss.

"You're not getting away with little snatched kisses," says Marcus.

"Marcus, we are in India, a most respectable place. People do not kiss in public here. We may get thrown out of this restaurant before I finish my lunch and especially because we have insulted the band."

"A respectable place?" says Marcus. "What about those statues?"

"That was a temple of love, Marcus. And I have got all of my arms and legs covered up because India is a place of contradictions. Respectable in the street, disgraceful in temples. I'm trying to keep to the rules. Tonight you're going to get the third position. Eat your lunch because you need the strength." She smiles at him and drinks her water. "I am a healthy girl," she says without explanation.

Each one of us is trying to take the lead, thinks Marcus. I think that I understand. I am, however, unsettled by the thought, which Kimberley has deliberately put into my head. Clever girl. Be gracious and most of all you are going to have to be strong. He thinks about the third position. Very athletic, he imagines, because although Kimberley is slim she is muscular and heavy. He thinks that she has excited me by telling me in advance.

"Do the band a favour, Marcus. Pay for lunch and then let the guys play their music whilst we leave," says Kimberley.

"All right," says Marcus.

272

They walk out of the restaurant into the street and Kimberley tucks her arm into Marcus's upper arm. They walk along companionably, looking at all the amazing sights. They walk for almost an hour and Kimberley goes into the different shops to look at what they are selling. At one shop she buys an extraordinary metal gadget.

"Whatever is that?" asks Marcus.

"It is a tin opener," answers Kimberley. "I buy one whenever I go to another country. I bought one in London and in South America and Haiti. I have a little collection of them. It is one of the only things left which every country makes differently. No country has dominated the tin opener market!"

"What are they like in America?" asks Marcus.

"Oh, we have electric tin openers fixed to the wall of the kitchen," says Kimberley. "Just to keep up the enormous energy bill of the USA."

"What about the other shops?" asks Marcus.

"They were interesting," says Kimberley. "One had a really cute little metal watering can, but I figured I couldn't get it into my luggage. I took a photograph of it instead. Then I went into a perfume shop."

Marcus takes a few photographs as they walk along. He mostly photographs people or animals, occasionally extravagant buildings.

They wave to a passing taxi, which stops, and they ride back to the hotel.

"I am going swimming," says Marcus.

"Okay," says Kimberley. "I have a lot of stretching exercises to do and then I will have a bath."

They gather what they need from the suite and Marcus leaves to go down to the pool in the hotel gardens. The pool is exceptionally large. Marcus judges it to be the same length as an Olympic swimming pool. It is made of white marble as usual and the water is very clear. Marcus starts swimming laps, aiming to do at least fifty. It is boring swimming strongly up and down the pool and there is nobody at the pool or in the gardens for Marcus to look at. His mind drifts to thoughts of Kimberley doing her stretching exercises in the hotel suite. He puts those thoughts out of his mind and swims six more laps. His next thought is about position number three. He pictures the statues in his mind and those thoughts last him for four more laps until he shakes his head to send the thoughts away. He begins to swim much faster to preoccupy himself and covers ten laps so energetically that his body becomes warm in the cold water. His mind then considers Kimberley's body for six more laps until he banishes the thought. Concentrate on your timing, Marcus, he tells himself. Increase your speed. The effort of this stops him from dreaming and his breathing is now deep and fast. His muscles begin to ache but it is a feeling he likes and he presses on to complete the fifty lengths at his fastest speed. He rests, holding on to the pool, too exhausted for five minutes to pull himself out. He eventually climbs out and lies on a sun bed using his towel as a pillow. He falls asleep.

Kimberley, meanwhile, is stretching excessively in the hotel suite. She is naked and is going through a rigorous routine, concentrating one after the other on her stomach and on her back, then her front and the backs of her legs. She does the splits three times, then concentrates on doing squats and then does pelvic floor exercises thoroughly. She stretches her arms, both biceps and forearms. She carries out each exercise for several minutes devotedly and then manages to hold the plank position for nearly three minutes. She ends by touching her toes twenty times and joining her hands together at the small of her back one arm stretched over a shoulder from her lower back. She then stretches her neck and looks left and right, ten times each.

Her body feels fluid and moves easily. There are no exercises in her regime which cause her any difficulties and she feels proud of herself, as she stands upright at the finish. Her body is shining with perspiration. She stands in front of a long mirror in the bedroom. She sighs and goes into the bathroom, where she has laid out the three products she bought in the shop today. She starts to run the bath with only slightly warm water because the air temperature is still hot. Kimberley wriggles her toes in the bath. She is relaxed. She is thinking about Marcus. He was terrific last night, she thinks. I don't think I have ever experienced such great sex. I have never lost myself like that before. The French call it 'petit mort', she remembers. She lost herself completely. It was fantastic. She shifts in the bath. I am twenty-seven years old, she thinks. My body at nineteen was perfect. Now I have to work at it every day. I have maybe eight more years to keep this body firm. After that it will change no matter how much I work out. Today it is okay and tonight I want to give Marcus a time to remember. She sighs. The oil I have put into the bath will make my skin slippery, providing that I pat myself dry with the towel.

She gets out of the bath and dries herself carefully. She puts on some lotion, which smells slightly of honeysuckle. He is swimming, she thinks. I hope that he will not be too tired. She wraps a clean dry towel around herself and goes outside to sit on the balcony. Maybe we should have alcohol, she thinks. She gets up and walks into the sitting room to ring room service.

"Do you have any French champagne?" she asks.

"Yes, madam, we have Bollinger," says the Indian at the other end of the line.

"Please send up two bottles on ice," says Kimberley, "and two glasses."

She goes back to the balcony to wait.

The champagne arrives at exactly the same time as Marcus comes into the suite. The man from room service is startled to see Kimberley in a towel.

"Hello, Marcus," says Kimberley. "Did you swim a long way?"

"I did," says Marcus. "A long way."

"Well, have some champagne," says Kimberley.

"What are we celebrating?" Marcus asks.

"A great holiday," answers Kimberley.

"Okay," says Marcus. "Let me take off my wet swimming costume and put on a fresh dressing gown."

Marcus is wearing a full-length towelling dressing gown, which he got from the pool attendant. He is carrying his clothes in a bundle. He leaves the room.

The man from room service is still waiting.

"Please open the champagne," says Kimberley, "and bring us some canapés like we had last night and two litre bottles of water."

"Yes, madam," says the Indian. He opens the champagne. "The canapés will be fifteen minutes, madam. I will bring the water at the same time. Would you like fruit as well, madam?"

"Yes, please," says Kimberley.

The man leaves and Marcus walks back into the room wearing a hotel cotton dressing gown. He sits on the balcony next to Kimberley. She pours two glasses of champagne.

"Here is to your health," says Marcus, and drinks half a glass.

"And to yours," says Kimberley, and drinks the same amount.

They sit comfortably side by side looking out at the garden.

"The Taj Mahal was fabulous," says Kimberley.

"Yes it was," says Marcus. "I liked it when it was pink in the light of the early sunset. I didn't care much for the yellow colour it changed into as the sun came up but then in full sunlight it was almost ecclesiastical, gleaming white."

"Oh, but I liked the blue colour from the moonlight," says Kimberley. "What a monument to a wife."

"Certainly," says Marcus. "She must have been some girl."

They sit quietly drinking their champagne and relaxing.

"You did not drink much alcohol at the start of the holiday," says Marcus. "Nor did I. Now we are letting ourselves go."

"I needed to keep my wits about me, Marcus," says Kimberley. "Strange country, different people, different food. A man I didn't know. I am more relaxed now, but I will stop drinking alcohol again from tomorrow. Too much sugar. But tonight is special."

Marcus looks at her. She has her legs up on the balustrading of the balcony and she is looking straight ahead. Her legs are shiny. So are her shoulders and arms, and her neck. She looks as if she has been slightly oiled by a masseuse or something. She looks very sexy. Marcus drinks some more champagne and they sit quietly.

There is a knock at the door of the suite.

"Canapés," says Kimberley, and gets up to let the man in. The waiter is prepared this time for the sight of Kimberley wearing a towel and he stares straight ahead, not looking at her at all whilst he pushes the trolley laden with food into the room. He has brought two bottles of water. He turns his back.

"Thank you, madam," he says as he leaves.

Kimberley walks back onto the balcony, sits down and puts her feet up onto the balustrade again.

"Now we can stay in the suite all night," she says, "with no interruptions."

"I welcome that," says Marcus.

Kimberley leans over Marcus and kisses him full on the lips. The kiss is passionate and changes into a fifteen-minute intimate encounter. Kimberley changes positions and kisses Marcus again, this time caressing his neck delicately with her hands. Then she places one hand onto his thigh outside the dressing gown. She strokes his leg through the cotton whilst she moves her lips down and deliberately gives him a big love bite on his neck. Marcus is startled.

"You are a teenager, Kimberley," he says.

"Yes," says Kimberley, "tonight." She sits back and puts her legs up again. "What shall we drink to now?" she asks.

Marcus is left with his heart beating faster and having to deal with the caressing and the kissing having stopped. He wants it to start again but because Kimberley has instigated it, he somehow feels reluctant to start kissing her. She has him off-balance and he would feel clumsy if he leaned across and started to kiss her. The initiative is hers.

"Let's drink to moonlight," he says.

"I like moonlight. I'll drink to that," says Kimberley.

Kimberley is sitting on Marcus's right hand side. She is sitting there because Kimberley learned to kiss in American cars and always from the front passenger seat on the right. The position now gives her confidence. She puts her left hand onto Marcus's right thigh.

"I thought that English boys were no good at kissing?" she says. "But you are okay."

"Okay?" says Marcus.

He leans over and starts to kiss Kimberley deeply.

"All right, a bit better than okay," she says, breaking away. "Let's try again."

This time they put their arms around each other, moving sideways to face each other.

"Wait," says Kimberley as their lips part. "Let's go inside because I'm afraid that we might shock the Indian people."

The move inside breaks the closeness which Kimberley has achieved and slightly cools things down. She sits on the sofa. I'm going to have to start it up again, thinks Kimberley, but I'll wait to see how much Marcus wants to.

Marcus does not wait very long before he puts his arms around Kimberley and pushes her gently backwards on the sofa. The sofa is seven feet long and wide enough for two but Kimberley wants to prolong matters for as long as possible. She kisses him back and then sits up.

"I need another drink," she says. "The champagne bucket is outside. Be a hero, Marcus, and bring it all inside."

Marcus does not know now when Kimberley intends to move on. He gets up and brings in the glasses and the heavy champagne bucket filled with iced water and two bottles of Bollinger.

"Would you like some ice, Kimberley?" he says, before quickly dropping three pieces down the front of her towel.

"You bad man," says Kimberley, and stands up with her back to Marcus as she loosens her towel to let the ice fall onto the carpet.

"You've cooled me down now, Marcus," she says and tightens her towel. "Pour me another glass to put me back into the frame of mind I was in before."

She kneels down in front of him. Marcus pours a glass of champagne and offers it to her.

She drinks it.

"More," she says.

Marcus refills the glass. She shakes her head and gracefully gets to her feet. Kimberley stretches her hands high above her head, revealing her shiny thighs, then touches her toes, revealing her cleavage very clearly to Marcus, and walks into the bedroom.

"Do you think this bed is too big, Marcus?" she says.

Marcus walks in and takes hold of her firmly with one arm around her waist. His free hand loosens her towel and pulls it from her. He throws it across the room.

Kimberley is not naked. She is wearing a bikini, which is white. The top is a bandeau style and is held together by a ribbon tied in a bow between her breasts. The bikini bottoms are tied together by string bows at the hips.

Kimberley wriggles away from Marcus's grasp and stands still, breathing in and out so as to draw attention to the swell in her breasts and the movements of her flat stomach. She supports her weight on one leg and slightly bends the other leg sideways.

Come on, Marcus, she thinks. Come and get it. Marcus looks hot.

"Didn't you just have a bath?" he asks.

"Yes, but then I had to wrap the present up."

"The present?" asks Marcus.

"Your present," says Kimberley. "I am your present tonight."

She smiles sweetly at him. Marcus walks towards her. She skips around to the other side of the bed.

She says, "You have to catch me before you can unwrap your present."

Marcus moves towards her. Kimberley walks onto the bed. Marcus follows.

"It is a big bed, Marcus," says Kimberley.

She somersaults onto the floor. Marcus grabs her and pulls her onto the bed again. Marcus pulls at the bow between Kimberley's breasts and the bikini top comes off all at once. Kimberley gasps. Marcus's hands move over Kimberley's splendid body and his lips move to her breasts. She twists her hips out of his reach, giggling and laughing, but she kisses him, then breaks away and jumps off the bed onto the carpet on the other side. Marcus springs across the bed and picks her up easily. He throws her onto the bed. Marcus rips off his dressing gown and throws it twenty feet away. He tears her bikini bottoms off. He throws them across the room.

"Position number three, Marcus," laughs Kimberley.

Kimberley loves his lack of control. It affirms all of her confidence in her attraction and it demolishes Marcus's detachment and coolness. He is moving now like a man possessed. Except that at this moment it is Kimberley who is possessed. He plunders her like a pirate. She makes no sound. She does not want to break the spell. She loves having Marcus ravish her like a wild man. It is overwhelmingly exciting. She stretches her legs to accommodate Marcus's approximation of position number three. Kimberley moves herself inches away from him. She breaks away. Marcus seizes her, pulls her back and uses her completely. She falls off the cliff again just as she hears Marcus growling like an animal and pulling her closer to him. She is falling again but this time so is he.

They both lie on the bed, their bodies intertwined and their breathing short. Kimberley thinks I couldn't have forgiven him if he had waited. It would have been insulting. She leans close to Marcus's right ear. She kisses it.

"You liked your present?" she asks.

"You know I did," says Marcus.

"I am flattered," she whispers.

"Your skin smells like honeysuckle," says Marcus quietly.

"Marcus, you make me feel special," says Kimberley.

"You are special," whispers Marcus and closes his eyes.

Kimberley is surprised by how sexually compatible she is with Marcus. They are completely natural together. He is a Brit, she thinks and yet they have some kind of sexual telepathy. Most men who Kimberley has known have been out of step with her. With Marcus it feels as if they have known each other for years. He is dominant. Exciting. Perfect, she thinks and then she falls asleep.

Later they are both wearing dressing gowns and sitting outside on the balcony again. They are eating cold canapés and drinking water. They both feel tranquil and satisfied. Both of them know that there has been a change but neither of them will talk about it.

"We're going somewhere else tomorrow," says Marcus.

"Oh yes, some place called Udaipur," says Kimberley. "Staying in a palace."

"A palace on a lake," says Marcus. "We are going there on another coach. I suppose that we will get to the Palace Hotel by boat."

"I hope that there are no more dancing bears," says Kimberley.

They sit quietly. It is four months since I last had sex, thinks Kimberley, and it was not as exciting as this. It was with an American football captain. She smiles. His dad had a big engineering company in Tampa. I thought he was a prospect but he had peculiar tastes. He always wanted me to keep my cheerleader's dress on. No underwear, just the dress with my white socks and trainers. Drove him crazy every time. She smiles again. Marcus is much better. Not a real prospect but one hell of a good lay. No strange tastes. Strong, lean, fantastic staying power. I'm glad we have broken the no sex rule. I was getting restless.

She puts her hand onto Marcus's forearm.

"Is there anything else you want, Marcus?" she asks.

Marcus looks at her and replies, "I'm sure that I will think of something."

Boy, what an answer that is, thinks Kimberley. I almost wish he was a prospect. He is all I've got for now but it sounds like I'm going to get it again. What a terrific holiday this is!

22
Udaipur

After a long sleep and breakfast they leave the hotel and get onto a coach to take them to Udaipur. They sit together and look at the countryside passing by the windows. Everything is greener and darker than it was further south. The country is jumping with wildlife, animals, birds, insects, snakes. There is an abundance of wild flowers. Although the population of India exceeds a billion people they don't seem to have overwhelmed the natural side of their country. Nature is predominant and people fit in. Marcus contemplates how the British local authorities like to cut down roadside trees so that they do not have to maintain them and how concrete is spreading all through the towns. Hard-wearing stone flagged pavements are pulled up in favour of little yellow concrete squares for the pavements, which changes the context of the eighteenth century buildings so that it is easier to replace frontages with aluminium and glass which matches the concrete. Here in India the people seem to live with nature. They respect it and consequently nature is everywhere. Trees, bushes, plants of every description and hundreds of birds. Birds everywhere.

Of course, some people like man-made places, thinks Marcus. Places like Las Vegas with no nature visible at all.

Places where people have forgotten the fact that they are part of nature themselves. The Indian people live with awareness that they are all part of nature and all here for a short time.

When they finally reach the outskirts of the city they watch the people. The coach stops at the edge of a lake. There are stone steps leading to the water and dozens of women and young girls are on the steps carefully doing their washing in the lake water. They soap the clothes and then bash them against the steps to get the dirt out before rinsing then thoroughly and squeezing them out, ringing them into twisted shapes before shaking them out and putting them into baskets to carry home on their heads where they will hang them up to dry before ironing them with simple irons, heated by the kitchen range.

"No washing machines here either," says Marcus.

"I guess not," says Kimberley.

The city is magnificent; fabulous intricate buildings the results of decades of skilled workmanship. There are many fountains in the streets and local people use them for their morning ablutions. They wash in the fountains, wearing thin cotton clothes, and although four or five people may be washing in the same place, they do not acknowledge each other. Each washes as if he or she were alone in their own bathroom.

"This may be the most beautiful city we have been to, Marcus," says Kimberley.

"It is stunning," says Marcus, "and it is the last city we are visiting, because after this we will go all the way back to the south to rest on the beach before going home."

"Let's make the most of it here then," says Kimberley. "We could go shopping and get some real Indian stuff."

"You know that all of the shopkeepers will post stuff home for you?" says Marcus. "They do it most carefully and it enables you to buy things which you couldn't fit into your luggage."

"Oh boy," says Kimberley. "My mother is going to be surprised when the mailman calls."

The coach driver is calling them to order. "Two people are staying at the Lake Palace Hotel," he says. "Who are those people, please?"

"It is Kimberley and me," says Marcus.

"Please to fetch your bags, sir, and to follow me."

The driver waits for them and then carries their bags alongside the lake to an ornate painted jetty. At the jetty waits an extraordinary ferry boat, almost banana shaped, with the bow and stern high in the air above the deck. The boat is painted red and gold. There are seats on board padded with red velvet and the crew of the boat are wearing white uniforms with dark red turbans and cummerbunds. On their feet are long shoes with curled toes.

"This is for you, sir, madam," the coach driver says and hands them their bags.

Marcus tips him and thanks him. Marcus and Kimberley walked down white painted steps, which lead directly onto the deck of the boat. They are the only passengers.

The boat has a big quiet motor and starts to leave the jetty and to proceed smoothly across the lake. The city recedes in the background and they notice trees surrounding the city and a small mountain in the distance. The lake is very large and gradually the boat approaches the Lake Palace Hotel. In Britain, castles in the lakes have walls which go straight down into the water and are secured at the base by heavy foundations. The same must be true of the Palace Hotel, except that an illusion has been achieved by creating a lip around the palace, so that from a distance it looks as if it is built on a saucer and as the wind ripples the surface of the lake the palace gives the impression that it is moving across the water on its saucer base. The palace is white and very ornate, with many patterned cupolas at intervals along the decorated outside walls. There is an extensive paved terrace in front of the palace entrance and the boat moors up at the start of that terrace, where there is a gatehouse and a heavy wooden door to be opened to gain access to the terrace, which they must walk through to reach the main entrance. The staff all have white uniforms and red turbans and Marcus and Kimberley are greeted with much formality at the discreet reception table in the main hallway. Marcus made special bookings months before and they are shown through carved marble passageways towards a grand staircase, which leads solely to the Maharaja Suite. This suite is enormous and appointed in the most elaborate and luxurious manner, although not in any way resembling a European or United States hotel, or an African or Australian one, for that matter. Here is pure seventeenth century Indian royal splendour. There are four separate rooms, which all open off a large entrance hall. The main bedroom has a large marble bathroom next to it with complicated plumbing arrangements. There are two other bathrooms, also in marble, and the toilet arrangements are quite separate in three hidden locations. The main bedroom has a bed, maybe twelve feet square, and two red velvet couches. In the room is a very comfortable looking swing with a double seat. It is suspended from the tall ceiling by two thick silver plated chains. Long tassels extend from either side of the velvet seat.

The porter places their small bags on the woven silk rug in the main bedroom.

"What is that for?" asks Kimberley, pointing to the swing.

"For sexual pleasure, madam," the porter answers, looking straight ahead.

"Okay," says Kimberley. "Thanks."

Marcus tips the porter, who leaves the suite.

"Shall we go downstairs and take a look around?" says Marcus. "I could do with some tea."

"Sure thing, Marcus," says Kimberley, "but I have to go shopping soon. These rooms are too good for my Annie Get Your Gun outfit."

"We will certainly go shopping," says Marcus, "but let's look and see where we are now."

They walk down the soft tread staircase from their suite and start to wander around. There is much marble decoration and murals of inlaid semi-precious stones, with ornate windows with no glass and little secret areas with simply two chairs and a table.

Eventually they walk into the gardens, which are laid out in an Elizabethan pattern. Maple leaf shaped ornate ponds and flowerbeds with water lilies and fish and tables and chairs widely separated by the various ponds. There are occasional fountains and a lot of greenery and what look like bougainvillea. There are cloisters along the sides of the gardens to provide shade and all of the stonework and marble is white to reflect the sun.

They walk through the gardens and into a large courtyard area, which contains a deep swimming pool. There are sunbeds arranged around it and there is a small bar with an Indian barman wearing a red turban.

"This would have been a fabulous palace," says Marcus.

"It is a fabulous hotel," says Kimberley. "It is going to make my apartment back home feel a bit tight, but we are here now. Alive today."

"Alive today," says Marcus. "That's right."

"Marcus, have you got any money?" asks Kimberley.

"Two or three thousand rupees probably," says Marcus.

"No, I mean money in real life," asks Kimberley.

"I don't count it often," says Marcus, "but okay, I have a house in the countryside possibly worth three million pounds. I have a flat in London. But it only has one bedroom but that is because I knocked three bedrooms into one. It still has two bathrooms. It may be worth one million pounds. And I have around one million pounds in cash which I keep for my next deal."

"Heavens, Marcus. You are loaded."

"England is very expensive you know," says Marcus. "A comfortable American family house would be less than a third of the price of my country place, and apartments in London cost a fortune plus the fact that everything else is expensive. You need around a hundred thousand pounds a year to live in or close to London."

"But you have done really well, Marcus," says Kimberley.

"I've been working since I was eighteen," says Marcus, "and I did not have to pay for a divorce. I guess that helped."

"Well okay," says Kimberley. "You are a good catch, Marcus."

"Don't tell me you like me now," says Marcus.

"I like you anyway," says Kimberley. "I was just wondering why you didn't have a job or a proper career but I got it wrong."

"I'm not a rock star or a movie star and I'm not a hedge fund manager and I don't have a plane. The real rich people compare what they have to other rich people all the time. That is why the very rich never look happy. Always angry."

"Richard Branson looks happy," says Kimberley, "and so does Mick Jagger."

"Well then, I give up. I don't understand human nature," says Marcus. "I have what you call, 'stuff you money'. If somebody asks you to do something you don't want to do, you can say 'stuff you' but of course you don't say it like that."

"I don't know why not," says Kimberley.

"Do you have any money, Kimberley?" asks Marcus. "Now we are asking each other personal questions."

"I'm younger than you, Marcus, and I went to college," says Kimberley, "but I don't spend a lot. I have a condominium. That is an apartment in a kind of complex. Tennis courts, swimming pool, car wash, laundry, that sort of thing. I nearly own it but I still have a mortgage. It is worth a hell of a lot less than your London place. I've got a few thousand in the bank and a Mustang Shelby. That is worth a lot of money. Plus I have a hell of a good body and I am lots of fun. I am rich, Marcus. Make a play for me."

"Every day," says Marcus, smiling. "Let's walk around the outside of this place a bit more."

They do and they find the palace to be wonderful. Alone on the water it offers privacy for the occupants and when there were Indian royalty they would have lived in isolated splendour.

Across the water several hundred yards away they see another isolated palace but it looks empty. Marcus walks around to the jetty to ask the boatman about the empty palace.

"Yes sir," says the boatman. "I can arrange to take you but there is nothing there, sir."

"I would like to go," says Marcus.

Kimberley, who is standing beside him, nods her head.

"Ten minutes, sir," says the Indian boatman.

Damn, thinks Kimberley, now Marcus is a prospect. He started as a travelling companion, then a sex partner and now he turns out to be eligible. I cannot think that. It will change my behaviour and Marcus will know because he is bright. I will have to ignore his money. Anyway I don't want to live in

Britain. Too cold. And I don't want my children to go through that terrible divisive education system. No. I will just have sex with him, for my own pleasure because he is good at it. Then I will go home and get an American man. Also Britain is too small, all of those tiny roads and nowhere to park. Today I am in India. An amazing country. Living in the past. Palaces and people living in the streets. Extraordinary.

A small boat arrives at the jetty. It is not as grand as the large boat which brought them to the Lake Palace Hotel, but it is very comfortable for two passengers. The boatman helps them aboard and they set off across the lake. There are many trees on three banks of the lake and one of them presents a wonderful picture, although strange. The tree is large and grey with grey leaves. All over the tree, on every branch there are birds perched; all the same species of bird. Large and almost crow-like in appearance. All sat in the tree. All looking in the same direction, and all silent.

"It is like an Alfred Hitchcock film," says Kimberley.

None of the trees close by have any birds in them at all. Only the grey tree, which does not have berries and does not look hospitable.

The birds all turn their heads in unison to watch the boat go past and Kimberley feels the eerie sensation that all of the birds are looking at her.

"Uh, Marcus. I don't like those birds. Put your arm round me quick," says Kimberley.

"They are just the departed souls of the people who once lived on this lake," says Marcus. "Probably the people from the abandoned palace we are going to."

"Oh Marcus, shut up," says Kimberley, "or I will start to believe you."

"I've never felt the atmosphere of death here in India," says Marcus. "Never witnessed a funeral or seen any signs of one. India is so teeming with life. It is so vibrant that you can only feel alive here. There seem to be no ghosts here. Everything is still alive. Everything is still going on."

"Talk about something else,' says Kimberley. "What do you think about that swing in our room? Shall we try it out?"

"The boatman speaks English," whispers Marcus into Kimberley's ear, "and the answer to your question," he whispers, "is that I don't see how we could possibly leave the place without trying it out."

"Marcus," says Kimberley, "that's thrilling."

At this point they begin to arrive at the deserted palace. The boatman knows exactly where they can tie up and disembark and he is very careful with the boat.

They step off the boat and onto a wide terrace similar to the one at their hotel, although overgrown. The walls of the building are no longer white but grey and flaking. The palace has no sinister feel to it; it is just resting quietly and happily in the lake. It has a good atmosphere. Marcus and Kimberley start to walk about. The views from the old palace to the shores in the distance are even more spectacular than from their hotel.

"I suppose that this palace was too small to be turned into a hotel," says Marcus, "and it is also much further away from the city."

"Make a good nightclub though, wouldn't it?" says Kimberley.

"Noise travels a long way over water," says Marcus. "Anyhow I don't think I have seen any sign of nightclubs anywhere we have visited. Not any sign of rock and roll music either. Apart from the surge of people and vehicles there is not a lot of noise in India."

"Okay then, a gambling den," says Kimberley, "or, all right, a children's orchestral school or a dance school or a yoga centre or, I know, I've got it, an abandoned palace."

"Bright idea," says Marcus, laughing. "Let's go inside. The front door is open."

They push open the door and step inside. The grandeur of the place is still present. The dimensions, ceiling heights, doors and windows are all splendid. The place is neglected and leaves have blown in. There are still ornate cupolas with domed tops and elaborate friezes all covered with moss and grass. Birds are everywhere. They walk around reverently looking into a vast ballroom and reception rooms and a curving staircase, which leads them up to a wonderful first floor terrace, which once again has fabulous romantic views of the lake. They look down onto neglected gardens, which still retain their formality of layout; lawns, ornamental trees and plants. The whole place is, in many ways, superior to the Lake Palace Hotel, but the spaces are so large and the layout so rigid, that Marcus can understand why it would not make a good hotel.

"It would make a grand casino," he says, "but there are no gambling places in India. At least, I don't think so."

"It would make a great summer palace," says Kimberley. "It is sad somehow, unloved."

"Democracy has left it behind," says Marcus. "A few people with all the money employing thousands of others. Now history has swept that all away and replaced it with the government having all of the money and thousands of people working for them."

"Sounds just the same," says Kimberley, "but without palaces and without polo played with elephants. Just drab hard work and lots of new rules."

"The United States looked like a free country in the 1950s and the 1960s," says Marcus, "but then the lobbyists and politicians and the big money taught themselves how to manipulate it all. It is very hard today for an ordinary hard-working American family to send a child to university. Prices are unreachable."

"Politics," says Kimberley. "Politics, governments keep taking more and more money and thinking of more and more things which are vital and which only they can do. You just can't worry about it."

Marcus puts his hand on Kimberley's back and softly turns her around, and then he kisses her long and gently and affectionately, holding her in his arms whilst he does so.

Kimberley draws her head back. "Marcus," she says.

"It's all right, the boatman is outside still in his boat," says Marcus and draws her close as he kisses her again.

He runs his hands down her back and caresses her lovely behind lasciviously. It is tight and muscled like a boy's. Kimberley pushes against him and raises her left knee to rub her thigh against his leg.

Marcus breaks off from kissing and whispers, "I'm just reminding myself."

He pulls her tightly to him and gently begins kissing her once more and for longer. He runs his strong hands firmly over her breasts, taking his time and holding them whilst he continues to kiss her.

Kimberley's heart is singing. Boy, what a holiday, she thinks, now I am being kissed and felt up by a goddamn British millionaire with a hot body. What the hell.

"You've forgotten?" she asks in a soft voice. "You are reminding yourself?"

Kimberley runs her hands down his back and takes hold of him. They have now moved from affectionate embraces to lust. Kimberley feels slightly giddy and both of them are beginning to develop an ache. A longing and an urgency. One of them must break it because it cannot progress on the dusty floor of an abandoned palace, although Kimberley is beginning to think it could. Kimberley pulls away and Marcus simultaneously releases her.

"Buy the place, Marcus," gasps Kimberley. "We could live in a summer palace."

"Can you cook?" asks Marcus.

"Cook? Sure I can cook," says Kimberley, "and I can sew and I can grow my own fruit and vegetables. What do you think? That I'm just some kind of blonde bimbo? I can give sports massages too," she grins at him wickedly, "and other kinds of massages. Oh, we could have a good time here, Marcus."

"Perfect," says Marcus. "You grow the fruit and vegetables. We keep chickens. I catch fish and gradually improve the place and you cook and wash up and sew and give me erotic evenings and because you can't swim too well, you couldn't leave. All right I agree but only if I can choose the uniform."

"Get outa here. I am not wearing a tight uniform to turn you on, whilst I'm doing all the work. No thanks," says Kimberley. "I'll get you some jeans and boots and one of those workman tool belts then I'll watch you do all the work."

"Come here." Marcus pulls Kimberley close again and they both increase each other's desire. Kimberley wants to take it somewhere fast but knows that he will not do it here. Marcus pulls away again and takes her hand to lead her back outside.

"The boatman has no one to kiss," he says.

"Don't you believe it," says Kimberley, "he looks like one of those fourteen children types."

They let go of each other's hand as they approach the boat. The man is waiting patiently.

"Nobody smokes here," says Kimberley. "Have you seen any Indian people smoking? I haven't. In the States the boatman would not be able to sit for an hour and a half on his own. He'd have to smoke or eat or drink coffee and probably all three. Here they are just tranquil."

"The guide at the Taj Mahal smoked," says Marcus. "The boatman, I don't know, maybe he was just thinking about his wife and the fourteen children, probably enjoying the peace and quiet in the middle of a lake."

"What do you think that he thinks that we have been doing?" asks Kimberley.

"He knows," says Marcus. "He knows that we have been necking. And he knows that you are the cause of it all. One look at you and he knows."

"Cheek!" whispers Kimberley, as they walk closer to the boat.

"I knew that you would be the cause of it all when I first saw you roller-skating," says Marcus.

"I didn't even like you then," hisses Kimberley.

"I didn't like you either," says Marcus.

"Oh shut up," says Kimberley, and punches him on the upper arm.

"Oww," says Marcus.

"Sir, madam, are you ready for the return journey?" says the boatman, getting up to help them aboard. "Did you enjoy yourselves?" he asks ambiguously.

"Yes," says Marcus, "we were measuring up."

"Yes sir," says the boatman, and starts the engine. The boat moves steadily away and the boatman steers towards the Lake Palace Hotel.

"Well, that was something," says Kimberley. She leans against him. "You're not going to buy it? Even if I wear the uniform?"

"I'm not going to buy it," says Marcus. "It is a long journey to work. Anyway I prefer you without a uniform."

"Marcus. You bad man," says Kimberley, smiling broadly. "I would miss my roller-skating but I could roller-skate all around the palace on the marble floors."

"We are not buying it," says Marcus. "Too lonely."

"Poor lonely Marcus," whispers Kimberley.

The boatman, who is staring ahead, knows that these tourists are crazy. The palace was appropriated many years ago by the new Indian democratic government and they will decide when is to be sold, that is certain. The boatman thinks to himself, funny people. Happy and polite, but funny. He steers the boat towards the hotel.

"Marcus, I am hungry," says Kimberley, as they step out of the boat. "It must be late. We have been out for hours."

Marcus is paying the boatman generously. The little acts of generosity in tipping are to the Indian recipient very welcome but to the giver amount only to a pound or perhaps two pounds. The goodwill which is created is incalculable, but Marcus does it to help in a tiny way the flood of poverty which exists in India. Democracy or kingdoms, it all has the same effect.

"We will go to the dining room," says Marcus, "see whether the restaurant is open."

They walk together. The restaurant is bustling with people. There is a long buffet arranged in the middle of the room and European guests are lined up to fill their plate with a variety of foodstuffs. They are given small plates.

Marcus talks to the head waiter, who tells him that à la carte service is available. Marcus and Kimberley are shown to a window table and given menus.

"This is like Russian roulette," says Marcus. "We have escaped unscathed so far but I wonder if our luck will hold. Surely they don't have a deep freeze here so we must go for vegetables and rice. Maybe chicken."

"You decide, Marcus," says Kimberley. "You have kept our stomachs settled for the past weeks. You can go on doing it."

"I'll try."

Marcus orders as usual something vegetarian with spices. No salads. Water in sealed bottles, and chutneys.

"Chutneys, Marcus?" asks Kimberley. "Could be made from squashed beetles or flies."

"Well, don't have any then," says Marcus, smiling. "They are bringing it separately."

As they look round the crowded room Kimberley sees a tall, handsome, famous US film star.

"Oh look, Marcus," she says. "It is Clifford Robertson."

"You mean the film star?" asks Marcus. "Look, he's coming over."

The man is rolling an ice-cold bottle of water over his forehead. His expression is a little dazed. He looks hung over. However, he has noticed Kimberley and wants to talk to her. He walks unsteadily across the dining room towards them.

He supports himself by leaning on their table when he arrives. He is painstakingly courteous. He introduces himself to both of them and apologises for disturbing them. At that moment the waiter arrives laden with food and begins to lay out all of the dishes on the table.

"I didn't see that on the buffet," Clifford says.

"It is not from the buffet," says Kimberley. "We ordered it specially so that it would be freshly cooked and less risk of food poisoning."

"Food poisoning?" says Clifford. "Yes, everybody warned me about that but the buffet looks okay."

"Twenty minutes outside in this heat and atmosphere," says Marcus.

"Well, thanks," says Clifford. "I'll order something freshly cooked. What do you recommend?"

"Lots of spices," says Kimberley. "Hot. It is good for your digestion in this heat."

"Thanks," says Clifford. "What are your names? Are you on your honeymoon?"

"Marcus and Kimberley," says Marcus.

"We are on our honeymoon," interrupts Kimberley before Marcus can say more. She stares at him. "This is our first time out of the room."

Clifford looks embarrassed. "Good luck to you both," he says, and walks unsteadily away.

"Poor man," says Marcus. "You embarrassed him and I'm sure that he only came over to talk to you."

They enjoy a delicious lunch and take time over it. Afterwards they ask the waiter to bring a pot of peppercorn tea to the ornamental gardens where they will be sitting. Once they are comfortably sat next to one of the fig leaf shaped ornamental pools, Marcus asks, "Kimberley, what is a Mustang Shelby?"

"You don't know?" says Kimberley. "Well okay. There is a man called Carroll Shelby. Sort of famous racing driver and mechanic and he went to the Ford Motor Company with a business proposition. He would turn their sports car, the Mustang, into a muscle car."

She puts up her hand to stop Marcus from asking.

"A muscle car is like the AC Cobra, and Shelby stripped down the standard Mustang and added tough suspension, wide wheels, competition clutch and different racing gearbox, stronger brakes and a bigger engine, very tuned up and lots of other things. Turned it into a mechanical fury car. It burns rubber when it accelerates away and it has a much higher top speed. It is like the Mustang used in the 1968 film, Bullitt. A mad car. I love it. Shelby has some deal with Ford over the sales and that is why it is officially called a Mustang Shelby. It is quite rare and that is why I said that mine might be worth a bit of money."

"I see," says Marcus. "Now I know something new."

Whilst they are chatting, and drinking the peppercorn tea which the waiter has brought them, two men stroll along the other side of the garden about fifty yards away. They sit down next to another ornamental pond. One of them is the movie star and the other is a tough-looking man expensively dressed. Maybe his agent or a film director or some other important person, thinks Kimberley, as she looks at them.

The tough-looking man takes a big cigar out of a leather case, clips the end off, and lights it thoroughly with a long match. The two of them sit quietly together and the tough-looking man enjoys his cigar.

There is a sudden crash from the dining room as a middle-aged woman rushes out of the glass doors and bangs them loudly behind her. She flies across the gardens muttering angrily. She is wearing flowing clothes in pink and yellow, with a scarf over her head. She arrives at the table of the two men and begins to shout.

"Your smoke is killing me," she shrieks. "Passive smoking is a crime. My family will sue you for every cent you have after I have died from your smoke."

"We are sitting one hundred yards away from the restaurant," says the film star reasonably.

"Smoking within my environment." The woman seems almost hysterical now. "Reckless endangerment. Manslaughter."

A little man in a formal jacket and striped trousers is hurrying along the path. He arrives at the smoker's table.

"What is the matter?" he asks. "I am the hotel manager. I could hear you screaming, madam. All guests of the hotel could hear you screaming. What is happening?"

"This man is smoking a cigar," shouts the woman, "risking our lives with his obnoxious weed."

"Oh dear, oh dear," says the manager. "Madam, these two gentlemen are staying at the hotel. They are occupying two of our very best rooms. They are treasured guests, madam. You are simply having a fixed price lunch. You are only here for two hours, of little value to the hotel, madam. I am the manager of the hotel, madam. I am responsible. You have upset treasured guests of the hotel. You will have to leave now, madam. I will arrange a small boat for you immediately. You will leave, madam."

He waves his arm at two men in white uniforms. They sprint over.

"The lady is leaving on the small boat immediately," says the manager. "Please ensure she leaves now. No questions. She must leave now."

The manager turns his back on the woman, who is purple with indignation.

"The hotel greatly apologises that your afternoon has been disturbed by an unwell person," the manager says to the two men.

"I shall go straight to the US embassy," says the woman, as she is led away by the two hotel servants, each of whom is holding one of her arms.

"Thank you," says the film star. "We are all right. Thank you."

"Yes sir, yes sir, yes sir," says the manager, as he bows to them whilst walking backwards towards the main hotel.

Marcus and Kimberley recognise the engine of the small boat as it speeds out into the lake.

"It is certainly not like California," says Kimberley.

"Good entertainment," says Marcus. "I wonder what else is going to happen?"

"We are going shopping," says Kimberley. "That is what is going to happen."

They ask the hotel reception to arrange a boat for them to go into town and the receptionist asks them to choose a time when they would wish to return so that she can ensure that the boat is waiting for them.

Kimberley and Marcus get into the ferry boat to find that there are two other passengers, a man and his wife.

Kimberley says, "Hi, how are you doing?"

And before Marcus can speak the Indian man, who speaks perfect English, says, "Americans. Ah, I like Americans. The country of freedom. Do you know that the British gave India its independence, gave India its independence after having first taken Indians' independence away by force of arms and killing? Then they plundered India's natural resources and changed its order of society and its court systems and its natural hierarchy. India used to have local police and a local court system, so that a man would be tried in his own town or village. The British smashed this and created their own district court system, a man from the British town of Bristol being tried in a place like Manchester, so that no local witnesses

302

could appear in the court because of the difficulties of travel and this gave the British judge total authority. So the natural, local, social justice system of India was damaged, smashed by the British, who then gave India its independence, having broken all of its customs first. They gave the independence with gracious condescending generosity and they sent an amateur English aristocrat to finally smash up the country. He called himself the last Viceroy of India. We did not call him that. And he decided as a parting poisonous gift to break up the country. The British invent words for bad actions. They called it the Partition. They split India from Pakistan, like splitting your Texas from your America. The British broke India just before they left and then they celebrated their leaving. They celebrated their generosity and they made India pay for it. Oh yes. I like Americans. I hope that India is treating you well."

"Certainly is," says Kimberley.

"Sure," says Marcus, not wanting to identify himself as British.

The boat is nearing the steps and the jetty of the main town. The boatman eases the boat gently against the jetty, ties up and then helps his passengers out onto the steps.

"Enjoy yourselves, please," says the Indian man and, taking his wife by the arm, walks into town.

Kimberley looks at Marcus.

"I think you got away with it," she laughs.

"I was brought up and educated with such conviction that Britain had given India clean water and sewage systems and all kinds of civilised benefits," says Marcus.

"He didn't think so," says Kimberley. "Come on, let's look about."

They walk up the lakeside steps and cross the road to walk into town. They are looking around them in all directions as they walk and Marcus sees a fabric shop with large bolts of cloth piled from floor to ceiling inside the shop. He takes Kimberley by the arm and they both walk into the shop.

"Are you going to make me a new outfit, Marcus?" asks Kimberley.

"No. I intend to send cloth home to cover my sofas and for cushions and curtains. First I will have a look around." Marcus speaks more loudly, "I will look at other shops to see if their prices are more reasonable. You can choose your own new cloth."

"Marcus, I am disappointed. Okay, I will look for some material."

They both stroll around the shop, which is quite big. Marcus looks at everything and Kimberley touches everything.

"Fine silk here, Marcus," she says.

"Oh, I think it is poor quality," says Marcus.

The owner emerges from a back room. "The silk is the very best silk, sir," he says. "Very fine quality, sir. May I show you?" He starts moving bolts of cloth from the shelves.

"Oh, thank you. No," says Marcus, "I do not think that I want to buy."

"Sir, feel the quality," says the owner. He reaches out to put a roll of silk into Marcus's hands.

"You are very kind," says Marcus. "Is this your shop?"

"Yes sir. My shop," says the owner.

"It is beautiful," says Marcus. "Everything is so well displayed and the shop is so clean and light. I like your shop."

"Thank you, sir," says the shopkeeper. "I have silks in every hue, sir."

"I have seen different silk in Hong Kong," says Marcus.

"Different, sir?"

"Yes, I believe they call it slubbed silk. Thick and rough to the touch."

"A created effect, sir," says the owner. "I have much better silk so that if you require slubs in the silk, it can be done, sir."

"How much would you charge me for a yard of your silk?" asks Marcus.

"Different colours can be more expensive," says the owner.

"Which colours are cheaper?" asks Marcus.

"Which colours do you like, sir?"

"I will probably like the expensive colours," says Marcus. "Please show me some of those."

The owner pulls down cloth from the shelves and arranges them on his central long table.

"Red, sir," says the owner, "scarlet red. Yellow, sir, and pale blue and pink, sir."

"So how much is a yard of any of these colours?" asks Marcus.

The owner answers, "Twenty pounds in your English money."

"Oh, thank you," says Marcus. "You are very helpful."

"Thank you, sir," says the owner.

"The other colours are the cheaper colours, you have said."

"I have shown you the expensive colours, which you said you liked, sir."

"Yes, that is true, but now I am thinking I want to compare prices in your excellent shop," says Marcus.

"Darker colours. Dark blue, purple, black and grey are sixteen of your English pounds for a yard, sir."

"And the slubbed silk, which you said was a different quality, that would be perhaps sixteen pounds for a yard?" asks Marcus.

"Oh no, sir, not sixteen pounds, sir. Perhaps twenty-four pounds or even," he looks carefully at Marcus, "for a gentleman like yourself, twenty-five pounds, sir."

"If I buy a larger quantity the price will be cheaper, yes?" asks Marcus.

"What the hell are you doing?" whispers Kimberley.

Marcus puts his arm around her and, as he kisses her cheek, he whispers, "Buying."

The owner says, "A large quantity, sir. I wish to avoid a long walk around the houses, sir. You tell me what you want and I will tell you the price, sir."

Marcus laughs. "Fair enough," he says.

"Before the price, sir, I will tell you that I travel to choose the silk most carefully. I oversee the dying process completely. I arrange transportation and supervision for the silks to arrive safely in my shop. These are the best silks, sir, and because of that I will not bargain like an Arab street trader. I will not talk of what is the most expensive colour, leaving myself to fall into your trap, sir. Tell me what you want and I will tell you how much it will cost. And I will not bargain, sir."

"I would like twenty yards of white slubbed silk, twenty yards of peacock blue smooth silk and ten yards of dark blue smooth silk and ten yards of primrose yellow, what you might call canary yellow, smooth silk and I would like it all posted to London, England," says Marcus.

The shop owner is writing as Marcus speaks. At the end of Marcus's words the owner takes a fresh sheet of paper and writes something new on it. He hands the paper to Marcus.

"This is the price, sir, and this is the cost of the postage."

Marcus has been made to feel rather cheap by the shop owner's careful rebuke of his attempts at bargaining, so he says, "I agree."

The owner then says, "I will give you three yards of the pale blue silk with no cost to you, so that your friend may have a dress made, sir, and I will recommend a dressmaker who is ten minutes walk away. Now I will arrange for my assistant to pack your silk so that it may be posted. Please let me have the name and address for the parcels, sir."

"May I buy three yards of rose pink and three yards of white silk, please?" asks Kimberley. "I want to have three dresses made by your friend the dressmaker."

"Yes, madam, and I will give you a bargain price." The owner writes the price onto a piece of paper and gives it to Kimberley, who promptly gives him the money without hesitation.

"Here," says the shop owner, "is the name and address of the dressmaker, madam. You walk in that direction, madam." He points with his hand. "Past the silversmith's."

"Silversmith's, Marcus," says Kimberley. "You can buy me a present with the money you nearly saved by bargaining so well." She laughs.

Marcus smiles and turns to pay the shop owner for all of his purchases.

"I apologise for attempting to bargain with you," he says. "Yours is an excellent shop and I am very pleased with the silk I have purchased."

"I accept your apology," says the shopkeeper. He turns to Kimberley. "The silk you have chosen will make fine dresses for your beauty, madam."

"Thank you, sir," says Kimberley, who takes the parcel from the owner and says to Marcus, "Come on, Marcus, before you say something else to offend him." She pulls Marcus out of the shop.

The owner looks after her, smiling. He thinks that she was delightful. Wearing strange pyjamas but delightful.

Marcus and Kimberley walk along the road towards the silversmith's. Inside the walls and shelves are hung with silver jewellery and trinkets, and objects like silver cigar cases and silver cufflinks and tie pins. There are silver chains of large thick links and also of small fine links.

"I had a friend who had a fine gold chain sealed around her waist," says Kimberley. "It fit her to within a quarter of an inch. She said it was to stop her putting on weight but it looked strange because a waist chain is supposed to rest on your hips. So it was too tight. What are those? They look big for bracelets."

"They are ankle chains," says Marcus.

"I thought that those showed men that you were a hooker," says Kimberley. "Oh look, Marcus. Toe rings with little bells on top. I'm gonna get me two or three of those."

She starts to look through the different shapes and bell types.

"How are you choosing them?" asked Marcus.

"I'm making sure that they are round and smooth so that they don't cut my toes," says Kimberley.

Marcus picks up some slightly bigger silver bells with silver loops on the top of them. "You could tie these into your roller-skating boot laces. So that children and others can hear you coming," he says.

"Good idea, Marcus," says Kimberley, and adds two of them to the four bell toe rings she has already chosen.

Marcus walks to the other side of the shop and buys something secretly, putting it into his shirt pocket.

"Marcus, are you going to buy a silver cigar case?" asks Kimberley.

"I don't smoke," says Marcus.

"Okay, so just a load of silk for your sofas," says Kimberley. "Not even a nose stud!" She laughs helplessly at the thought of Marcus with a nose stud.

After a little more time in the shop Kimberley purchases her bells and they walk out and further down the road to the dressmaker's.

"You can leave me here, Marcus," says Kimberley. "I will be a while."

"All right," says Marcus. "I'll walk further and come back in forty-five minutes. Is that enough time?"

"Sure," says Kimberley, and walks inside to meet the dressmaker.

She has particular ideas of what she wants made for her and in which colours. She uses the dressmaker's pad and pencil to draw what she wants, and when the dressmaker frowns and attempts alterations, Kimberley firmly puts strong pencil lines through the alterations and draws again what she wants. For one dress she emphasises on her thighs how short she wants the dress to be. On another she draws a low, scooped neckline and on the third a spoon-shaped backless area of the dress. Marcus will want me when he sees me in any of these dresses, she thinks. How exciting. The Indian dressmaker is scandalised but not altogether surprised. She has seen the clothes which some foreigners wear.

After detailed descriptions Kimberley arranges to collect the dresses tomorrow morning and agrees a price for the work.

"Nine thirty in the morning," the dressmaker says.

Kimberley thanks her and walks out of the place to look for Marcus. She walked slowly up the road in the direction he took.

I am in India, she thinks, an astonishing place but I am managing okay. Having dresses made how I want them and bells for my toes. I get a warm feeling when I think of Marcus.

This realisation surprises her. I last felt like that when I was sixteen. Billy Joe MacArthur. His dad was a farmer and now Billy Joe has the farm and has bought two more. Married and has children, I last heard. He must be nearly thirty now, but when I first started dating him I used to ache when I saw him, and feel butterflies in my stomach when I realised that he had his dad's car with the big back seat. It was because I liked the feeling that he wanted me. He was the first man I ever attracted. Maybe I loved him. We used to park in the woods and fool around. He used to make me cry. I don't know why. Growing up, perhaps. Leaving my childhood behind. Trying to keep something, which I knew was moving on by. The back seat of that car used to excite me if I saw the empty car parked in town. An awful sort of longing. To be wanted again. I didn't understand. It was security. A feeling of wanting someone to wait for me. It was painful and powerful and transient. It did not have to be transient. Billy Joe wanted to marry me. Part of me wanted to marry him. Maybe the best part of me. The sensible part.

After I broke up with Billy Joe, boys did what I wanted if I wanted them to. I slimmed down and filled out in all the right places and I took gymnastic classes. The boys were not as simple and honest as Billy Joe. He was a pure soul. The next boys were handsome and sure of themselves so I played them against each other. I toughened up. Got smart. Strong. I became the person I am now.

She sees Marcus walking towards her. I am a tough, fit cheerleader. I am a male fantasy, not a farmer's wife or a Brit's girlfriend. I have a life plan. I have aims. I have goals.

"Hello, Marcus," she says as he walks up to her.

"Did you order the dresses you want?" he says.

"Yes," says Kimberley, "and I am going to throw all of my cowgirl outfits away. They are scratchy and full of Indian dust."

"That is why we got them," says Marcus. "Because the travelling we have done is so dusty. We don't need them now. We are going back to the sea. To the beach. The day after tomorrow. Five days there and then we go back to London. Then you fly home to Florida."

"So quick," says Kimberley. "Like the school holidays. I always thought that the clocks changed during the school holidays. Long time at school, short time at the holidays. This has been just the same."

"That is because we have done so much. Seen so much," says Marcus. "School days are all the same. That is why they seem so long."

"I guess so," says Kimberley, "but it is not over yet. We still have time here and then more time at the beach. We are still here, Marcus. Did you see anything interesting?"

"A lot of people. A lot of extravagant buildings. Unusual and different," says Marcus. "Are you glad that we came?"

"Marcus," Kimberley hesitates. "It has been wonderful. Thank you."

"Thank you for being my travelling companion, Kimberley. You have been the best," says Marcus. "Are you ready to go back on the boat? It will be waiting for us in fifteen minutes."

"I am ready," says Kimberley. "But I have to come back tomorrow morning to collect my dresses."

"That's fine," says Marcus. "I'll come with you."

They walk to the jetty and Marcus takes Kimberley's arm. The boat is waiting for them. The boatman helps them aboard. They cross the lake. The Palace Hotel is waiting for them. The Maharishi suite is waiting, thinks Kimberley. I am excited. It must be a holiday mood. Holiday sex. The boat arrives and they both get out onto the terrace and walk into the hotel. The reception staff greet them warmly. They are the most extravagant guests, after all.

It is late afternoon and Kimberley wants a bath to get rid of all the dust. Marcus says that he will go swimming in the hotel pool.

"It is not very big," he says. "I will have to do more lengths."

They prepare for the evening. Marcus swims and Kimberley bathes and then they go to the restaurant for another cautious meal. They are happy together. They both laugh.

"Shall we have an early night?" asks Marcus.

At the doorway of the suite Marcus kisses her. It reminds her of kissing at the abandoned palace on the lake. She returns his kisses and brushes his back with her fingertips. She wants him to want her. It excites her the most.

They kiss for longer and then Kimberley tears at his clothes. She rips off his shirt and she pulls it off him and she unlocks the door, pulls him inside and locks it behind them. Inside the suite, Marcus treats her gently. He removes each piece of her clothing, slowly kissing the bare skin underneath. Kimberley's skin is satin smooth and café au lait in colour all over. She must sunbathe at some secret place on the roof of her apartment building, thinks Marcus. Sunbathe in the nude. Marcus carries her into the bedroom.

Pretty corny, thinks Kimberley, but I like it.

He places her on the bed and looks at her almost reverently.

"You look as if you were designed by an overenthusiastic group of fourteen year old boy scouts," Marcus says. "You are the sexiest girl I've ever known."

Kimberley rolls slightly from side to side, putting one knee up.

"Well, don't waste it then," she says. "We are going home soon."

Marcus leans down and begins to kiss and stroke and caress her body carefully. He is slow and tantalising and Kimberley moves underneath him.

"I won't break," she says softly, to urge him on.

He lowers his head. "You taste of wild honey," he says.

Kimberley wants a man to want her. It is what she has worked at for years. For men to want her even if she doesn't want them. But she wants Marcus. Her body aches with longing. She has to speed him up. Kimberley is completely unselfconscious about her body. There is no part of it which she doesn't like. She seeks no enhancements. She knows that she is smooth and firm everywhere. So she starts to use it to urge Marcus on. He begins to make love to her but still he moves at his own pace, like a slow bass drummer in a band.

Lose control, dammit, thinks Kimberley. I am going to fall over the edge soon.

She gets active, wraps her legs around his back, and then his hips. She scratches his back lightly. She squeezes her thighs together and paws at his shoulders.

"Don't be separate, Marcus," she cries, "be with me."

Immediately he is and as they move they feel compatible and together. Their bodies increase the drumbeat and speed it up. They are soon temporarily exhausted and complete. They lie still together. After a few minutes Marcus speaks quietly.

"I am going to get onto that swing, Kimberley, and I would like you to get on top of me."

"Would you like me to, Marcus?" asks Kimberley.

"I would like you to very much," says Marcus.

"Then I will," says Kimberley.

Minutes later they are swinging backwards and forwards, their bodies tightly entwined.

"If the chains break we are going to fly out of those big open windows," says Kimberley.

"I am going to fly out of them any second now," gasps Marcus.

Kimberley cradles his head, pulling his face towards her. "You fly," she whispers. "I'll hang on tight."

Later they are asleep on the bed with their arms around each other. Superman, thinks Kimberley as she sleeps.

The morning sun streams into the room. Kimberley wakes up slowly. Marcus is kissing her neck. Half asleep, she likes it. Fully awake, she stops him and sits up.

"Breakfast," she says. "I have to go into town."

They have eggs and bread and fruit and strange-tasting coffee before they take a little boat across the lake again and ask the boatman to wait half an hour for them. Kimberley walks to the dressmaker and Marcus strolls along the lakeside stone terrace.

The dresses are provocative, thinks Kimberley. I really like them. Already I am thinking about sex. The dressmaker wraps them up. Kimberley pays her. She walks out of the shop and back to the boat to meet Marcus. The boat takes them back to the Palace Hotel. Kimberley asks a porter to put her parcels into the suite. They go into the garden for peppercorn tea.

"I like it here," say Kimberley, "in these gardens. Quiet and restful."

"It is a luxurious place," answers Marcus. "Pity that we have to move on tomorrow."

"Long journey back," says Kimberley.

"We are taking a plane," says Marcus. "One flight and we have first class seats."

314

"What is the airline?" asks Kimberley.

"Indian Airlines, I suppose," says Marcus. "It is an internal flight."

"I wonder if the pilot will have a handlebar moustache?" says Kimberley.

"Part of the uniform, I expect," answers Marcus. "Is there anything you would like to do this afternoon?"

"I'm thinking about that, Marcus," says Kimberley. "I could watch you water-skiing on the lake?"

"They don't have water-skiing here," says Marcus.

"Pity," says Kimberley. "Can we just stay here? Would you mind doing nothing today?"

"I would like it," says Marcus. "I will send a picture postcard of the hotel to my secretary. Tell her about the film stars here."

"Only one," says Kimberley.

"With postcards you have to exaggerate a little," says Marcus. "She will enjoy the thought of it."

"I believed that you were an honest man, Marcus. Now I am shocked."

"Send one to your law firm," says Marcus. "Exaggerate what you have seen."

"If I just tell the truth about this trip they will not believe it," says Kimberley. "I will have to tone it down."

Marcus smiles. They sit quietly together. The fountains are the only sound.

Kimberley looks carefully at Marcus's profile. Maybe it is the place having an effect on me. What my friend Karen calls the desert island effect. On an island for a long time with only one man, eventually you find him attractive. Marcus is attractive.

"I want another cup," she says. "Be generous, Marcus, pour me another."

He laughs and picks up the silver teapot. "I should have bought a silver teapot at the silversmiths' market," he says. "Silver keeps the tea warm."

"You would have to fit it into your luggage," says Kimberley, "and then it would not fit into your old English house."

"You are right," says Marcus. "I don't regret anything about this trip. Everything has been perfect."

He is silent for five minutes and then he says, "Kimberley. When I make love to you, I am slow because I don't want it to end. I was like that with my favourite ice cream when I was a boy."

"Oh, so I am an ice cream now," says Kimberley. "Marcus, slow or fast, it is going to end. The moment I step onto the plane to Florida it will end."

Marcus says nothing.

"That sounded a little sharp, Marcus. I am sorry."

"It sounded a little true," says Marcus.

"But we are here now," says Kimberley. "A person can only live in the present. Come on, let's go to bed and go fast." She pulls him to his feet.

23
Dangerous Waters

They are quiet on the morning that they leave the Lake Palace Hotel at Udaipur. In the boat they are both sad. Kimberley was so uninhibited and carnal last night with such unbridled passion that they are not strangers any more. They feel as if they have known each other for years. For each of them it is a strange feeling. For Kimberley, because she has a tough exterior and does not allow people to get close. For Marcus, because he uses charm and humour to keep his distance and to keep his secrets. Now, like strangers on a train who have told each other everything, they find themselves familiar. Mind you, thinks Marcus, you wouldn't make love to a stranger on a train the way that Kimberley did last night. And me too, if I admit it. Most people don't make love like that even on their honeymoon. She is irreplaceable, thinks Marcus wistfully. Tough and strong and humorous and we don't even argue. Best girl in the world. The boat reaches the shore and there is a taxi waiting. They get into the taxi with their bags and with Kimberley's parcels and a taxi proceeds to the airport.

They check in at the first class desk and are told where the first class lounge is. They walk there and wait. Kimberley drinks fruit juice and Marcus has bottled water. The airport terminal is very hot but the first class lounge is cooled by one air conditioning unit.

Eventually there is an announcement in several languages telling them to proceed to the departure gate. They have not spoken very much and the plane reminds them of their eventual journey to London, and for Kimberley her eventual journey home to Florida.

They take their seats and the plane takes off rather clumsily from a long runway.

During the flight there is turbulence and the plane shakes about a lot. Kimberley takes Marcus's hand, which he finds to be as intimate as their lovemaking last night. He squeezes her hand, remembering that Kimberley does not like flying.

The stewardesses bring them drinks and some Indian food in plastic containers. Neither of them eats the food but Kimberley has some fruit, which she shares with Marcus. The flight is long and uncomfortable. The plane begins its descent on the way to Goa and Kimberley holds Marcus's hand again.

They land hard with a noisy crash and the jet engines go into reverse until the plane stops. There is a delay until the steps are brought to the exits on the plane and the first class passengers, only six of them, are let out first. The temperature outside is oven hot and they remember again the red earth and the dust in the air. There are no immigration formalities or customs because it is an internal flight and they walk outside the terminal into the heat. Marcus hails a taxi.

They have booked a bungalow on the beach and an Indian woman to cook and clean for them. Marcus has the address written down. The drive to the beach bungalow is long and slow. Kimberley still looks sad.

"You can work on your suntan," says Marcus, "and rest."

"Everything went by so quickly," says Kimberley.

"We still have five days left," says Marcus. "For five days more we are still in India."

"I know," says Kimberley, who tries to smile. "Thank you, Marcus, for bringing me with you."

"It is the greatest pleasure I have ever had," answers Marcus.

"Me too," says Kimberley quietly.

They arrive at the bungalow, which has a large veranda around it and a dining table at the sea side of the veranda with steps down onto the sand.

The bungalow has two small bedrooms and one large bedroom.

Marcus carries their bags into the large double bedroom and walks back to pay the taxi driver.

"We are in a different place from last time," says Kimberley. "A different village."

Marcus hugs her and says nothing. She clings to him and says nothing either. They both feel desperate but do not want to speak.

Their suitcases from the hotel they first stayed at in Goa have been delivered to the bungalow and are standing in the sitting room.

"I can throw away my travelling clothes," says Kimberley. "They were a good idea, Marcus." She smiles at him. "Everything which you arranged was a good idea."

"Most of it was arranged by a travel agent in London," says Marcus. "I just added a few details."

Kimberley puts her suitcase onto the low coffee table in the sitting room. She opens it and looks through the contents.

"Just as if we have never been away," she says.

"There is a hotel up the road a little way," says Marcus. "It has a restaurant. We could eat there tonight if you would like to and tomorrow we can find places on the beach for lunch and tell the woman who is looking after us what we would like for dinner each night."

"Perfect," says Kimberley. "Give me a few minutes. I will have a shower and change and I will be more cheerful."

"You don't have to be cheerful for me," says Marcus, "perhaps just for you."

"I'll be all right soon, Marcus. I just felt a bit devastated when I realised that the holiday was nearly over," says Kimberley.

"Live for today," says Marcus. "That is what you taught me. Today is all we have."

They both shower and change into clothes from their suitcases. Then they walk up the road towards the brightly lit hotel. They can hear music playing. They are given a good table in the restaurant. The menu describes international dishes with some Indian dishes. They both choose Indian dishes. They both choose Indian vegetarian food with rice. Marcus orders a bottle of French Chablis and two bottles of sealed water. The wine is served in an ice bucket and is very good.

The guests in the hotel are mostly English, here on expensive package holidays; escaping from the cold English weather.

"I am proud to be seen here with you," says Marcus. "You look beautiful."

"And you look handsome," says Kimberley. "You could work in Florida, you know. Real estate in the US is a very good business to be in, Marcus. You can offset lots of expenses against tax and you can defer your taxes for years. If you worked in the States you could see more of me."

Thoughts flashed through Marcus's mind of last night and the fact that it would be difficult to see more of Kimberley than he had already seen.

320

"If you bought land in America," says Kimberley, "you might find oil or gold or something precious and be rich."

"The United States are really free, aren't they?" says Marcus. "If an English person finds oil or gold or silver in the United Kingdom it doesn't belong to him. It belongs to the Crown, which means the Queen, which means the government. I think possibly that the finder may get ten percent but I'm not sure."

"Even if it is on your own land?" says Kimberley.

"Ownership of land in Britain does not include the mineral rights," says Marcus. "So there can be no Beverly Hillbillies striking oil and getting rich in Britain."

"There are a lot of complexities in your country, Marcus," says Kimberley.

"Most European countries, I think," says Marcus.

"There is so much ancient treasure in the Aegean sea around the Greek islands that the government there has banned scuba diving. They want to wait until they have enough government money to fetch it up themselves. The Greek people don't pay their taxes very well so the government never has enough money."

"Why do you know all these things, Marcus? They are all depressing facts. Don't you know anything cheerful?"

Marcus looks at Kimberley. "Lots of cheerful things," he says. "I am saving them all up to tell you later."

"Tell me something now," says Kimberley.

"Aeronautical engineers say that bumble bees can't fly but they do. And honeybees produce honey that cannot be analysed. Scientists cannot tell us what is in honey. They don't understand it."

"When you try to tell me something cheerful, Marcus, it comes out weird," says Kimberley. "Try again."

"You can walk all over Britain without asking the land owner's permission, except in people's gardens, of course. British people have the right to roam," says Marcus.

"The right to roam," says Kimberley. "That is a little bit cheerful. A person can't do that in the States. Private land is private but we do have lots of enormous public parks where a person can walk and camp and things, Marcus." Kimberley looks at him. "Marcus, would you kiss me, please?"

Marcus kisses Kimberley with great affection and tenderness and their waiter hesitates before he brings their food to the table. He has waited for Marcus and Kimberley to stop kissing. Honeymooners, he thinks.

"I am going to drink this wine and then ask for another bottle," says Kimberley. "I want to go to sleep drunk tonight."

"All right," says Marcus, who is a little concerned. "I will order more of this wine and tomorrow we can enjoy the sunshine and the beach."

"Yes," says Kimberley, and drinks a full glass of the delicious French wine.

She drinks more as she eats and she enjoys most of the second bottle as well. Marcus is only drinking wine to preserve some of it away from Kimberley who seems determined to blot out the night. Later, she drinks tequilas. French wine is not a good foundation for tequila, thinks Marcus, but he cannot stop her. When everything has been eaten and drunk (although Marcus has eaten more than Kimberley and drunk more water), Marcus helps Kimberley to her feet and discreetly holds her up as they leave the restaurant and then the hotel.

The hot fresh air outside is too soporific to revive Kimberley and as they walk down the road to the bungalow, Kimberley starts to sing. "These boots are made for walking, dum, dum, dum, dum, dum, all over you." She leans sideways against Marcus as they walk and puts her head on his shoulder. "These boots are made for walking."

Suddenly she pulls at Marcus. "I am not wearing boots," she says and starts to laugh. "No boots for walking. Dum, dum, dum. No boots."

She falls silent and although they are both still walking forwards and nearing the bungalow, Marcus is convinced that Kimberley is asleep; walking in her sleep. They reach the bungalow and Marcus lifts Kimberley up the steps, onto the veranda. He unlocks the front door with difficulty and, because the door is not very wide, holds Kimberley tightly as she walks in. Her breathing is now deep and steady. She is asleep, thinks Marcus, now I have to get her into bed. He simply picks her up and carries her into the biggest bedroom. He puts her gently onto the bed and then methodically takes all of her clothes off. Then he rolls her sideways and props her with a pillow so that she cannot roll onto her back. He positions her face at the edge of the bed and then covers her with a sheet. Too hot for anything more. Keeping his eyes on her, Marcus moves about the room taking his own clothes off and then goes into the bathroom. He emerges a few minutes later. His breath smells of toothpaste and he checks on Kimberley. She has not moved. Everything is deep and regular and her heart is beating slowly. Carefully Marcus gets into the same bed from the other side and vows to stay awake. He does not.

In the morning he hears the shower running and hears Kimberley singing 'Somewhere over the Rainbow'. She sounds okay, thinks Marcus. He dresses in beach clothes and goes into the kitchen to make tea and carry it out onto the veranda overlooking the sea. He finds some fresh Indian bread and fruit in the kitchen so he carries that out with plates. He has barely sat down when a warm mouth meets his lips and a wet arm encircles his shoulders. Kimberley is wearing a thin short yellow sundress. Her hair is wet but brushed and her face has a bruised look.

"I feel like hell this morning, Marcus," she says, "Give me some tea, or anything to drink except alcohol."

Marcus pours out the tea and Kimberley sips from the cup.

"No peppercorns," she says. "Why not?"

"I couldn't find any," says Marcus.

"Don't worry, you can't do anything wrong today, Marcus," says Kimberley, "because we are on a lovely beach, in lovely sunshine, with a lovely sea. I have a headache," she frowns. "If I go swimming, will it make my headache go away?"

"Probably," says Marcus. "But have some breakfast first. That will help as well."

Kimberley feels better after breakfast and they take two bottles of water from the fridge, collect their beach towels and walk out onto the sand. Kimberley has a beach bag over her shoulder.

"Oww," she says. "The sand is hot." She pulls sandals out of her bag and, hopping to brush sand from her feet, she puts them on. "Ooh, that is better."

They walk away from the small crowd of people who are on the beach near to the hotel. Marcus and Kimberley find a deserted spot one hundred yards from anyone else and throw their towels down to make places to lay down. Underneath her sundress Kimberley is wearing a white bikini and Marcus undresses to reveal dark blue swimming shorts. They both lay down.

"Was it this hot last time?" asks Kimberley.

"I can't remember. I had come from London so it seemed hot to me," answers Marcus.

"I think it is hotter," says Kimberley.

324

Marcus will remember her next words for years to come.

"I am going swimming," says Kimberley, "to cool down and cure my headache."

"All right," says Marcus. "Don't go out deep. Stay close to shore. I will stay here."

Twenty minutes later Marcus sits up. He cannot see Kimberley. He puts on his sandals and walks to the water's edge. He looks up and down the beach.

"Lady drown." He looks around and there is a small Indian boy. "Lady drown in current," says the boy.

Marcus crouches down to the boy's level. "What do you mean? What current? Has lady already drowned? Please." He looks into the boy's innocent brown eyes.

"Current very strong. Underneath top of water. Strong current. There." The boy points to the right hand side of the beach. There are no swimmers there.

"And the lady?" Marcus looks at the boy.

"Lady go out. Whoosh. Very fast," says the boy.

"When?" asks Marcus, shaking with anxiety.

"Now," says the boy. "Whoosh, there now."

Marcus throws off his sandals and runs down the beach into the sea. He swims powerfully straight ahead, avoiding the right-hand side of the beach. His idea is to get ahead of Kimberley by swimming on the left and then cut across to the right-hand side where the deep water might have weakened the current. He swims steadily and fast. Fifty yards. One hundred yards. One hundred and fifty yards. He cuts across to the right and moments later he sees blonde hair. As he gets closer he can see that Kimberley is keeping her head and part of her shoulders out of the waves by treading water furiously. He swims as quickly as he possibly can towards her. He sees her head go beneath the surface. Too long. She pops up again coughing, water coming out of her mouth. Marcus powers himself through the water. He is ten yards away when she disappears again. He swims frantically towards the spot. A person drowns in only three minutes, thinks Marcus. That was the second time that I saw her going down but it might have happened before. Blonde hair appears close to the surface. Marcus grasps the hair and pulls it up. The head and neck appear. Her mouth is in a paroxysm of coughing, water coming out in drops. Marcus grabs Kimberley underneath her arms and from behind. He shouts at her loudly in case she is in a state of shock.

"I am going to tow you in, Kimberley. On your back. I will tow you. You do nothing. Just breathe, Kimberley. Breathe steadily in and out."

Marcus cups a hand beneath her chin and begins to swim sideways away from the current. Sixty yards away he turns towards the shore.

"Breathe Kimberley, breathe," he shouts in a ragged voice.

He is now swimming in a complete panic. His speed increases. He is driven entirely by adrenaline. Is she breathing? He thinks. She must stay alive.

On the beach people have stood up to watch the impossibly dramatic rescue. Three Indian men are standing at the shoreline with a life belt and a long length of rope tied to it. Two other Indian men are running down the beach towards them. The little boy who spoke to Marcus is running up and down the beach behind the man with the lifebelt.

Marcus is swimming in powerful jerks towards the shore. He is scissoring his legs beneath Kimberley's inert body and yard by yard he gets closer to the land.

A lifebelt is thrown just beyond him and pulled by the men on the beach until it reaches him. Marcus holds it tightly with one hand and holds Kimberley around her body with his other arm. Five men on the beach are now pulling on the rope, walking backwards up the beach.

The little boy is running up and down excitedly. "Pull, pull," he shouts.

Marcus and Kimberley are pulled into shallow water and then onto the sand. Marcus immediately rolls Kimberley onto her stomach and begins to give her artificial respiration. Over and over again he pumps at her. She starts to cough weakly.

"Lady is alive," shouts the little boy, jumping up and down.

Marcus persists with Kimberley. "Come on. You are a gymnast," he says.

She starts coughing a little more strongly and a lot of water comes out of her onto the sand.

A white-haired elderly gentleman walks up to Marcus and Kimberley. He is wearing big khaki shorts, a Hawaiian shirt and Hush Puppy shoes. "I am a doctor," he says. "Retired, but still a doctor. Carry on exactly as you are doing. Perfect technique."

Kimberley is struggling now and coughing more.

"Doctor, I have heard that people can die if they have water in their lungs. They can die in their sleep. But how do I get all of the water out of her lungs?"

"You are right young man," says the doctor. "I practiced on the coast. I have known holidaymakers die in the night after a partial drowning. It does happen. We will have to drain her lungs, get her to hospital."

Surprisingly the old doctor turns and shouts in perfect Hindu to the Indians who had helped in the rescue.

"Called for an ambulance. Told them to tell the hospital. Half-drowned woman."

"You speak the language?" Marcus says.

327

"Live here," says the doctor. "Got to speak the language. Let's sit the girl up. Pat her back. Keep her coughing up the Indian Ocean, what?"

Marcus keeps coaxing Kimberley to recover and after some minutes he hears the ambulance.

The doctor shouts at the Indian men who then pick up Kimberley and carry her to the beach entrance road. Marcus and the doctor follow. The ambulance reverses to the edge of the sand and two paramedics in clean white uniforms jump out and open the ambulance doors. Kimberley is carried in and put on a stretcher. The doctor follows, and then Marcus. A paramedic is fitting an oxygen mask to Kimberley's mouth and nose.

Marcus says, "Excuse me. Do you mind if I lie down for a moment?" The doctor helps him onto the other stretcher and Marcus passes out cold.

He wakes up on a hospital bed fully clothed. He even has his shoes on. Somebody must have brought his clothes up from the beach. He is on top of the bed and next to him in a neat little pile is Kimberley's sundress, her shoes and her beach bag. Marcus looks around. Kimberley is in the next bed, with a drip in her arm and a long tube coming out of her mouth. She is sedated and is sleeping.

The old doctor walks in. "Good looking girl," he says. "Are you going to marry her?"

"I don't know," says Marcus.

"Marry her, old boy. Have lots of children. Invest in life. Marry the girl. She owes you something now. Good basis for marriage. Doesn't work if the man owes the girl. This way round is best. What's wrong with her that you say you don't know if you want to marry her? Is she difficult? Bitchy, moody, lazy, no good in bed, what is it?"

"She is perfect," says Marcus.

"Marry her then," says the old doctor. "Have a good life."

"Is she going to be all right, doctor?" asks Marcus.

"Of course she is," says the doctor. "We got a lot of seawater out of her. She must have a strong will to live. Fought on whilst she was actually drowning. Tough girl."

"Yes. She is a tough girl," says Marcus.

"She will be fine," says the doctor. "We can let you both leave this evening. You need a rest. God knows how you did it, but you did. Good man."

"Thank you, doctor," shouts Marcus, as the door to the room closes. Marcus looks over at Kimberley and then he falls asleep again.

When Marcus wakes up it is nearly five o'clock and Kimberley is awake. There is no drip in her arm and no tube in her throat.

"Hello, Marcus," she says. "I need ice cream for my throat. Had a tube stuck down it. Do you think there is ice cream in India?"

"The hotel had that American brand, is it Ben and Jerry's?" answers Marcus.

"Oh, that is very good ice cream, Marcus. Let's check out of this place and go and eat ice cream. Then you can tell me what happened because I don't know for sure. Or maybe I don't want to remember, but you'll tell me, Marcus, won't you?"

"I'll tell you," says Marcus. "Meanwhile I think that we should tell the nurse or somebody that we are leaving."

The hospital is spotless; light and airy, old-fashioned and run with great dedication by an enthusiastic and happy staff.

Marcus arranges to come back tomorrow and pay the bill. The hospital arranges a taxi and Marcus and Kimberley go to the hotel for ice cream.

"Banana and chocolate, please," says Kimberley to the waiter, after Marcus has explained that they want ice cream.

"Yes sir," says the waiter, and walks away.

Marcus and Kimberley are sitting in the hotel gardens looking at the swimming pool.

"So, what happened, Marcus?" asks Kimberley.

"You floated out too far and some men had to throw you a lifebelt and pulled you back in. You swallowed a bit of water on the way back," says Marcus calmly.

"That is not what the doctor said," says Kimberley, "or the nurses or the little boy with brown eyes who came to see me and brought me flowers; all while you were asleep, Marcus."

"There may be a little more to it than I told you," says Marcus. "I did not want to wake up bad memories for you. You went out to sea, came back and now we are getting ice cream."

The waiter places two dishes of ice cream on the table between them, banana and chocolate for Kimberley and vanilla for Marcus.

Kimberley takes a spoonful of the super ice cream and looks at Marcus.

"Heroic, they said. Impossible, they said. Unbelievably brave, they said. I know what happened, Marcus. I was there, remember? I just wanted to know what you were going to tell me. You said nothing that praises yourself, Marcus, nothing at all."

"It was not heroic," says Marcus. "It was more a matter of desperation. I was frightened of your mother, you see."

"You don't know my mother," says Kimberley.

"That is why I was frightened of her. Her daughter drifted out to sea while I was asleep. Bad story."

"What you are telling me now is a bad story, Marcus; rip tides, stormy seas, towing me two hundred yards, artificial

330

respiration. You left all that out. I cannot tell you off, Marcus. I cannot be impatient with you. I never had my own real life hero before. You are the best man I've ever known."

"Oh, shut up, Kimberley. If I had drifted out you would have swum out to me, I know," says Marcus.

"The hell I would," says Kimberley, "and I didn't drift out. I was pulled out fast and strongly. You are a hero, Marcus, so don't argue. And you can do anything you like with me tonight and I will enjoy it. That is what happens to the hero in storybooks. I will wear my smallest dress and you can tear it off me. We are eating at the bungalow tonight?"

"Yes, we are," says Marcus, "and you are shameless and bold and beautiful, Kimberley, and you must read the most unusual storybooks, and I have a present for you."

"A present. What? A seashell from the ocean depths?"

"You'll have to wait. I have to wrap it up first," says Marcus. "Hey, look over there."

Kimberley turns her head. Marcus steals a spoonful of her ice cream. She sees him. "You cheat," she says. "Oh, there is the little boy." She looks over Marcus's shoulder and smiles. "More flowers."

The second that Marcus turns his head, Kimberley tosses his ice cream over her shoulder into the flowerbed. When Marcus turns back his dish is empty.

"Oh Marcus, your ice cream is gone," says Kimberley. "Never mind, you can lick more ice cream off me tonight. I'll buy a big tub and take it to the bungalow."

"You are a bad girl," says Marcus.

"You like me though, don't you?" says Kimberley and blows him a kiss.

"I suppose so," says Marcus and smiles at her. "Come on, let's go for a walk. I am going to keep you on dry land."

He pays the waiter and Kimberley runs into the restaurant behind his back and persuades the maître d' to sell her a tub of vanilla ice cream. She wraps it in a towel and puts it into her beach bag and hopes that it will not have turned to liquid by the time they get to the bungalow.

They leave the hotel and wander arm in arm into the small village. There are hens pecking about at the base of the untidy hedgerows and goats placidly eating the hedgerows.

"How do animals know which plants are poisonous and which ones are good to eat?" asks Kimberley.

"They get a book out of the animal library," says Marcus.

"Get outta here," says Kimberley. "They must just watch to see which animals die before they eat."

"That is a horrible idea," says Marcus. "I think it is all instinct and smell."

Four small children approach them. "Hello," says Marcus. "Can you all swim?"

The children don't speak English. They smile and hold their hands out.

"What are we going to do, Marcus?" asks Kimberley.

"Give them money I suppose," says Marcus. "We have money. They don't have money. The story of the world."

"Okay," says Kimberley. "It's my turn. I'll give them money." She bends down and gives each child twenty rupees and then to their horror she kisses each of them on the cheek. They all run away screaming.

"Losing your touch, Kimberley," says Marcus.

"Wait until tonight," says Kimberley. "And then tell me."

Marcus hugs her. "You don't owe me anything," he says.

Marcus finds Kimberley's adulation very awkward. It makes him feel uncomfortable and he does not know how to receive it. He kicks a stone along the road. Kimberley senses his embarrassment and does not know how to undo it. He is English, she thinks. He is modest.

"How do you feel, Marcus?" she asks. "Are you still tired?"

"I think part of it is shock," answers Marcus. "I feel calm and rested now and I feel happy. Right this minute I feel really happy."

"So do I, Marcus," says Kimberley. "Shall we walk back? There are going to be lots of children all around us soon wanting twenty rupees each and I haven't got enough with me. I'll buy a lot of fruit tomorrow."

"Yes," says Marcus. "Fruit is a good idea."

The Indian woman who is paid to housekeep for them has heard about the drama and has made a special effort. She is laying the dining table on the veranda when they walk in through the front door. Smells from the kitchen are delicious. Marcus walks out and greets the housekeeper warmly and formally. He shakes her hand. She nods back at him and carries on working. Kimberley is putting the ice cream in the fridge freezer and then she goes into the big bedroom to shower, wash her hair to get rid of the sea salt, clean her teeth and change her clothes.

Marcus looks in the kitchen cupboards and in the fridge and later in the sitting room sideboard.

He finds a considerable quantity of alcohol and four bottles of wine in the fridge. He fills a wide short glass with ice from the large American fridge freezer and pours himself a large whisky. He doesn't usually drink spirits, but tonight he feels the need of it. He walks outside to sit in a comfortable basket chair, which has cushions on it. He sips his drink indulgently.

"I'll have one of those," says Kimberley, as she walks out onto the veranda. "Then I won't smell it on your breath.

Anyway, I deserve one. Stay where you are. I'll get it. Whisky, right?"

She prepares one and comes out and sits down in the only other basket chair. "I have just thrown my white bikini into the trash," she says. "Never want to see it again. Do you like my dress?" Her dress is very tight and revealing. "It will probably split when I eat dinner," she says. She takes a large sip from her drink. "Have you tried yours?"

"Yes, I am enjoying it," says Marcus.

"I was just waiting for the taste," says Kimberley. She leans over and kisses Marcus openly on the lips with passion.

"The housekeeper is in the kitchen," says Marcus.

"Good," says Kimberley, "because I am hungry. I think I can smell curry." She gets back into her chair.

"I believe that it is curried chicken," says Marcus. "There are all sorts of exotic vegetables as well as a spicy rice dish being prepared."

"Wow," says Kimberley. She drinks deeply and sighs. "First time we have had our own little homestead. No more hotels. I like it here."

"What's the time, Kimberley?" asks Marcus.

"It's only seven o'clock," says Kimberley.

"Dinner is served at eight o'clock, according to the bungalow schedule," says Marcus.

"We have a schedule?" says Kimberley.

"We have everything," answers Marcus.

Where they are in southern India, the sun sets into the sea because they are so far south, and the sun sets quickly. Kimberley and Marcus watch the great red ball of distant fire as it disappears into the sea. There are outside lights and Marcus gets up to turn them on. They soon attracted moths, which whirr around their heads and bump against light bulbs.

There are a row of other bungalows on the beach but Marcus and Kimberley feel pleasantly alone.

Soon the housekeeper starts bringing out the white plates and then steaming dishes of food. She says a word to both of them and then walks back to the kitchen.

"What did she say?" asks Marcus.

"I think it was, wuk abrambla," says Kimberley. "Which means eat your dinner while it is hot."

"You are very good at languages," says Marcus.

"It is a gift," says Kimberley. "And talking of gifts, you told me I have a present."

"It is right there on the chair next to you," says Marcus.

"What is it?" says Kimberley, as she snatches it up. "I'm going to unwrap it." She tears the paper and reveals a wooden box. "Oh my God," she says. "It is a wooden box." She starts to laugh. "I've always wanted a wooden box."

"Open it, you twerp," says Marcus.

"Twerp? What is a twerp?" says Kimberley. "All right, all right."

She leans away as Marcus reaches to snatch the box from her hands. She opens it and inside, wrapped in a piece of purple material, there is an ornate silver filigree necklace made from thick broad links and long enough to reach Kimberley's cleavage. It is polished silver and sparkles in the evening light.

"It is a souvenir from India," says Marcus. "I'm glad I did not give it to you before. It would have sunk you to the bottom of the Indian Ocean."

Kimberley takes his hand and squeezes it. "Okay," she says.

This man is special, she thinks. I wish that there was something wet about him so that I could hate him a bit but there isn't. He is cool. What am I going to do about him? Damn well risking his life to rescue me and then pretending that he didn't. And now he comes up with a lovely Indian silver necklace, which I may never take off again. Damn. I hate him.

They eat in silence. The only sounds are the moths and the housekeeper washing up in the kitchen. The housekeeper watches until they have finished and then comes out and takes their plates to wash up.

"Draclonovitch," says Kimberley with a smile. The housekeeper looks puzzled as she walks back to the kitchen.

"What does that mean?" asks Marcus.

"Delicious," says Kimberley confidently.

They sit a while longer and the housekeeper comes out to say goodbye. Marcus thanks her profusely and once again she looks puzzled. He is paying for her, she thinks. She walks out of the front door and Marcus locks it behind her. He comes back to the veranda. Kimberley is sitting in a basket chair with her long shiny legs up on the partial balustrading. Marcus looks at her.

"Are you going to kiss me?" she says.

"Do you deserve it?" says Marcus.

"Hell, no. People don't get what they deserve. They get what they aim for. And tonight, Marcus? I am a certainty."

"Get up," says Marcus. "Follow me."

He walks through the bungalow and into their bedroom. He has never made Kimberley follow him before. It makes her feel a little smaller somehow. Marcus pushes the bedroom door shut.

"Take off the necklace," he tells her. She takes it off carefully and puts it on the dressing table top. As soon as her fingertips have left the necklace, Marcus turns her around to face him and, with each hand at a shoulder of her small dress, he rips it from top to bottom, leaving her standing naked. I told him I was a certainty, thinks Kimberley, but it seems that he can't wait. Kimberley is clearly not in charge of events. Marcus sits on a nearby chair and pulls Kimberley over his knee and with a lot of strength he holds her there with his left arm. With his right hand he smacks her behind. "That is for going too deep," he says. He smacks her again. "That is for nearly drowning." He smacks her again. "That is because I had to rescue you." He smacks her again. "And that is because of the ambulance and the hospital." His last smack is very hard. "And that is because I love you," he says.

Nothing like this has ever happened to Kimberley before. She always controls her sexual encounters and no man has ever struck her. She thought that she would shoot a man if he did but tonight a thought deep inside her head believes that she deserves it. The next thought is that it is warming her up. The next thought is that she feels turned on.

Marcus gets up, holding her by the waist, and throws her onto the bed. He takes his shirt off. "Don't make me do that again," he says and without lead up or play he starts to make love to her. Kimberley feels totally possessed. She ought to feel humiliated but she is frantic with excitement and the feeling that Marcus owns her tonight. Nobody has ever taken charge of Kimberley before but tonight it means that no decisions are hers and she has not had to make a move or coax Marcus to make a move. He is like an unprepared for hurricane, and she is shaking from her head to her toes which are now pointing straight downwards. She lets out a loud long scream.

Marcus waits for her breathing to subside and then says, "Now you don't owe me anything."

Kimberley feels as if he has slapped her face. Doesn't he want her to owe him everything? Doesn't he want her now? Didn't he say that he loved her? Unexpectedly for a tough character like Kimberley she involuntarily starts to cry. Great sobs rack her slender frame and her eyes become red.

"English bully," she says between sobs. "Rescue a different girl next time."

Marcus puts his arm around her. "I don't want a different girl," he says.

"Then why push me away?" gasps Kimberley.

"I don't want you to owe me anything," says Marcus. "I want you to want me all by yourself."

"Stupid English man," says Kimberley. "I want you all the time."

Marcus spreads Kimberley out on the bed. He starts to lick her body. "Draclonovitch," he says.

Kimberley stops crying and starts laughing. Marcus is increasing her temperature again.

Later Kimberley is lying on the bed, totally depleted. What is the matter with me, she thinks. This guy beats me up, tells me he loves me, and then treats me like a hooker. And I like it. Am I kinky? What has he awoken in me? Do I think that I do belong to him, like Red Indians believe when somebody saves their life? Bringing me to orgasm with his tongue. I like the smell of him. I like the taste of his skin. Damn. I feel further out to sea than I did yesterday. How am I going to get myself back again? How am I going to become me again? Maybe I should go home to America; I will know myself there and I can forget about all this. About him.

Marcus is on the balcony, drinking whisky. Do I love this girl, he thinks. Or is it just that it cost me so much effort to save her that I think I love her? I am lost. When I am back in London, back in England again, maybe I can forget her. I like the taste of her. I like the smell of her skin, but that is an animal thing. That is not practical. And we are in a fantasy place here. No relevance to either of our lives.

Kimberley gets off the bed and puts on a dressing gown. She walks onto the veranda outside the sitting room to see Marcus sitting there. She takes his glass of whisky from him and takes a sip and gives it back to him.

"I missed you," she says, kisses him then she sits in the other basket chair.

"We have two days left," says Marcus. "What are you going to do when you get back to Florida?"

"Get professional swimming lessons," says Kimberley. "And roller-skate. I've missed my roller-skating. I do it every day back home. What about you?"

"Meeting with my secretary and lawyers, I suppose," says Marcus. "Then I might go and look at my house in the country. See how the garden is doing."

"Okay," says Kimberley, thinking at the same time, oh boy that sounds boring. I could never live in England.

"What would you like to do in the final two days?" asks Marcus.

"The final two days?" says Kimberley. "That sounds really sinister, Marcus. Final days. Uugh! Anyway I thought that you would have it all planned out. Shark fishing or helicopter rides over the local wildlife or shooting tigers, that sort of thing."

"We are doing all that before breakfast tomorrow," says Marcus. "I just wondered if you wanted something special?"

"I've already had something special," says Kimberley. "Let me have some of your drink."

"Get your own drink," says Marcus.

"Yours tastes better," says Kimberley.

"All right, have mine and I'll get another," says Marcus, getting up.

"You are a genius, Marcus," says Kimberley. "A hero and a genius. Can you cook?"

"Shut up," says Marcus from the sitting room.

Whilst Marcus is pouring himself another drink, Kimberley starts thinking. I guess I have put on three pounds in weight since I've been here. No salads. No raw vegetables. Too much rice and alcohol. Not enough tough exercise. I have lost the perfectly concave stomach that I had and, because I am not roller-skating five miles every day, my butt is not as tight as it should be and my legs are not so firm. I have not done fifty press ups every morning either. Nor have I kept my pectoral muscles hard, so my breasts don't sit up as much as they did. No gyms in the hotels in India. I have let my body fall into neglect.

Kimberley's body is her most valuable asset (it should be for everybody but it's not); she expects to be looked at when she walks into a restaurant or onto a beach or roller-skating. She wants men to want her. She is lucky to be tall and have even features but she has worked hard on everything else and she undoubtedly believes that she is destined to marry a successful man. Even the man she went to Haiti and Venezuela with, the man she described to Marcus as a mistake, was in fact a famous rock star earning millions of dollars a year. Kimberley discovered what he liked and gave it to him, or more accurately rationed it to him, for financial favours. He was the man who gave her the Mustang Shelby. She broke up with him because he started doing drugs and his concerts became half empty venues and his records began to fail. Kimberley disappeared.

Her whole raison d'être is that men want her and the man who is lucky enough to get her has to be successful and on his way to more. The last two days have shaken the foundations of her life beliefs. She finds Marcus attractive. He seems to be able to do what he likes with her and unfeasibly she is beginning to become addicted to it. She is not the person

340

calling the shots in the relationship and she is not mindlessly adored. Marcus gives her very considered compliments and not a reckless infatuation. He is secure about himself and at the same time self-contained and self-effacing. He did say he loved her but he said it whilst he was hitting her, punishing her for being careless. He also said, don't make me do that again, implying that he would do it again if he thought that she deserved it.

This was all contrary to Kimberley's experience; puppy dog love, swaggering tough guy love, possessive love, but always respectful love. That was what Kimberley was used to and she wants it back. She wants her pedestal back.

Marcus is successful but he doesn't keep at it. No American takes more than one week for a holiday. Marcus seems to take two or three months a year. Why isn't he driving to build up a company he can sell on the stock exchange? Why is he not pushing his success further and further? He is not conventional. He is almost bohemian. He seems detached from standard middle class aims and acquisitions. He misses the usual patterns of behaviour. A girl could not rely upon him to keep trying materially. She has to pull back from him. She cannot keep on sliding down the slope of love with him. He would be a let-down, she sighs. He is rich, she thinks, and good at sex. I would say the best ever, but I can always get sex, she thinks. Maybe not very good sex. They either peak too soon or run out of steam and they all follow her directions. Marcus does not even ask her for directions. What shall I do?

Marcus walks back onto the veranda.

"What are we going to do, Marcus?" ask Kimberley.

"Well, I thought you mentioned something about ice cream," says Marcus, who knows what Kimberley wants to talk about and wishes to avoid it.

A shiver is going through Kimberley's body. Marcus, ice cream, his tongue. Damn, how weak am I? All physical indulgence, but I guess that is exactly what I created this body for, and now I have a man who knows how to make it work.

"Tonight, Marcus?" she asks.

"I'm ready," says Marcus, glad to find a way to delay the inevitable conversation. "I saw you buy the ice cream."

Whoa, thinks Kimberley, this man has some stamina. I wonder how much sex I would need to burn off three pounds? Is this still payback time for the lifesaving? He told me I didn't owe him anything. So shall I refuse him? Hell no, thinks Kimberley, I want to make the most of him while I have still got him.

"I'll get the ice cream," she says.

Two trembling heavenly hours later, Kimberley is lying on top of the bed exhausted. Her body is covered with streaks of drying ice cream, even on the soles of her feet. She is fast asleep.

In the morning Kimberley wakes up to find Marcus beside her and an empty tub of ice cream on the floor.

She gets out of bed and takes a shower. Whilst she is drying herself she sees, in the mirror, bite marks on her bottom, which is sore enough as it is.

She walks back to the bedroom to Marcus. "Did you bite my arse last night?" she asks.

"You shouldn't look like that if you don't want me to taste you," says Marcus. "And you are delicious."

"And you are a pervert," says Kimberley.

"You are not hurt," says Marcus. "You are a tough girl. The doctor told me. You are also irresistibly sexy. I couldn't resist you."

This appeals to Kimberley, who likes the idea that she is irresistible, even if he is a peculiar Brit.

"So, Kimberley," Marcus says. "What are we going to do?"

"We are doing what we came here to do," says Kimberley. "We are going to enjoy ourselves on the beach. Like two young people on holiday for the next two days. Then we are going home, you to England and me to the States. You could not live in the States with me, Marcus. And I could not live in England. So we are going home to live our lives. For the next two days it can be sandcastles on the beach. Fruit for the children. And sex. After that it is all over. Is that what you think?"

"When I asked what are we going to do," says Marcus, "I meant breakfast. Where shall we have breakfast? I didn't think about plans for the rest of our lives. That is God's job or fate or destiny or whatever you call it."

"Darling Marcus, I'll buy you breakfast at the hotel. Go and shave and shower and get dressed," says Kimberley. "I won't let you starve. The next two mornings I'll cook you breakfast."

Whilst he was in the shower Marcus reflected upon Kimberley's attitude and her decision for the future. He had not brought Kimberley to India for romance, he had brought her for companionship, but she is a wonderful companion. Life without her will feel empty. Even if I have the temporary excitement of another exotic girlfriend, as I have in the past, I shall miss Kimberley's character. I will miss everything about her. Well, what do you want? Do you want to marry her?

Outside on the beach Kimberley is crying. He did not fight for me, she thinks. He did not disagree with me. I pushed everything into the open because I wanted to know how he saw things. What he wanted. He doesn't seem to want anything. And I know now that I love him to distraction. Damn. What do I want? Do I want to marry him? What would

I say if he asked? What would he say if I asked? I am not going to ask a damn man to marry me. He should want me already.

She hears Marcus coming out onto the veranda and, standing on the beach with her back to him, she dries her eyes with her fingertips. "Hi Marcus," she shouts. "Hungry?"

"I certainly am," says Marcus. "I had an unusually energetic day yesterday."

"Unusually?" says Kimberley. "You should exercise more, Marcus. Toughen up."

Marcus takes Kimberley around the waist and then walks down the sandy beach towards the hotel. Kimberley has made Marcus think about his life. Mid-thirties. Not married but he has a house and apartment. What are his plans? He knows that his plans are to create enough rental income for him to live on. Shops, offices, warehouses, industrial estates. Safe tenants. Long leases. Why does he want all of this? Because when he has children, he does not seem to doubt that he will have children, he wants to have the time to enjoy them. Well, why has he not worked longer and harder earlier? His answer to that is that he was almost painfully aware of the ecstasy of youth and he wanted to savour it more than just working indoors in an office. He has still been successful but his choice of girlfriends has been mistaken; exciting, honest and committed, but not good life partners. Maybe Kimberley is like that, exciting and honest, but there is more. She is humorous, clever and strong. Besides which he just likes her. Were his previous girlfriends not humorous and clever and strong? Maybe they were. So why didn't he propose to any of them? He doesn't know.

They walk back into the hotel restaurant and both order different breakfasts. Kimberley walks out to the reception for a few minutes, returning just before breakfast arrives.

They are both a bit shell shocked that the truth about their future has been spoken about. Neither of them has anything else to say at breakfast today.

Later they walk down the beach together to find a secluded spot.

"I want to top up my sun tan," says Kimberley. "You should do the same. England is grey, at least Florida is sunny."

They strip down to their swimming costumes. Marcus has a small pair of shorts and the lithe body of Kimberley is splendidly displayed in a small polka dot bikini. They lie in the sunshine on the smooth sand.

"What do you do, Marcus? I know that it involves property but please tell me all about it."

"All about it?" says Marcus.

"Yes please," says Kimberley.

"Well, I build houses and apartments and sometimes shops and offices. Foolishly I am always trying to get the English buyers to enjoy space, but they are only interested in value."

"What do you mean?"

"Well, English buyers expect to make money from their houses or apartments. I have mistakenly made efforts in the past to get them to live differently and to enjoy space. I built a small number of two-bedroomed houses in Sussex, south of London, and I left out the second bedroom. I put the electric sockets in and the windows and everything but I left the floor out to create an open space looking down at the living room. I took the ceiling out so that you looked right up to the rafters and the single bedroom was a gallery room. I gave the buyers plans so that they could put in the second bedroom when they had their first child. I was wrong. They all wanted the second bedroom before they moved in and they all wanted the ceiling back. They were thinking of value, you see. How much they can sell the house for. It is like my London apartment. It is big enough to have three bedrooms but I knocked it all out to make a very big living room and one grand bedroom suite. If I wanted to sell it I would have to put all of the bedrooms back."

"So do you have a gang of workmen on your payroll?" asks Kimberley.

"No. I give fixed-price contracts to builders. Each development is in a different company with different architects, engineers, builders and a different merchant bank financing each deal. Spread the risk."

"Are you successful, Marcus? Or do you always mess up? Try to give people what they don't want?"

"I am successful. I don't mess up," says Marcus. "The Sussex deal was profitable, it just taught me the basic lesson that you have to always give buyers what they want and they want what they know. You cannot educate them."

"How do you get the money?" asks Kimberley.

"I borrow around seventy-five percent of the whole deal," says Marcus.

"The money is easier in the States, Marcus, you can get private investors as well who take a profit share and help you to get all of the finance."

"It all sounds like a lot of hard work and I would have to find my way around," says Marcus.

"It seems to me that you have already found your way around pretty well, because you have bought buildings in Florida already."

"I had to find somewhere to store my old clothes," says Marcus.

"Bullshit, Marcus," says Kimberley. "You knew what you were doing. And I have studied contracts, remember. Specialised in building contracts. I could help you. Oliver Gateskill, the lawyer who employed me in Florida, the one I

346

used to work for. I did all the work for you. He just put his name to it. You bought the property in a company you formed in Delaware in the US. I know what I am doing, Marcus. I can help you."

"Okay," says Marcus. "I can help you too. You need suntan lotion or you will burn. I can rub it into you. Prevent you from getting too hot."

"That is your answer?" says Kimberley.

"No, I'm thinking about my answer," says Marcus. "Meanwhile let me cool you down."

"You are a big thinker, Marcus," says Kimberley, "and having you rub suntan lotion into my body is not going to cool me down. You know that it will stop me from talking. Okay Marcus, go ahead, but prepare yourself for one hot girl. Will it help you to make up your mind?"

"I'm looking forward to it," says Marcus.

"When you told me how much money you have, Marcus, you did not mention the corporation in Delaware. You borrowed the money from the First National Bank. Nor did you mention the deals you may have in Britain," says Kimberley.

"Borrowed money," says Marcus. "It does not count. Anyway I did not know that it was a full audit. We were just chatting, I thought. Roll over. I'll start on your back."

Marcus undoes the strings which hold the top of her bikini on. He spreads them out so that her back is bare. Then he starts to rub in the suntan lotion.

"Is anybody close to us?" asks Kimberley.

"Nobody within one hundred yards," says Marcus.

"Good," says Kimberley. "Go ahead."

Marcus works his way down and undoes her bikini bottoms. "You sunbathe with no clothes on at home, don't you?" he says.

"Sure. I hate strap marks," says Kimberley. "I sunbathe on my roof."

Marcus pulls her bikini bottoms off and smooths more lotion into her.

"Marcus, you are a turn on," says Kimberley.

"I am just doing a thorough job," says Marcus.

"Don't you always," sighs Kimberley.

"I want you to remember me," says Marcus.

"I will," says Kimberley.

Marcus smooths the lotion into Kimberley and then tells her to turn over.

"What are we doing, Marcus?" asks Kimberley.

"Playing around," says Marcus. "We only have two days left, remember?"

"Are we still one hundred yards away from anybody?" asks Kimberley.

"One hundred and fifty yards," says Marcus.

"Make love to me, Marcus. As if you really mean it," says Kimberley.

Afterwards they cling to each other. They don't speak, they just hold each other for a long time. Kimberley wants to cry but she does not know why. She has already booked her onward flight to the States from when they arrive at London airport. She does not want to spend time in Britain with Marcus. It would be too difficult to leave. She will tell him that she is flying straight on to the States when they get to London. She is not going to tell him before. She is going to have a great time with him over the next few hours.

"In that direction is one of those snack and drink huts," says Marcus. "Shall we tidy ourselves up and then walk over there to see if they have anything to eat?"

"We haven't got food poisoning yet," says Kimberley, "but I'm still not going to risk it. If they have something fresh, which they can barbecue, then we could try it, but I have to get back here this afternoon, Marcus. I want to make a sandcastle. You and your property building, my sandcastle is going to be prettier than any of your houses."

"Okay," says Marcus. "I'll walk over there first to see what they have and then I'll come back and tell you."

"Great service, Marcus," says Kimberley. "See you in a while." She turns over onto her back to tan the front of her naked body. She gives a big sexy sigh as Marcus walks away and as he looks back she gives him a conspiratorial wink.

Marcus waves a hand at her and walks on, thinking that she looks like a washed-up mermaid with no tail and big breasts.

Ten minutes later he walks back. Kimberley has put her bikini on.

"They have fresh fish," he says, "and rice and some vegetables. They will barbecue the fish and vegetables and cook the rice on a small stove."

"When you say fresh fish?" asks Kimberley.

"Live fish," says Marcus. "They are keeping them in a net in the sea. You can choose which one you want to eat."

"Let's go then," says Kimberley, and puts her sundress over her head and slips on her sandals.

They walk up the beach. Kimberley leans against Marcus as they walk. The afternoon is agony for both of them because they are thinking about the end of the holiday and being apart from each other. They do not talk very much. Kimberley makes a sandcastle on the beach with a drawbridge made from driftwood and four towers, one at each corner. The little brown-eyed boy sits and watches her construct it carefully from sand, wetting portions of it to mould it accurately.

Afterwards the little boy asks Kimberley who the sandcastle belongs to. "You are going home soon, miss," he says.

Kimberley tells him that the sandcastle belongs to him and that it is called Kimberley's Palace.

"Kimberley's Palace," says the boy. "A very clever name, miss."

Marcus has gone into the sea and is swimming up and down parallel to the beach. He enjoys the clean feeling of the salt water. The thought of being back in Britain and having to say goodbye to Kimberley is a black spot in the future. He does not want it to happen. He swims ashore and walks up the beach towards Kimberley and the boy. Kimberley is like sunshine, he thinks, as he looks at her.

"I have forgotten to pay the hospital," he says. "I will get a taxi and then come straight back. Will you be all right on your own?"

"I am not on my own," says Kimberley. "I am with my friend." The little boy suddenly looks very proud.

Marcus puts on his trousers, shirt and shoes and walks up the beach to find a taxi at the hotel.

He pays the receptionist at the hospital and asks to see the nurses. He thanks each of them and they all smile very brightly. "Strong lady," the sister says.

As Marcus is walking out of the hospital he sees the retired doctor who had been so helpful to Kimberley.

"Doctor," calls Marcus. "Please wait."

The doctor turns to look at him. "Mr Field," he says.

"Please, call me Marcus. I am sorry but I do not know your name."

"Harry Elliot," says the doctor. "How is the girl?"

"She seems to be completely recovered," says Marcus. "She is on the beach making sandcastles. Would you join me for a tea or coffee?"

"Where are you going?" asks the doctor.

"The hotel," Marcus tells him.

"Certainly. That is convenient. Near to my house. Yes, I will join you."

Soon they are seated in the hotel gardens with a pot of tea between them.

"What are you going to do about the girl?" asks the doctor.

"I'm still thinking about it," answers Marcus.

"Oh, thinking about it," says the doctor. "And what do your emotions tell you?"

"Emotionally I would like to stay with her forever, but logically and practically I have to face the fact she is American and I am English. We live in different countries and I don't think that things can possibly work out between us. I will have to leave it as the greatest romance and say goodbye."

"When do you leave?"

"Tomorrow," says Marcus, sadly.

"Not much time," says the doctor. "You may have to rely on your emotions."

"I am very upset by it all," says Marcus. "I don't know what to do."

"I am a doctor," says Harry. "Not an agony aunt. I will tell you one thing which I have learned, something which old patients tell me often. You seldom regret the things, which you do in life, but you do regret the things which you do not do. At the end of your life it matters if you lived it to the full and if you didn't do something you wanted to do then you cannot go back."

"That is a little frightening," says Marcus.

"Life is frightening," says the doctor. "You will make the right decision. You are young, intelligent, brave. You cannot go wrong."

"Thank you, Harry," says Marcus. "It is selfish of me to talk about my own dilemma. How is your life?"

"I am old," says Harry. "Clockwork running down. I have four children and seven grandchildren. The grandchildren are fun but they all live in different countries. I try to get them out here once a year for a big holiday. Myself, I keep a garden. I paint and I help out at the hospital part-time. Keeps me alive. Life doesn't stop you know, Marcus, and it is not slow. It is racing along. Grab hold of happiness and cling on for the ride. There is nothing else."

"Thank you, Harry. Thank you for all of your help. I must go now. I have left the girl on the beach."

"Let me know how you get on, my boy. Here is my card. A rescued drowning girl and a heroic swimmer make a good story for our local newspaper."

Marcus walks outside and onto the beach. He sees Kimberley in the distance teaching the boy how to do cartwheels on the sand. Marcus feels terrible pain. Well idiot, go up to her and ask her to marry you, thinks Marcus. She has already said that we cannot live in each other's country. She has told me that this day is for sandcastles, sunbathing and sex. Marcus walks towards her and when he gets close enough he says, "Put your arms around me, Kimberley."

"What's the matter, Marcus?" she says. "Do you feel faint? I can't hold you up. I've got a new man now."

The little boy stands up straight. "Me," he says. "I am an acrobat now."

"A very good acrobat," says Marcus. "You have a very good teacher. She is a champion in the United States."

The boy turns to Kimberley. "I have to go home now, I must help my mother."

"Okay," says Kimberley and bends down to kiss his cheek. "Take care of yourself."

"Oh I will, most assuredly," says the boy and runs away up the beach.

"What is the matter with you, Marcus?" asks Kimberley.

Her demeanour is unsympathetic, almost combative. Certainly not warm. Marcus feels alone.

"Are we eating at the bungalow on our last night?" asks Kimberley. "Is the housekeeper cooking for us? Why don't we call her the bungalow keeper? What time do we have to leave in the morning? We get a taxi to the airport, I guess? Are your clothes all washed and ironed and ready to pack?"

Marcus says, "The taxi picks us up at eight o'clock tomorrow morning."

"How was the hospital? Did they say that I could still drown? On the plane for example?"

"I saw the old doctor," says Marcus. "His name is Harry Elliot. He says that you are fine. Healthy. A tough girl, he said. I had tea with him."

"That's why you were so long," says Kimberley. "What did you talk about?"

"Life," says Marcus. "He has seven grandchildren and four children. Do you want children, Kimberley?"

"Sure thing," says Kimberley. "You don't get a complete life without them. I thought maybe four. To make a big gang. What is the time?"

"You have that big diver's watch, Kimberley, but you always ask me for the time," says Marcus.

"Easier," says Kimberley. "Means that we both know."

"Six thirty," says Marcus.

353

"So it will be dark soon," says Kimberley. "I wonder if this beach has crabs as well."

"Are you going to jump on me?" asks Marcus.

"Feeling like I do now, I guess I'll jump on them," answers Kimberley, who has turned her back on Marcus and is putting things into a beach bag.

Marcus's normal cheerfulness has evaporated and Kimberley is not giving him an opportunity to create closeness on this, their last night. Protecting herself. She is closing up and becoming again the roller-skater he first met.

Kimberley turns around and looks at him. "Ready for the cold, Marcus?" she says.

Marcus is startled by the comment and looks hurt.

"Britain," says Kimberley. "Cold country. Cold people."

"You can fly anywhere in the world from London," says Marcus.

"You'll only find warmth in certain places," says Kimberley.

They walk up the beach side by side, separated by their thoughts. Kimberley is seething with anger and she doesn't know why. Marcus is turning over in his mind the words Kimberley used when she said they were parting. 'You could not live in the States and I could not live in England'. She had been considering both options. Considering the two of them staying together. Should I take that as encouraging or has she decided now that we are no good together? And what do I want?

They are getting close to the bungalow and the prospect of being alone together is disturbing each of them. Kimberley keeps talking trivia to avoid anything real being said. Marcus is fighting against unusual shyness.

The housekeeper is inside and both Marcus and Kimberley are pleased to see her.

"What time do we have to get up?" asks Kimberley, "if the taxi is arriving at eight o'clock? Around six thirty or seven? I reckon we both pack tonight and put out our travelling clothes to wear in the morning."

"Yes," says Marcus.

"So let's play cards tonight and drink wine," says Kimberley.

"Okay," says Marcus.

"Dinner is at eight o'clock. That is the schedule," says Kimberley. "So we can play a few hands and drink a bottle before bedtime. It will help us to sleep and it will stop us talking."

"Talking?" says Marcus.

"In the past weeks," says Kimberley, "we have done all of our talking. Now we have to pull apart before we go to our homes."

"Pull apart?" says Marcus.

"Get the cards," says Kimberley. "They are in the cupboard there?" she points. "I'll open the wine. We must sleep in separate bedrooms tonight, so that we can wake up on time."

"Okay," says Marcus. "What shall we play cards for?"

"For fun," says Kimberley, "and to pass the time before dinner. After dinner I am going to walk on the beach. Say goodbye to India."

"What game are we playing?"

"I don't care," says Kimberley. "You decide."

They play until the housekeeper tells them that the dinner is ready. Marcus puts away the cards and they both walk inside.

The dinner is goat and vegetables. "I am looking forward to American food. Salads and raw vegetables I can trust. Then

I can lose the weight I have put on in India and start exercising again."

"I have not noticed that you have put on weight," says Marcus.

"You're right. You have not noticed," says Kimberley. "But I have."

"I think you look perfect," says Marcus.

"Maybe you do, Marcus," says Kimberley, "or maybe you have not looked at me lately. Do not know me at all."

Marcus says nothing, just eats his dinner slowly.

The housekeeper clears the table and Kimberley walks outside onto the beach. She does not look back and Marcus does not follow her. He goes inside to pack. It was dark when Kimberley left and when she returns it is pitch black.

"Have you packed?" she asks Marcus, who is sitting on the veranda.

"Yes," says Marcus.

"I am going to pack now," says Kimberley, and walks inside.

Marcus sits alone outside with his thoughts.

Kimberley takes a long time and then at about nine thirty she comes out and says, "I am going to bed early. I will see you in the morning."

"Okay," says Marcus.

24
Going Home

The next day they are hurried in their arrangements. Marcus makes breakfast but Kimberley doesn't want any.

"Where is the taxi?" she says.

"Ten minutes yet," says Marcus.

"Okay, I'm going to check my things," says Kimberley.

At the airport they wait in silence for the London flight. They check in and go to the departure gate together. Kimberley walks apart from Marcus until they are told to board. She takes the window seat and tells Marcus that she is going to sleep. She closes her eyes. It is a long flight to Dubai, where the plane refuels. Once again Kimberley walks separately from Marcus until they board again. There is a frost between them on the final leg of the flight to London. They do not speak at all. Kimberley has brought fruit again and wordlessly shares it with Marcus. Afterwards she feigns sleep again until the plane begins its long descent into London Airport.

The plane lands and this time Kimberley doesn't hold Marcus's hand. She clasps her own hands together in her nervousness at flying. The plane taxies to the landing bay. The stewardess indicates that they may unfasten their safety belts and Marcus gets up first and makes room for Kimberley to get her bag down from the overhead locker. Fetches his afterwards and they walk off the plane and into the long corridors that lead to immigration. Kimberley goes through first and then stands waiting for Marcus.

"I am saying goodbye here Marcus. I cannot go into London with you. Let us just part here. I had a wonderful time. A wonderful time."

"Do you think that you could live in England Kimberly?"

"You know that I couldn't Marcus. And I don't think that you could live in the USA."

"I don't know," says Marcus.

"We could go to Africa," says Kimberly.

"Africa would be different," says Marcus. "But you live in paradise."

"What?" says Kimberley.

"That is what they say about Florida, Welcome to Paradise," says Marcus.

Kimberly pulls Marcus into her arms.

"You took me to paradise Marcus. You have a good life, and Marcus,"

"Yes," he says.

"Marcus, I will love you until the minute I die. I am going now. Goodbye. I will miss you Marcus," she says and then runs away towards the baggage reclaim carousel to get her bags and go onwards before Marcus can catch her up. When he gets to the baggage reclaim area she has gone.

Kimberley snatches her baggage from the luggage carousel and then rushes towards a gate marked transfers. She becomes lost and more and more impatient. She runs in the other direction but still cannot ascertain where she should check in to the flight to Florida. She looks at departure boards. She asks someone in a uniform. He directs Kimberley to an

358

information desk where a patient young man draws Kimberley a simple map on a piece of white paper.

"I suggest you walk carefully so as not to get lost," he says.

After more trouble and delay Kimberley sits in a window seat on the flight to Miami. I have avoided confrontation, she thinks. I avoided disagreements and bad feelings. I am going home. She has a long flight ahead of her and then another long drive in her car to get to Jacksonville and her apartment. I'll be all right when I'm home, she thinks. I will not miss him.

When she does get home she throws down her bags and does not feel all right. I miss him, she realises. Then she takes a shower and changes and rings her next door neighbour to ask if she wants to have dinner out.

Her next door neighbour's name is Mary Beth. She is a happy person who works with children. The two girls go to the beachside restaurant and Kimberley orders a steak.

"I haven't had a steak since I left Florida," she says.

Mary Beth orders lobster salad and starts to ask Kimberley about her trip. "What was India like?"

"India is not like anywhere you can imagine," answers Kimberley. "Now I think about it I believe that it is just magical; a jumble of humanity and contradictions. Extraordinary."

"What about your companion? The Englishman?" asks Mary Beth.

"He is wonderful," says Kimberley, "but he is not the kind of man I have ever thought I would want. He does not fit in with my plans."

"I didn't ask you if you wanted him," says Mary Beth. "I asked you what he was like."

"Mary Beth, I do want him and I deliberately let him go. I left him very suddenly at London Airport. I said nothing to

359

encourage him at all. I thought that once I was here I could forget him."

"But you can't," says Mary Beth. "Maybe it was all part of India. An unreal experience."

"A lot of the experience was very real," says Kimberley.

"Kimberley," says Mary Beth, "did you get close to him?"

"Oh yeah," says Kimberley. "Close."

"What are you going to do about him?" asks Mary Beth.

"There is nothing I can do," says Kimberley. "He is a Brit and he is going to stay there. I guess that I will never see him again and the idea of that hurts me real bad."

"Have some key lime pie," says Mary Beth. "To welcome you home."

Kimberley's expression is very bleak.

Marcus stands at the London airport without knowing where to go next. He gets his bags and walks to the long stay car park, fetches his car and drives into London. He spends the night in his ridiculously large London apartment.

The next day Marcus telephones Alistair and makes an appointment to see him in two days' time.

They meet at Alistair's office.

"How was the trip?" asks Alistair.

"Spectacular," answers Marcus. "Unrepeatable."

"And the girl? How was she?" asks Alistair.

"My world is toppling," says Marcus. "She has changed my convictions on life. She has unsettled me. I have come to see you to make some new arrangements. I need your help, Alistair."

"Of course," says Alistair. "I will do everything I can."

Marcus makes a lot of plans and Alistair prepares documents for him to sign the next day.

Marcus visits his accountants and instigates changes in his company structures. He signs documents and then goes to his

London apartment and packs a bag. He locks the apartment and drives to London Airport. He gets on a flight to Florida. He has no doubts. He feels relieved.

Once he is in Miami, he gets a private car to drive him to Jacksonville and books into the Hilton Hotel, where he showers, eats and sleeps.

The next day is Sunday and after breakfast he takes a cab to the address which Kimberley gave him ten weeks ago. He walks up to the door of her condominium apartment and rings the bell. No answer. He knocks. No answer. The next door neighbour, Mary Beth, comes out of her apartment.

"I am looking for Kimberley Judd," says Marcus.

"She is not in," says the girl. "She has gone roller-skating on the promenade. She has been very angry this week and is out trying to burn off energy."

Marcus takes the same cab, which he had paid to wait for him, down to the beach and walked along the promenade. Eventually he sits on a bench. Maybe it is the same bench where the child ran out in front of Kimberley before he knew who she was. He sits patiently looking left and right until he sees a girl in white shorts and a red top roller-skating towards him. He recognises Kimberley and he stands up. His heart is pounding. He walks to the middle of the promenade and puts his arms out wide. Kimberley sees him and begins to accelerate towards him faster and faster. When she is within six feet of him she leaps up and collides with his chest, wrapping her arms and legs around him. She knocks him to the ground and only because she has her hands around his head does he avoid hitting his skull on the hard surface of the promenade. He is completely winded and cannot breathe at all.

I've killed him, thinks Kimberley. I had better do something. Kimberley gives him rough and overenthusiastic mouth-to-mouth resuscitation, blowing into his mouth until he begins to cough. She pulls him into a seated position with her legs still wrapped around him. He continues to cough and gasp.

"What are you doing here?" demands Kimberley. "Have you forgotten something?"

Marcus gasps a bit more and then says, "Yes, I have forgotten something. You told me to have a good life so I came here to ask you to marry me."

Kimberley is silent for a whole minute and then says, "You mean that you want me to be your girl, be your fiancée, be your wife and you want me to have your children, Marcus? Have you thought about it all?" says Kimberley, remembering that Marcus had said on their flight to India that he never understood men who wanted that.

"Of course I have thought about it. From the first week I have thought about it and that is all I want," says Marcus.

"All you want? Well, ask me then," says Kimberley. "Ask me what you came here to ask me."

"Kimberley Judd," says Marcus. "Will you marry me?"

Kimberley looks at him seriously. She looks at his face and his hair, which is ruffled from the fall and she looks at his body, which is sitting on the promenade with her legs around him. She feels as if a wall has broken down and the sun is shining through.

"Sure," she says. "What took you so long?"

"I had arrangements to make," says Marcus. "I will be an alien in the States. I only have a three-month visa."

"Marry me and give me children and you can be a resident," says Kimberley. "Where are you staying?"

"The Hilton," says Marcus.

"The hell with that," says Kimberley. "You are staying with me." She starts to laugh and laugh and then kisses him long and hungrily. "I've missed you. I want a pre-nup

362

agreement. Everything you have now, you keep. Everything we make together, we share. You and I are going to be a big success."

"I thought you wanted to be a trophy wife?" says Marcus.

"No," says Kimberley. "I want a trophy husband. You'll do."